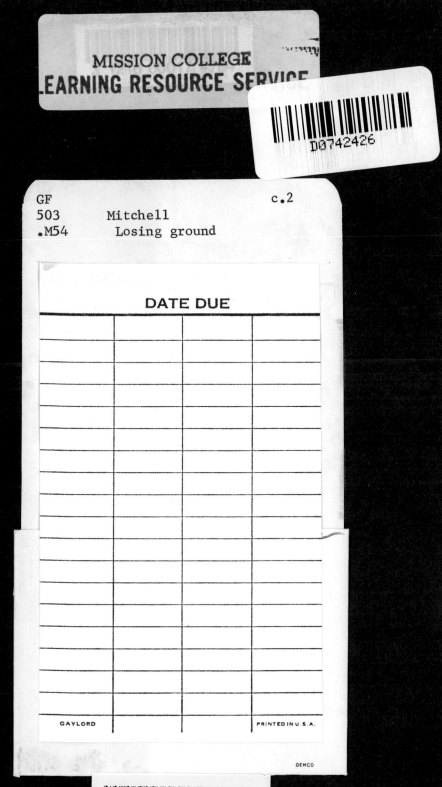

DATE DUE

GAYLORD			PRINTED IN U.S.A.

DEMCO

LOSING GROUND

JOHN G. MITCHELL

LOSING GROUND

Sierra Club Books · San Francisco · 1975

The Sierra Club, founded in 1892 by John Muir, has devoted itself to the study and protection of the nation's scenic and ecological resources —mountains, wetlands, woodlands, wild shores and rivers. All Club publications are part of the nonprofit effort the Club carries on as a public trust. There are some 50 chapters coast to coast, in Canada, Hawaii and Alaska. Participation is invited in the Club's program to enjoy and preserve wilderness everywhere. Address: 1050 Mills Tower, San Francisco, California 94103.

Mitchell, John G
 Losing ground.

 1. Human ecology—United States. 2. Environment protection—United States. 3. Nature conservation—United States. I. Title.
✓GF503.M54   333.7'2   75-1073
 ISBN 0-87156-128-X

Printed in the United States of America.
Design and composition by Zoe Brown.
Production by Charlsen + Johansen & Others.

"The Asbestos Gitche Gumee" and "The Selling of the Shelf" have appeared, in somewhat different forms, in *Audubon* magazine.

CONTENTS

For Ms. Blatz and the Big Dogs

ACKNOWLEDGMENTS

A lot of people out there helped me put this book together. Knowledgable about this or that, they generously shared with me the information I was after, and I hope they will have no regrets when they see how I have used it. Some of them are named in the book where specific identities seemed appropriate and prudent; others for various reasons are not, but not because they were any less valuable as sources. There are friends to thank also, unassuming types whom I shall not presume to embarrass here except to say that their encouragement and counsel were most helpful, especially the benedictions they offered to me in San Francisco, under the griffin's head, the sign of the eagle, as it appears in a certain waterfront establishment there. More specifically, I am obliged to the wordmen who not only determined my beat over the past twenty years but gave me the rope to pace it off with some freedom: Larry McSwain, James D. (Red) Horan, Edwin Diamond, Charles E. Little, August Fruge, Paul Brooks, and Les Line.

JGM

It is not quite true that you can't go home again . . . . But it gets less likely.

Wallace Stegner
Angle of Repose

GREETINGS

Today in the mail I received greetings from Uncle Harry. He is not a blood uncle. He is a printer in New York who likes to celebrate obscure occasions, as the faithful observe feast days. This time Harry's card says *Happy Ground-hog's Day,* and he adds that "a light is visible at the tunnel's end." Harry is a fine printer but an unconvincing optimist.

Once upon a time, and not so long ago at that, I too celebrated an obscure occasion. The date was April 22, 1970. The occasion was Earth Day. To friend and foe alike I dispatched greetings: *Happy Earth Day,* a drawing of a pig with human hands strewing garbage, and a phrase by cartoonist Walt Kelly that would soon become the most redundant cliche of the new-born environmental movement: "We have met the enemy, and he is us." And on the day of the occasion I stood in Manhattan's Union Square with thousands of ebullient young people and graying old-school-tie conservationists and we saw light at the end of the tunnel. The Great Revolution had come at last. Victory was soon to be ours. But of course we were wrong. We were only fooling ourselves, as others in the Sixties were deluded into thinking that rallies and marches could somehow overcome racial prejudice at home and genocide abroad. We are still in the tunnel. Our marches have simply moved us from the streets of Selma to the school buses of South Boston, from My Lai massacre to mail-order mayhem, from the blowout at Santa Barbara to the prospect of oil rigs off all our beaches, a price we are told we must now pay in order to stop the Arabs from owning the world. Sorry, Uncle Harry. I'm all for the ground-hog, but I don't see the light. Only shadows.

For the better part of the past year, I have been poking at shadows here and there across America, trying to find out

1

how certain places are getting along in these stringent ener-
getic times, and how certain people in them are relating to
their environment, and to what extent the bloom is on or off
the yellow rose of Earth Day. I attempted no sweeping survey, no "in-depth" demographic "blockbuster," as the old
city editors used to say, but rather, for the most part, a selec-
tive revisiting of some places I had known as a newspaper
reporter, or in which I had lived for some small or large part
of my life. I would like to say that I returned to old haunts in
a mobile camper, a converted bus perhaps, with loyal dog and
folding chair and a lamp to read by in the lonely evenings; on
the road for a full cycle of seasons, touring the country, taking my own sweet time. No such luck. I would like to say
that I filled my notebooks with the wisdom of potentates
and laureates. Not bloody likely. I went by conventional
modes, arriving at dreadful hours in the company of commission salesmen and insurance adjusters; and I filled my
notebooks with the wisdom of farmers and fishermen and
housewives and cops and assorted other types who, for better or worse, are close to the issues I wished to explore.

I also traveled with a bias in the heart and mind, for it is
no longer possible for me to be as objective as people like to
think a reporter should be. The painful truth, if you have not
guessed it, is that by habit and conviction I am a person
whose bias runs toward natural things. I am fascinated by
rivers and lakes and woods and swamps, by storks and pelicans and trout, by oak and maple and spruce, by the way
these things fit into people's lives, or don't fit, depending on
circumstance and attitudes. Conversely, I am intrigued by
some of the things that now and then get between people
and nature, such as dams and penstocks and nuclear reactors
and pelletizing plants and absolute kill zones, among other
shadowy cultural artifacts described in this book.

There is a hazard in doubling back over country you have
already been through. If you aren't careful you can take a
wrong turn into the maze called nostalgia, wherein lie the
bleached bones of the lost ones who languished there in

search of some personal truth. I don't know how many times we have been warned that you can't go home again. By and large, it is fairly sane advice, especially for those whose bias runs toward natural things and whose memory of them goes back to a time before suburban sprawl, off-road recreational vehicles, and the interstate highway system. But if there are hazards in going "home" again, there can be benefits as well. Time sharpens perception; and though you may not be demonstrably the wiser, at least you are not so easily fooled by surface appearances. You begin to see some stories you missed, the details you overlooked, the relationships you ignored. And if environment is your beat, you soon discover that the significant issue is not always the one that is riding under the boldest headline; that the loss of a scraggly urban greenbelt, for example, can count as much against the scheme of things as the destruction of a redwood forest.

The reader will encounter bad news and a little anger in this book. Unlike Uncle Harry, I am no optimist. I have spent too many years looking at the undersides of rocks, and have come to believe, however perversely, that bad news is what keeps us on our toes. I understand also that pessimism has no survival value, as someone once remarked. But survival is not what I set out to write about, though I think it may figure here and there between the lines, discreetly, like the shadow of a groundhog on a partly overcast day.

As for the anger, I have tried to keep it muted. The world is already too shrill, and the pulpits are overcrowded with prophets of doom. If at times I seem to be a member of that unworthy clergy, forgive me. I have witnessed much in the past year to infuriate and sadden: the reluctance of people to adapt their attitudes and practices to the clear reality of diminishing resources; a myopic trust in the nation's ability to walk the waters of continued growth; the sanctity of corporate profits at the expense of public health; the blight and the benign neglect. But the prospect I see is not altogether dark and enraging, for on occasion I also encountered some positive signs: the ability of nature to heal itself; the courage of people believing in unpopular causes; the tenacity of endangered species; the beauty of unexploited country; the way truth, if there is such a thing, keeps emerging from the lessons of the past.

Someone in a fortune-cookie factory is trying to tell me that the past is unimportant. I know this because of what happened to me in Hanford, California, when I went back there last year to see what I had missed two decades earlier. I was having dinner at a restaurant on Hanford's China Alley. California is full of surprises. The cuisine was Continental. Yet everything else about the place was Chinese, from the decor and the staff to the fortune cookie they served with my coffee. The message inside my fortune cookie said: "Forget the past—and look towards a harmonious future." I was amused and brought the message home; and now it is tacked to my bulletin board, and Uncle Harry's groundhog card is hanging next to it.

The trouble is, I cannot embrace the fortune cookie's forward-looking message any more readily than I can accept Uncle Harry's promise of a light at the end of the tunnel. Certainly I shall forget the past, some day. Some day I shall have to. I would forget it now if only the present could yield evidence that we have learned our lessons—from the past—and are now capable of a future in which humankind and nature are at peace. I cannot say for sure that this will ever happen. It is a far piece off, and it may never happen. But for heaven's sake, for perpetuity's sake, for Uncle Harry's sake, for yours and mine, for groundhogs and pelicans, it had better happen. Don't you think?

J.G.M.
The Saltbox
Staten Island, New York
February 1975

FEEDING THE GRIFFINS

. . . we cannot hope to escape the great law of compen-
sation which exacts some loss for every gain . . . . The
California of the new era will be greater, richer, more
powerful than the California of the past; but will she be
still the same California whom her adopted children . . .
love better than their own mother lands? . . . . Amid all
our rejoicing and our gratulations, let us see clearly
whither we are tending . . . . The future of our State
looks fair and bright; perhaps the future looked so to
the philosophers who once sat in the porches of Athens.
. . . Our modern civilization strikes broad and deep and
looks high. So did the tower which men once built
almost unto heaven.

—Henry George, 1868

Among my eccentric acquaintances is a metaphysician who
denies the existence of California. The trouble seems to be
that my friend was born in California, near Los Angeles, and
grew up reading the wrong sort of books, books such as
Nathaniel West's *Day of the Locust*, in which Tod Hackett,
the protagonist, dreams of painting a huge canvas of Los
Angeles in flames. My friend is no painter himself, but I am
certain his view of California was profoundly colored by that
book. Bye and bye he took leave of California to obtain a
college education in Connecticut, and later he settled down
in New York. There, apparently, California ceased to exist as
a state of the Union and became instead a state of his mind.

One day in New York this friend telephoned as I was
rushing to catch a taxi to the airport. He asked where I was
going. I said I was going to San Francisco.

"Well, good luck," he replied cheerily. "I hope you can find it."

"I hope the pilot can," I said.

"You will come down in a fog," said my friend, "and when you step out of your plane, San Francisco, California, will be gone."

I told him he had a good imagination but no faith.

"And you lack vision," he said. "You are flying to a fiction." Suddenly he was quoting the Spaniard de Montalvo, a spinner of tall tales, who in 1510 had written of an island called California, near the Terrestial Paradise, where robust women with golden arms fed to ravenous griffins the men whom they had borne. "So you see," he said finally, "it is all a myth."

"Even the griffins?"

"No," he said. "Perhaps not the griffins. The griffins may be the only thing about California that is absolutely authentic."

The weather was dense over most of the country. I saw the Missouri through a hole in the clouds, but the Plains were shrouded and only the taller peaks of the Rockies broke through to the sky. For all I knew, the Republic had vanished. And then, somewhere west of Walker Lake, Nevada, the clouds shredded out in wisps and tassles, and the Boeing jet banked sharply into open skies over the parched brown eastern slope of the High Sierra. In a few minutes Yosemite was under the left wing. The soft gray granite was dusted with snow, but the valley was green and the Merced River sparkled like a hot wire twisting down the long western slope toward the larger valley below. Then we were over sapphire reservoirs in the foothills and soon the land flattened out and the rivers ran straight across the checkerboard of the San Joaquin, and here were Merced and Los Banos and the great aqueduct running on poured concrete down the edge of the Diablo Hills to the faucets and fire hydrants of Los Angeles. The plane banked sharply again, over water. Now the flaps came down, then the wheels. The terraced hills of San Mateo were on the left, Oakland was on the right, and in between, dead ahead, was the jagged skyline of San Francisco without fog. The wheels touched. We rolled down the runway. The doors opened. The stewardesses waved goodbye.

"What brings you here?" asked a friend who is not as eccentric as the one in New York. I said I had come back to visit old haunts with a pencil and notebook.

"Looking for what?"

"For griffins," I said.

And later that evening, in front of a television set, I watched the shootout between the Symbionese Liberation Army and the Los Angeles Police. A great pall of smoke darkened the sky above the burning bungalow where the fugitives were trapped. It looked as if the entire city were ablaze, as if the fire and the smoke and all the violent faces had been reconstructed from the unfinished canvas of Todd Hackett's dream.

All the Kings' Horses

Water is the key to California. I refused to see that when I lived there in the Fifties; and on the two newspapers which employed me then I winced each time an editor ordered from my typewriter another twist in the tangled riparian affairs of the Colorado River or the Central Valley Project. I thought it especially unfair that a young man so clearly destined to fill an urban niche should have to squander his apprenticeship on a subject of interest to farmers only. "No damn more about water," I snarled at the publisher in Santa Maria the day I departed for a job in New York; yet I have been sinking or swimming in news about water ever since.

The other place in California was Hanford, about halfway between the lemon groves of the lower Sierra and the oil rigs in the Kettleman Hills. In Hanford, we rented a house on Van Zante Street. It was a small house with a long yard trailing out behind it, and at the end of the yard was more damn water, which flowed sluggishly in a trench called the People's Ditch. While our cat stalked lizards in the tall grass that grew along its banks, I stared darkly at the opaque flowage and cursed it for the mosquitoes it sent through the holes in our flyscreens. But that was before I got into the mountains to see where the water in the People's Ditch came from, and how the sound of it thundered down the canyons, each converging on the next until the whole great river swept broad and deep into the valley, where pumps and siphons and ditches were waiting to disperse its waters into calculable allotments of acre-feet.

Later, when people asked where I had lived in California, I would reply that I had lived on a branch of a strange and beautiful mountain river. And in great detail I would describe the Kings: how the South Fork began in ice fields on the 14,000-foot Palisades of the High Sierra crest and tumbled down through Le Conte Canyon to join the Middle Fork at the Monarch Divide; and how the two rushed on together to Rodgers Crossing to gather the waters of the North Fork, which, if one wished (and I always did), could be traced to such wonderful places as Hell-for-Sure Pass and Six Shooter Lake and Post Corral Meadow and Blackcap Basin and Indian Springs.

Invariably, my listener would interrupt with a question: "On which of these forks did *you* live?" And I would have to explain that I had lived on none of them, but downstream in the City of Hanford, at an elevation of 242 feet above sea level, on the lizard-infested banks of a Kings canal, on the seamy shore of the People's Ditch. And finally I would explain how a funny thing happens to the Kings on its way to the salty forum of the sea, after the People's Ditch and a dozen like it have sucked their allotments from its tired teat. The funny thing is that the Kings disappears.

Not far from Hanford, a clay plug rises imperceptibly across the flat bed of the river, and here, according to maps, the Kings divides. Part of it curves north into the Fresno Slough, which joins the San Joaquin River near Mendota, and from there the San Joaquin rolls on toward the great delta at San Francisco Bay. The other part of the Kings curves south toward a large square which is colored blue on the maps and identified as Tulare Lake. But the maps lie, for except at times of heavy flood, the Kings no longer flows to the Fresno Slough; and to the south, in the furrowed fields of the very last farmer entitled to it, the mighty river expires under the hot valley sun, a trickle sopped up in a flash of evapotranspiration. As for Tulare Lake, it was once considered the largest fresh-water body in the west, covering some 500 square miles at its greatest pool. But in 1898, with people upstream getting busy in water associations and ditch companies, the lake went dry. From time to time, when High Sierra snowpacks are deep and the runoff comes fast, the old lake bed is flooded. So the cartographers, in self-defense, keep coloring it blue. They had *me* fooled; I brought a bathing suit to Hanford. And to this day, the locals down in Corcoran still have fun when tourists from Los Angeles appear in town, with yachting caps above their sunglasses and motorboats on trailers behind their cars. "Hey there, fella," the tourist says, "could you direct me to the nearest marina?" The cocky local loiterer points the way down Whitley Avenue. Five minutes later, at the dead end of a dirt road, the gullible admiral from Los Angeles gets out of his car, scratches his head, and stares across a sea of cotton to the distant shores of J.G. Boswell's big, sprawling, dry-docked Boston Ranch. Otherwise known as Tulare Lake.

There are several rivers in California longer than the Kings; some whose flowing volume is greater by the cubic foot; and it is possible that those who know the mountains better might argue that there are one or two rivers whose upper reaches are more striking to the eye. However that may be, people nowadays are less inclined to measure rivers by their scenic value than by their proven and potential capacity to do work. And I suspect that, by this measure, mile for mile and gallon for gallon, the River of the Holy Kings—*El Rio de los Santos Reyes*—is without parallel. In short, El Rio works its tail off.

In days gone by, the river's job was easy. It simply obeyed the law of gravity and ran downhill, free as the freshets that fed it. The farmers in the valley knew what to do next, because most of them were refugees from the played-out gold mines up north and were good with shovels. What they did was dig ditches. This allowed the river water to spread out across sown fields, and soon the whole valley was green with crops. But then the farmer's life became complicated by alternating floods and droughts. Even between such bad times, with more and more settlers, barely enough water came downhill to keep the valley as green as the farmers would have liked it. So they began digging wells. But the wells needed pumps to draw the water against the law of gravity. And the pumps needed what the old-fashioned windmills could not adequately deliver: the pumps needed kilowatts. So the farmers turned to the engineers, and the engineers came up with a solution. They would go to the great mountain staircase of the Kings and, by building dams to hold back the floods and store up the water against the droughty days, with penstocks and powerhouses and turbines and tailraces and transformers to generate the kilowatts, they would increase the capacity of the river to do work. To be specific, they would impound in reservoirs some 1,250,000 acre-feet of water (nearly half a trillion gallons) and, at the same time, deliver unto the valley a constant quantity of energy that would equal the power of 400,000 horses, each pulling the weight of an adult human male two-thirds the length of a football field in one minute. And all of this power would come from the majestic force of the falling Kings.

In the early autumn of 1956, I had occasion to visit the North Fork Kings Project as a guest of the Pacific Gas and Electric Company. Several reporters and editors from other valley newspapers were aboard as well, and, from a rendezvous at Sanger, we drove up along the Kings to the huge Pine Flat Dam which had been topped out just two years earlier by the Army Corps of Engineers. The reservoir behind the dam was already half full. Canyons were now coves, and from one bend in the road we saw a farmhouse chimney rising out of the water like a channel marker. Someone asked why the Army had left the house to be flooded. "Because," said another, "houses are good for the fish to live in." More relevant questions and answers were in our press kits. As we twisted up the interminable staircase, I was impressed to read that the Pacific Gas and Electric Company was operating under a "Magna Charta of science and economics" to help reclaim the greatest agricultural empire in the world. By curbing the regal whims and destructive rampages of the river, by tapping the benign affluence of its waters, all the Kings' horses and PG&E's men would put humpty dumpty together again.

I was more than impressed; I was awed. I saw where the new Balch penstock would plunge 2,400 vertical feet down the precipice at Patterson Bluff, and how the Haas Powerhouse was being carved out of bedrock 500 feet underground; the two newest reservoirs upstream, Wishon and Courtright, with their rock-fill dams rising 300 feet above streambed; the slash burning in windrows at Coolidge Meadows and the quarriers taking the mountains apart in ten-ton blocks with dynamite. The public relations man from San Francisco said it would all be over in six years. The dust would settle. The mountains would heal. Except for the roar of the water and the hum of the generators, there would be blissful silence. High-tension wires would carry the kilowatts down to the valley, where no man ever again would want for the power to make things grow, including his social communities. Such was my bright perception of the future as I returned to the porches of Hanford. I had swallowed it whole.

As anyone with a passing memory of the Fifties may recall, the projections and predictions of those halcyon years were not long to stand the test of time. Especially the projections of energy supply and demand in the coming decades. And so it was, on September 24, 1973, as the nation swaggered toward its first, and by no means last, crisis in power, that the Pacific Gas and Electric Company filed an application with the Federal Power Commission for a license to interrupt the blissful silence on the North Fork Kings River with construction of yet another hydroelectric project. This one, installed near the top of the staircase, would deliver a generating capacity three times greater than that of all the plumbing facilities inserted along the river during the Fifties. In other words, more horses—more than 1,200,000 of them.

Seventeen years appeared to have brought little change to the staircase of the Kings as I drove up the twisting road from Sanger in the spring of 1974. Behind the high dam at Pine Flat, the impounded waters were a brilliant blue against the straw-colored foothills. I saw small boats instead of chimneys and imagined the bass were sitting pretty in the parlors of the flooded farmhouses. Overhead the wires came down along the road suspended from steel towers, like a procession of skeletons roped together for mountain safety. Far to the east, between the valleys of the South and Middle forks, I could see the peaks of the High Sierra Primitive Area bright and snowcapped in the sunlight.

At Balch Camp I stopped to visit the Pacific Gas and Electric Company's operations headquarters. I said I had come to learn about the proposed hydroelectric project. The dispatcher introduced me to an engineer, and the engineer showed me into a hallway between two offices. Stretched out along one of the walls was a schematic drawing of the top of the North Fork staircase.

"This," said the engineer, "is a picture of the Helms Pumped Storage Project—$235 million, about 1,050,000 kilowatts. We expect we'll have to build about six miles of new roads, starting next summer. The underground excavation would begin in the spring of 1976. They expect about 117,000 cubic yards of spoil will come out of the powerplant and surge chambers alone. It's all underground, you see. Now. We have a difference in elevation of more than 1,600 feet between the two reservoirs—Courtright up here, and Wishon down here. That's what you call *high head.* This tunnel here will come out of Courtright to Lost Canyon, 4,875 feet long. This next tunnel from Lost Canyon to the penstock will be 8,864 feet long. And then the penstock slants down about 3,000 feet—now that's the running length, not the drop in elevation—to the underground powerplant here. And finally this tunnel runs out into Wishon, about

4,000 feet. Now the powerplant will be 1,000 feet below ground level. It will have three reversible pump-turbines. During periods of peak demand, weekday mornings mostly, water from Courtright will be released through the powerhouse into Wishon. During off-peak hours, mostly at night, water from Wishon will be pumped back into Courtright, so it can be released again. That's called recycling your energy."

"But don't you have to borrow energy from somewhere else to pump Wishon back uphill into Courtright?"

"That's right," said the engineer. "We can draw on high-efficiency plants in the system that otherwise would be idle at night, or just throwing off kilowatts that you can't store up."

"You mean nuclear plants?"

The engineer nodded.

"Like the one on the coast at Diablo Canyon?"

Again the engineer nodded.

"And what will they do with all the spoil from the excavations?"

"Dump it," said the engineer. "If we get the permit, mostly in Lost Canyon."

"Perfect," I said. "When the canyon is all filled up, you won't even have to change its name."

I had wanted to take a look at Lost Canyon, but eight inches of new snow had fallen overnight above Wishon, and when I got up there the trails into the Helms area were shin-deep in slush. "Don't advise goin' up there, mister," said a man in a yellow PG&E hard hat. "If it's swimmin' you want, you'll find plenty of that in Wishon Lake." I declined with thanks and turned back down the mountain road toward Balch and the valley. I wanted to see something else: the underground Haas powerhouse, the prototype for the one they proposed to build at Helms Creek.

They gave me a hard hat and we walked past the three transformers to the elevator access shed. These, and the surrounding chain-link fence and the wires going away, were all that showed of the plant above ground. The transformers

were tall and surreal, with so many loops and coils and sym-
metrical appendages that they looked to me as if they might
have been designed by the art director of a science-fiction
magazine. "There are two generators down below," said the
man from PG&E. "The power leaves the generators at 14,400
volts and shoots up a copper cable into these transformers.
They boost it to 230,000 volts." I said I would take his word
for it, that what I really wanted to see was the water, and
what happens to *that*.

An elevator lowered us down the vertical shaft, 400 feet
to the control room. Everything computerized, fully automatic, and everything humming. From the control room we
descended into the cavernous chamber of the generators,
with walls of naked granite cold to the touch and etched
with secrets a billion years old. Construction crews had been
digging here when I passed by in 1956. They had started at
the tailrace down by Black Rock Reservoir, blasting and
drilling their way into the powerhouse chamber and then
straight up the elevator shaft. I do not know what happened
to all the spoil. I suppose it made a secret of some other lost
canyon. Then we descended another flight of stairs into a
chamber where the turbines were spinning. Here my guide
showed me how the penstock, buried in a tunnel for the final
760 feet of its descent, fired the falling water under pressure
of one thousand pounds per square inch into the blades of
the turbines, how the turbines whirled the electromagnetic
rotors in the generator shafts, and so on—power up the copper cable, through the transformers, and out along the wires
to the valley.

"What happens to the water?" I asked.

The man from PG&E opened a trap door in the floor of
the chamber and suddenly we were both engulfed in a great
gust of cold air. I looked down into the opening. The water
had been pounded to a white froth. Thousands of gallons
rushed by each second, pinched in the tailrace, fighting the
friction, the water bellows to its own wind as it roared on
toward Black Rock and Balch, toward the other tunnels and
penstocks and turbines waiting, then out into the reservoir

at Pine Flat and through the flood gates falling, and down the natural riverbed into the valley, across the checkerboard to the People's Ditch, to the Boston Ranch, to the hot sun beating on the shimmering surface of the cotton sea. And I wondered, in foolish disregard of scientific fact: in a hundred miles, how many times can a quantity of water be made to do work?

On the way back to the elevator I noticed water seeping down one of the granite walls of the generator chamber. High on the wall, the seep was defined by a long thin deposit of lime. "That seems to be quite natural," the man from PG&E explained. "The ground water in these granitic formations tends to be calcareous, and sometimes it percolates through. That's why we treat the ceiling with a sealing compound to reduce the moisture."

"Well," I said. "I think you have a problem. Some of my friends tell me that one of these days all your reservoirs are going to fill up with silt. And now it looks to me as if some of your powerhouses are going to fill up with stalactites."

"It can't happen here," he said.

"But just suppose it could."

"Well," he said, "we wouldn't be around to know the difference."

As we got into the elevator, I conceded that at the rate we were going he was probably right.

Salt of the Earth

The County of Kings, which takes its name from the river, is located about halfway on a curved line between Los Angeles and San Francisco. From Hanford, the county seat, you can drive to either metropolitan marketplace in just under four hours. This happenstance is very good for business in Kings—since the people of those big cities must feed and clothe themselves—because the business of Kings is food and fiber.

Seventy thousand people live in Kings County, or did when I drove down there from the mountains in the spring of 1974. The size of the county is 1,400 square miles. This is also good for business because it means that the population density is only fifty people to the square mile, which leaves a lot of room to grow crops and graze cows; even more room when you consider that most of the people are concentrated in Hanford and Corcoran and Lemoore and Armona and Stratford and Kettleman City and Avenal, therein occupying less than 10 percent of the land. With the exceptions of Lemoore, sustained by the presence of a Naval Air Station, and Avenal, which subsists on the memory of oil, the towns of Kings County owe their existence to the relatively few men and women who live on the other 90 percent with their crops and their cows. The crops and the cows owe their existence to water.

Of the fifty-eight counties of California, Kings ranks thirty-fifth in size, but it is fourth in total irrigated acres and, against formidable competition, fourteenth in the cash value of its crops. The most notable competitor is Fresno County, directly to the north. Fresno is not only tops in crops for California; it is the wealthiest agricultural county in the United States. It surpasses its downstate neighbor for a number of reasons, and chief among these is the fact that, with taps on both the San Joaquin *and* the Kings River, it has access to more water.

The Kings River supplies about 40 percent of Kings County's present water needs, or some 542,000 acre-feet per year. Another 60,000 acre-feet are siphoned from the Kaweah and Tule rivers to the south. From the Friant-Kern Canal of the Central Valley Project, at times of surplus flow, comes 43,000 acre-feet; from the California Aqueduct, 196,000 acre-feet; and from the San Luis Project into the Westlands Water District, 23,000 acre-feet. Effective precipitation—that is, the portion of annual rainfall that percolates into the soil before it can evaporate—bestows on the county about 114,000 acre-feet, assuming a total annual rainfall of eight inches. And that is a large assumption. Whatever additional quantities of water the county requires for its towns and farms must be pumped from wells.

With its hot sun, its long growing season, and all that water sloshing around in the fields, the cornucopia of Kings County spills forth lettuce and tomatoes, cantalope, olives, pistachios, almonds and apricots, peaches and plums, walnuts, beans, corn, rice, safflower, sorghum, sugarbeets and wheat. Sixty thousand acres are planted to alfalfa; 115,000 to barley. There are more than three million chickens and turkeys. And the bovine population, exploding in Kings as scores of Southern California dairymen seek refuge from the preemptive assessments and suburban sprawl of Greater Los Angeles, may soon outnumber the human two to one. The leading crop is long-staple cotton—172,000 acres of it, valued at $90 million on the bale, enough cotton in a year to weave a midiskirt for every mizz in America. The Kings County Economic Development Commission, with offices in Hanford, issues a report elaborating on some of these statistics. To the commissioners, the future of the county looks fair and bright. The cover of their report shows a boll of cotton and the head of a cow emerging from a king's crown. The report states that Kings County has "the basic requirements for almost unlimited growth." One of these, according to the commissioners, is "abundant" water.

The illusion of abundance is everywhere. In the early morning, before the sun gets up too far in the sky, the people of Hanford arise and go forth to their green lawns to uncoil the hoses, set the sprinklers, and turn on the taps. Soon the city is showered and scrubbed and the air is spiced with the sweet smell of grass after rain. In the fields beyond the city, long jets of water spurt from the nozzles of pump-fed irrigators, tracing arcs that sparkle in the sun. The canals and the ditches run full toward Armona and Lemoore. Anyone can see for himself this prodigious use of water because it is out in the open. It is on the surface, and one may assume that what one sees on the surface is all there is to see. One may also assume that prodigious use is somehow evidence of abundance. After all, it is a free country, especially for economic developers. The laws prohibiting myopia haven't been written yet.

Gerald Schumacher is director of the Kings County Water District, which embraces 143,000 acres in the county's northeast corner and supplies to its members groundwater from 350 operating wells. Schumacher's water is not on the surface. In fact, over the years he has been digging deeper and deeper beneath the surface to get it. I asked him to explain the problem.

"It's very simple," he said. "There's more acreage under irrigation. And the intensity of farming practices has increased. The family farms have been selling out to the big operators, who can afford deep wells, and the big operators are shifting to crops requiring more water. When you were here back in the Fifties, wheat and alfalfa were the leaders. Now it's cotton, and cotton can require as much as two more feet of water to the acre."

Schumacher picked up a blackboard pointer and went to the wall behind his desk. He directed my attention to a sequence of charts, done up in red and green tints. "These are groundwater analyses," he said. "They go back to 1940. You can see what's been happening. Look at the green. That's the hundred-foot lift line. That's where you have to go down a hundred feet or more to reach groundwater. Now in each decade shown here, you see the green blob growing larger. Here it is, then, coming in from the southeast. And here it is in 1970. We're mining it too fast. We're not giving it a chance to recharge."

"It looks like a Rorschach series," I said. "What do you see in those blobs?"

"What I see," said Schumacher, "are the jaws of a shark."

The Environmental Resources Management Element of the Kings County General Plan is an unusual document—unusual in that one does not readily expect to encounter realism at any official level in a county whose Economic Development Commission, with apparent impunity, promotes the impossible dream of unlimited growth. Planners, of course, as opposed to developers, are radical by nature. Some of them had long hair even before long hair became fashionable. And I suspect that nearly all of them spend their evenings reading wild books instead of sitting in front of television sets watching the burning of Los Angeles. One planner in Kings County evidently spent a few evenings reading the works of John Muir, an incurable radical. The inside front cover of the Environmental Element carries Muir's great pronunciamento on ecology: *When we try to pick up anything by itself we find it attached to everything in the universe.* After which, citing critical resource shortfalls, the Element goes on to say that, when we try to pick all the groundwater out of the aquifers under Kings County, Kings County is hell-for-sure up buffalo chip creek without a paddle, plain and simple.

According to the Element, groundwater extraction is the difference between total demand and surface supplies—that is, what rain clouds, rivers, and canals can't deliver, you pump from the ground. In 1970, groundwater extraction in Kings County totaled more than 400,000 acre-feet, almost a foot of water for every irrigated acre in the county. By 1990, county planners estimate the groundwater draft will increase to 680,000 acre-feet. And the wells, perforce, will have to go deeper. "Although the aquifers in the valley have a tremendous water-holding capacity," the Element warns, "extensive pumping has caused some areas in the County to experience a drop in groundwater levels of up to fifty feet in a single year."

Aquifers, unfortunately, do not respect geopolitical boundaries; and so, when we try to pick up Kings by itself we find it attached to the Tulare Basin Hydrologic Area, which also includes Fresno, Tulare, and Kern counties. The farmers of Fresno, Tulare, and Kern counties have wells, too, and there are no pikers among them when it comes to extracting groundwater. But now there are these long-haired planners saying that the ground can render only so much water— saying, more specifically, that the safe groundwater yield of the entire Tulare Basin Hydrologic Area is only 600,000 acre-feet a year. Not just for one county; for *four* counties. And they are noting that since Kings County accounts for

16 percent of the Basin's irrigated acreage, its fair share of the safe groundwater yield should be about 98,000 acre-feet—not the 400,000 it is taking now and most certainly not the 680,000 it may be counting on in 1990.

The Environmental Element, with its serious warnings of a groundwater overdraft, had already received wide distribution when I arrived in Hanford last time out. Making the rounds of official agencies, I expected to be told that a state of emergency had been declared, that some bold and daring strategy would soon be announced, like rationing, with padlocks on well heads and meters on pumps. Instead, I discovered that the only course of action on which everyone agreed was that Kings County should import huge additional quantities of surface water. From where? Why, from the River of the Holy Kings, of course. From the Eel and the Klamath and the Mad. From anywhere and everywhere, more water. More dams. More tunnels. More irrigated acres. More intensive practices. More cotton. More cows. More money. To be sure, a few water managers like Schumacher would use the additional flow to recharge the thirsty aquifers. But most would use it to make more things grow bigger and better and faster than ever before.

At the Kings County Planning Department, I talked with a young man who had worked on the Environmental Element. His name was Hardisty. "Don't people around here take the groundwater situation seriously?" I asked. "Don't they know there has to be a limit?"

"Some know it," said Hardisty. "But *some* isn't enough." And then he said something that suddenly reminded me of silt and stalactites and the man upstream from PG&E. He said: "The trouble is, people just can't believe that the aquifers could run dry in their lifetimes."

I asked Ernest Eaton of the Soil Conservation Service how he felt about that. "It's going to happen, all right, and sooner than most people think," Eaton said. "I'm just sorry I won't be around to see it, because when it does happen, this valley's going to be one helluva beautiful place. If you like deserts."

Soluble salts are present in all soils, but more so in some than in others; more so, for example, in the soils of the San Joaquin Valley. Where rainfall is insufficient to leach the salts from the soil and carry them by stream to the sea—as in Kings County—a white crust of alkali may form on the earth such that nothing will grow. Not even a weed. And so those who wish to make productive use of the soil are obliged, periodically, to flood it with water. As the water drains down through the soil, it leaches the old salt to a level below the root zone of crops. The more salt you have, the more water you must use to keep the salt below that zone. But there is a catch, for it is also true that the more water you use, the more salts you must ultimately dispose of—with more water. Even the freshest water is not wholly salt free. The minute it starts moving over rocks and soil on its way from here to there, water picks up salt. An acre-foot arriving in Kings County can contain up to 300 pounds of salt. So if more salt demands more water, more water will ultimately result in more salt. Some times, some places, you just can't win.

George Ferry was talking now. He is the University of California agricultural extension agent in Hanford. His specialty is salt, and he believes that the presence of salt is inhibiting the full capacity of the San Joaquin Valley to grow crops. "We have to flush it out," he told me. "We need a drainage system to carry off the saline water after leaching. And if we don't get a system, we're going to salt out." How soon? "Anywhere from twenty to two hundred years." The system Ferry favors, as do most of his valley colleagues, is a proposed 280-mile sewer called the San Joaquin Master Drain. At full load, the Drain would collect nearly 400,000 acre-feet of waste water annually and transport it north to the San Joaquin-Sacramento Delta and San Francisco Bay.

Predictably, not all Californians are in agreement as to the benefits of constructing a San Joaquin Master Drain. San Franciscans and north coast folk are especially dubious. For them, it is one thing to share their wet mountain waters with the farmers of the dry San Joaquin, but quite another to have some of that water come back later in second-hand condition, laden, as it would be, with dissolved salts, nitrogen fertilizers, and organophosphate pesticides. The nutrients, some critics have pointed out, could bring eutrophication to the Delta. The salts could upset its delicate estuarine balance of fresh and saline water. And the pesticides could deliver massive punishment to the marine life of San Francisco Bay. As one observer described it, the Drain, if built, would be nothing less than California's *Cloaca Maxima*.

George Ferry dismissed these objections. "All this concern for the Delta is ridiculous," he said. "The Delta is a mosquito factory." However relevant that may be, the voices of restraint so far have prevailed, and the Drain now only simmers on the back burners of the California Department of Water Resources and the United States Bureau of Reclamation, its sponsoring agencies. Both are biding their time. "The Vietnam war," said George Ferry, "slowed down the momentum of water development in this country. And the environmental movement stepped into the gap. Well, there's a saying that those with clout get what they can for as long as they can. And I have a feeling that it will soon be agriculture's time once again."

Among the many water development proposals brewing, like the Master Drain, on one back burner or another is a project that would add four new dams to the Kings River and thereby greatly increase its proven capacity to perform work. I had heard rumors of this plan in the mountains, and as I made the rounds in Hanford, the details began to fall into place. I learned, among other things, that the board of directors of the Kings River Conservation District had adopted the following resolution:

> *WHEREAS, Kings River Conservation District is a public district covering approximately 1,100,000 acres located in the Counties of Fresno, Kings and Tulare in the State of California, said area within its boundaries*

being commonly known as the Kings River Service Area; and

WHEREAS, the District . . . entered into a contract with International Engineering Company, Inc., for a comprehensive study of the water problems of the Kings River Service Area and the potential solutions of such problems; and

WHEREAS, such study will include and encompass studies of the availability and feasibility of additional storage on Kings River and the potential for power development at various locations on said River or its tributaries, including but not limited to Dinkey Creek, Rodgers Crossing, Mill Creek, Pine Flat and Piedra; and

WHEREAS, it is deemed to be in the best interests of the District and the inhabitants thereof that in conjunction with said overall study, this District file an application to the Federal Power Commission for a preliminary permit covering the study of potential power development at said sites and the feasibility thereof;

NOW, THEREFORE, BE IT RESOLVED that Kings River Conservation District execute and file with the Federal Power Commission an application for preliminary permit . . . .

Said preliminary permit having been granted, the Kings River Conservation District and the International Engineering Company are now embarked on a five-year study. Their goal is to justify the impoundment in new reservoirs of one million acre-feet of water—nearly as much as is now contained at Courtright, Wishon, and Pine Flat; and to extract from that water, as it falls from dam to tunnel to penstock to turbine, the power of 475,000 horses—more energy than PG&E harnesses on the North Fork, without Helms. About 11,000 acres of Sierra and Sequoia national forests would fall within the project's boundaries. Exactly how many of those acres would be flooded behind dams is not yet known, although just one reservoir, on Mill Creek, is expected to have a surface area of 2,650 acres.

The Kings River Conservation District is managed by practical men who know that such a prize will not be won easily.
They understand the environmental movement still has clout,
that the kind of people who can delay, or possibly even defeat, construction of a San Joaquin Master Drain are also
fully capable of delaying or defeating further development of
the Kings River. So they are going about their business in a
very quiet, professional way, not saying too much, keeping
their chins tucked close to their chests as they listen politely
to consultants who have been retained to anticipate the impact of more dams on the river. Are the managers worried?
A little, perhaps. But I do not believe that men and women
who must measure water by the acre-foot can afford much
personal fuss over what an afterbay to regulate irrigation-
releases at Piedra might do to one of the best stretches of
trout-fishing water in Central California. I expect that J.G.
Boswell and all the others who are growing cotton and such
on the flats once known as Tulare Lake will only remember
the floods of 1969, when a snowpack two-and-a-half times
deeper and wetter than normal came roaring down the staircase of the Kings. Even the dam at Pine Flat failed to hold
all that water, and it spilled out across the valley, drowning
cotton and barley and melons, inflicting $30 million in agri-
cultural losses on Kings County alone. These are the things
the farmers will remember when there is talk of a new dam
600 feet high at Rodgers Crossing, with the canyon behind
it six miles long and wide enough to store up 200 billion
gallons of runoff. These are the things that count for the
people of the valley—not the fact that the Kings above
Rodgers Crossing is a Class VI whitewater stream, or that
back toward Garlic Falls you can watch eagles and falcons
and maybe a condor now and then high above its canyon
roost, or that the North Kings deer herd has dwindled to a
precious few and in all likelihood will not survive the loss of
any additional stream-bank habitat. O, yes—it will be too bad
about the kayaks and the condors and the deer. No question
about that. In wildness is the preservation of the world and
all that sort of thing, and three hearty cheers for John Muir

and Henry David Thoreau. But men must be about their business, and the business of the Kings is food and fiber. And kilowatts.

"Why kilowatts?" I asked an official in Hanford familiar with the plan. "I can understand the part about water storage, but where does an association of farmers get off selling electricity?"

The official leaned back in his chair and smiled. "You are missing the whole point," he said. "The water these dams will impound is a drop in the bucket. But spin the turbines in the bottom of the bucket and you have a commodity that is worth a great deal of money. We will sell our kilowatts to public utilities. Then we will use the revenues to buy more water."

"From northern California?"

"That's for starters," he said. "The amount of water that's going to waste in the Pacific is criminal. Why, do you know that 140 million acre-feet goes out the mouth of the Columbia every year?"

No, I said, I didn't.

"Well," said the official, "doesn't it seem only logical that we should be able to put some of that water to good use?"

From Hanford, I drove out across the valley toward Kettleman City and the golden hills of the Westside. This had been rough country once, good only for cows and alfalfa. But now the aqueduct carrying water from the north was turning the panoche and lethent clays green with summer crops of okra and cucumbers and eggplant and safflower and water melons. The sun was hot. The land shimmered at the edge of the sky.

I turned off the highway and followed a dirt road into the hills to a place where you can look back across the full width of the valley. I had been here once on a day so clear the view extended to the frosted escarpment of the High Sierra; but this time the mountains were lost in a pulsing gray mist. The valley rolled on vaguely without limit. I got out of the car and walked. I began to wonder about those people out there in their small towns and large associations trading water entitlements like stocks and bonds, and the pumps humming at the well heads and the turbines spinning, and the runoff rising slowly behind rock-fill dams, and the salt of the earth coming down the ditches 300 pounds to the acre-foot. I remembered what the river and the valley of the Kings had been like nearly two decades earlier; I wondered what they would be like two decades hence. Would there be new dams at Piedra and Dinkey Creek and Rodgers Crossing? Probably. And would that be the end of it? Probably not. Men and women would be about their business yet. And after they had tamed the Kings' horses at Piedra and Rodgers Crossing, they would surely be into Dusy Creek below Hot Springs Pass. And then Bench Valley, right up to the Roman Four. And when even these proved insufficient, there would be Blackcap Basin, waiting to be filled with water to the 9,000-foot contour of Reinstein Peak. Why not? Why not flood the wild useless country beyond the Le Conte Divide? Why not turn the entire Evolution Valley into a reservoir for water siphoned from the Eel, Klamath, Trinity, Rogue, and Columbia, with a giant pumped-storage plant reamed into the bowels of Mt. Goddard, so that more kilowatts could be traded for dollars to purchase more water? And in my mind's eye I saw the green valley turning white with salt until it glittered in the sun as brightly as the snow-capped mountains. It was, as Ernest Eaton put it, one helluva beautiful sight. If you like deserts.

"They Drive Cars, Don't They?"

Interstate Five skewers some lonely country on its way from Stockton to Los Angeles. On the long middle stretch there are no towns to speak of for 150 miles, except for Three Rocks, Avenal, Lost Hills, and Kettleman City. I don't know much about the others, but as for Kettleman City, it is a good thing the highway came along when it did. The highway has put Kettleman City, with its convenient gasoline stations, back on the map; and it is said there hasn't been so much action since before the oil wells went dry in the hills behind town in the 1950s. So here is a town that Crude built, subsisting in its old age on the retail proceeds from refined tetraethyl. Almost every stranger who drives into town has the same curt comment. What do they all say? What else *is* there to say but "fill 'er up"?

"All the way?" asked the young man at the pump.

"All the way," I said. "And while you're at it, check the oil."

While he was at it, he also checked the stranger. "Visiting," he asked, "or just passing through?"

"A little of both," I said. "I'm looking for a place that used to be known as Milham City."

"Never heard of it."

"No reason you should have," I said; and adopting the approach of my metaphysical New York colleague, I quickly added, "since, as a matter of fact, it never really existed."

The attendant pulled his head out from under the hood and straightened up with a series of quick torso rolls, like a fighter warming up in his corner. His eyes were wary. "Well, then," he said, "what's the point of going?"

"To see what happens to people's dreams," I said. "They were going to build a big city. Boom town. They only got as far as the hotel. At least, there were the foundations of a hotel back in the Fifties."

"Where?"

"I've forgotten. Not far from here. Just off the road from Hanford, I think. I was there once."

"Nothing but a hotel, huh?"

"Foundations," I said.

"Then how come you call it a city?"

"Someone else called it a city. I didn't. How come you call *this* a city?"

The young man closed the hood of the car. "I don't call this nothing," he said. "I just work here."

My recollection of the details of the Milham oil discovery of 1928 is sketchy. Some musty volume once revealed them to me, but now, in the little library at Kettleman City, I could find only a passing reference to Milham, to his wildcat operation, to his dream of creating a new town that would outshine and outlast Kettleman and Coalinga and Taft and all the other viscous villages that were then prospering with development of oil fields in the hills of the Westside. I did find a map, yellowed and dog-eared, and there was Milham City sure enough, all laid out on a neat grid, with the streets already named, about three miles northeast of Kettleman City. And I remembered having read how, after the first big gushers came in, a syndicate had taken space in the Los Angeles newspapers, touting the glorious opportunities of Milham City and the fantastic bargains to be had in the purchase of land there. To house and entertain their prospective customers, the promoters had planned an elaborate hotel at the townsite. I am not sure whether the edifice was ever completed, but the foundations were laid. They were there yet in the mid-Fifties, cracked with weather and age, rising like some half-finished fortification from a field of wild grasses. The syndicate apparently had not considered the possibility that the accessible deposits of oil in the Kettleman Hills might soon run dry, or that the prosperity of the Twenties might shortly collapse under the weight of a national depression.

Out Highway 41 and then north on Quail Avenue along the foot of the hills, I kept looking for landmarks to guide me to the ruins. I looked in particular for the old water tank I had once climbed to obtain a better view, but it was gone. The only structures of any height out there were the steel towers supporting the power lines that parallel Interstate Five down the length of the valley. On either side of the road, fields of ripe barley rippled in the wind, not the wild rangeland I remembered. Water from the north had changed all that. I turned the car back toward Highway 41. A short distance down the road I noticed piles of earth at the edge of the barley, the kind of piles you see around demolition sites. Mixed with the earth were slabs of broken concrete. So there it was. How sensible: the foundations demolished to make way for something more profitable than history and grass. Now there was nothing left of Milham's great dream except the dog-eared map in the Kettleman City library.

Returning through town on my way west to Santa Maria that afternoon, I stopped and told the librarian of my discovery. "They've put the first and last of Milham City under barley," I said. "For history's sake you'd better hang on to that map."

"I will," she said. "And isn't the barley beautiful this time of year?"

Oil. I never thought much about it when I was tooting around Central California as a cub reporter. To tell the truth, I never thought much about it at all, except for the stuff that spilled out of tankers and offshore wells. I didn't have time to think about oil until the winter of 1974. Then I had plenty of time to think about it, along with everyone else owning an automobile, as I waited in line down the street from the gas pumps; and when I got to the pump I didn't dare say "fill 'er up" because, for a while, the limit was five dollars. Under normal circumstances five dollars *would* have filled 'er up. But that was the kind of normalcy which prevailed before American petroleum executives decided that if the Saudis could live like sheiks, why shouldn't they?

I didn't think a lot about it then, but I certainly heard about it, especially in Santa Maria, where, as it happened, some of my best friends had been oilmen. Well, not exactly. Oil geologists. The finger-men of the whole messy business. We used to meet them in a little place off Broadway where everyone assembled for coffee at ten o'clock in the morning. There were always two or three of them. I forget their names, except for one with whom I have stayed in touch over the years; and since we are still friends, for present purposes I shall forget his name, too. Besides, he is out of the messy business, now a professor of geology in Oregon, and I happen to know that he loves trees and clean beaches and no longer believes that in Crude is the preservation of the world.

They were a serious bunch, those geologists. They meant business, and since their business was finding new sources of oil for a competitive market, they were reluctant to discuss their work with the press, however friendly and disinterested. You would come upon them at their booth in the hash house and they would scoop up their field notes, like kids retrieving dirty pictures at the approach of a priest. What might have been an intense discussion of a specific syncline would suddenly become innocent chitchat, and "pass the sugar please" was repeated so regularly on such occasions that I am sure it was code for "shut up" to those whose backs were to the door.

"Hear you guys have been up to Cuyama," George Jones would bluff. Jones, the wire editor. My beatnik friend from San Bruno who worshipped Kerouac and confounded readers of his occasional column with tales of rhinoceros-like monsters and fictitious Greek poets frequenting the then-lonely dunes at Nipomo. Jones, who cloaked his own personal intensity with whimsy and fun. The geologists didn't like him.

"Who says we've been up to Cuyama?"

Jones was a master of the straight-faced put-on. "It's all over town," he said. "They're saying you got a new field up there."

"You're crazy, Jones."

"Well, anyway, we got the story," he said and turned to me for confirmation of the lie. "Right?"

"That's right," I said.

"You're both crazy."

"It's plain as day you've been to Cuyama," said Jones. "And I can prove it."

"So prove it," said the geologist with the Stanford crewcut.

"That your jeep parked outside?" said Jones. The geologists nodded. "Well, I hate to tell you but the tires are covered with red mud. And red mud's Cuyama."

The one with the crewcut slid out of the booth and through the door. In a moment he was back, scowling. "You're off your rocker, Jones," he said. "Those tires are clean as a whistle."

"Aha," Jones said. "That proves it right there. Now the question is, why *are* the tires clean? And the answer, if I may be allowed to supply it, is because you washed them. Right? To obliterate traces of red Cuyama clay. Right?"

"As a matter of fact, wrong," said one of the geologists. "We've been down to Santa Barbara."

"There's oil in Santa Barbara?" asked Jones.

"You're getting warmer," another geologist said. "Let's say there's plenty of oil. If you don't mind getting your feet wet."

This was in 1957, and though we didn't know it at the time—and wouldn't have cared much if we had—the big oil companies were scrambling for their pieces of action in the Santa Barbara Channel. It would be another ten years before the federal government began granting leases to drill wells into the outer continental shelf; twelve years until the floor of the ocean would buckle around Union Oil Company's Platform A, spewing forth three million gallons of Crude to stain fifty miles of beachfront, to kill God only knows how many creatures that squirm or wiggle or spread their wings at the edge of the sea.

Most of our other friends in Santa Maria that year seemed to be Air Force professionals, transferred out from Redstone Arsenal and Cape Canaveral to convert an old army stockade and armor training center, down the coast between Casmalia and Lompoc, into a launching pad for intercontinental ballistic missiles. The place is called Vandenberg Air Force Base today, but we knew it then as Camp Cooke. The airmen liked martinis. So did the geologists. So did George Jones. So, what else was there to do? We had a party.

For openers, it was dreadful, as most cocktail parties tend to be. There was Texaco at one end of the room. There was the Air Force at the other: two majors, a captain and three wives. And there was Jones on his best behavior, shuttling back and forth with a voluminous pitcher of Six-to-Ones. After half an hour, the opposing camps advanced. The missile gap had been bridged by the martini.

"It's madness," one of the geologists was saying some time later. His elbow was crooked on the mantlepiece.

The major was sitting on the arm of a stuffed chair and his

eyelids were heavy. "I really don't think it's that bad," he said. "You're talking about a one-in-a-million probability."

"The hell I am," said the geologist. "I'm talking about you guys shooting missiles over the most valuable oil find in the West. And that's a risk that shouldn't be taken."

The major closed his eyes and took a deep breath. "Wait," he said, and the eyes popped open to see Jones approaching with the pitcher. He extended his glass. "Let's take this one step at a time," he said. "In the first place, nobody's drilling much out there in the channel."

"But they will be," said the geologist.

"In the second place, our launches will be to the west and north. Without warheads. You talk as if we're going to be shooting live stuff."

"What about San Nicolas Island?" said the geologist.

"That's a Navy operation," the major said. "Regulus guided missiles. Buzz bombs from Point Mugu to San Nicolas. That's something altogether different."

"Still," the geologist persisted, "one of those babies can go down in the drink and it's whamo. It would crack a pipeline. Have you ever dropped a cherry-bomb in a bathtub?"

The major closed his eyes again. "No," he said. "Have you ever found a needle in a haystack?"

"The thing you're missing here," said the geologist, "is that you guys need that oil. You can't get off the ground without it."

"We'll get off the ground with liquid oxygen, mostly. And a little kerosene, I suppose."

"Okay," the geologist said. "I don't care whether it's you and the ICBM or some admiral and the Regulus. There's a shelf out there that's full of oil and in a few years the industry is going to be drilling the bejezus out of it. There'll be platforms and pipelines from Anacapa all the way to Point Conception."

"Be our guest," said the major, and now his eyes were wide and clear and he was standing. "But let me give you a word of advice. I don't know much about geology, but I know enough to say that if you're really going to drill for

oil in that ocean then you'd better stop fretting about mis-
guided missiles and start worrying about rocks."

"What d'ya mean, rocks?"

"I mean there aren't any," said the major. "I mean you're
going to be punching holes in the sand. I mean the shelf under the Santa Barbara Channel is porous. I mean, once you
drill the well, can you contain the oil?"

The geologist laughed. "We know all that," he said. "What
d'ya think we are? A bunch of amateurs?"

Jones was standing by with an empty pitcher. "Who could
possibly think that?" he said. "But all the same, isn't it funny
you asked?"

That afternoon in Santa Maria brings to mind another discussion of oil years later in San Francisco. There were three of
us—strangers—in the bar of the Palace Hotel, and as men
alone at bars are wont to do, we were soon exchanging casual
observations on this and that, including the unusual density
of the evening fog. One of the gentlemen was an engineer.
He was on his way to Korea for the Bechtel Corporation, to
build a fertilizer factory near Seoul. The other was a petroleum geologist (yes, another geologist) for the Standard Oil
Company of California. "And what's your line?" the engineer
inquired of me across the corner of the bar.

"You've got me outnumbered," I said, explaining that I
did some writing and editing now and then for the Sierra
Club.

It was pleasant enough. They wanted to talk about *ecology*. The man from Standard Oil especially wanted to know
how I felt about the proposed Trans-Alaskan oil pipeline.

"I don't like it very much," I said.

"Do you really feel the pipeline will interfere with caribou
migrations?" asked the engineer.

"I don't know," I said. "Some people think it might. But
it's not the pipe that worries me as much as the delivery by
tanker down the coast."

"But that's the easiest part of it," said the man from
Standard Oil.

"Not the way I hear it," I said. "Those are treacherous waters south of Valdez."

"And you're worried about spills," said the engineer.

"You bet I am."

"Well, sure we have to worry about spills," said the oil-man. "We've all been worrying since the *Torrey Canyon.* We've been worrying so much we've got the margin of risk down next to nothing. We've got the kind of technology now that makes it possible to say that kind of thing will never happen again."

I said nothing. You cannot argue with certitude. The talk shifted to other things. And even as we sat there in the Palace Hotel, a tanker under lease to the Standard Oil Company of California was slipping through the fog beneath the Golden Gate Bridge, bearing a cargo of oil on a collision course with the freighter *Name Tokum.* And at precisely 1:08 A.M., January 11, 1971, the impossible happened. I learned about it on television the next morning, and that afternoon I watched volunteers on the beach in Pacifica sponging the goo into beer cartons. I had wanted to telephone regards to my friend at Standard Oil, to tell him what a small world this surely must be. I couldn't reach him. His phone was busy all day.

Santa Maria was not the town I remembered. The small Victorian house on South McClelland Street, where Jones had helped the major across the oil gap, was long gone, replaced by an awesome medical building which smelled of ether even from the sidewalk. The hash house off Broadway where we bedeviled the Texaco finger-men was gone, too. The town had grown up, split its britches and spilled out into the countryside. The industrial park was bustling with a dozen light manufacturing plants, and out at the brand-new airport there was jet service to San Francisco and Los Angeles three times a day. I stopped by the newspaper plant on West Main, the *Times,* with its red tile roof and fine Spanish arches. A few months later I would have found it empty and boarded up, for even the paper was moving on to bigger and better things.

"It's all happening right here," said a *Times*man I remembered from my own days. "Take what there was when you were here and multiply by two. And that's what we've got."

"That's quite a lot," I said. "Are you sure you can handle it?"

"You bet we can," he said, "Except for the traffic, maybe."

"Getting bad?"

"Getting so bad some days you'd swear you were down in Los Angeles."

"One solution to that," I said, "is another energy crunch."

"Oh, that," he said. "It barely touched us here. We had plenty of gas."

"You did?"

"The whole thing was a hoax. Why hell, there's oil to burn in this country if only we'll tap it."

"There is?"

"Now that they've got the go-ahead on Alaska, all they have to do is open up those new offshore deposits down south."

"After what happened at Santa Barbara? You think people in Santa Monica and Palos Verdes and all those other towns are going to stand for that?"

"They've got no choice," he said. "They drive cars, don't they?"

I was turning that conversation over in my mind later as I drove north on the freeway toward Avila Beach. Near Pismo, I pulled off for gas. A grease monkey came to the window. "What can we do you for?" he asked.

I said: "Fill 'er up." Dammit.

Your Friendly Nuclear Neighbor

According to the Pacific Gas and Electric Company, one of the brightest tourist attractions on the entire central coast of California is the company's Nuclear Information Center near Avila Beach—that and the 2.2-million-kilowatt powerplant at the mouth of Diablo Canyon. Some people are easy to please.

It was a fine spring day when I stopped by there, heading north. The parking lot was filled with cars, many from out-of-state, and a company jitney waited in front of the large ranch-style building, ready to shuttle the next load of sight-seers out to the canyon. I went inside and registered for the trip.

"There's a briefing film first," said the receptionist. "We'll be starting in a few minutes."

While I waited for the curtain to go up, I wandered down the hall into a museum-like room filled with models of pow-erplants and cross-sections of generators, with charts and graphs and larger-than-life photographs of flora and fauna. Perhaps my first impression was mistaken, but for all the technology on display, I had a distinct feeling that PG&E was trying hard to appear to be selling ecology along with its electricity. In one of the windows a sign proclaimed:

> *The life of Diablo Cove . . . (a) pageant older than Man, goes on unharmed and abiding in its perpetual pace through time, close alongside its nuclear neighbor.*

Another visual display announced that the "powerful instal-lation will operate in complete harmony with the natural life." And a third, poetically describing the ancient oaks and "ferny glens" of Diablo Canyon, promised that these, too, would continue "undisturbed by their friendly nuclear neigh-bor." Suddenly I felt warm and safe, for it was good to be assured of such things and to know that, whatever others might say about nuclear radiation and thermal pollution, PG&E had the situation well in hand. Howdy, neighbor.

Then the lights were growing dim in the screening room, the projector was whirring behind our heads, and here came Eeyore, straight out of *Winnie the Pooh,* exclaiming in full animation: "It won't work!" And as quickly as he said it, so help me, there was a failure in the sound track. The image on the screen stuttered and vanished. We sat in the darkness, waiting. "How's that for perfect timing?" said a woman somewhere in front of me.

"Is there more?" someone inquired of the darkness.

The lights went on and a man in a blue blazer, looking official and apologetic, slipped past us into the projection booth. "We'll be with you in a second," he said over his shoulder. The second turned into minutes. Finally, the man reappeared and stood smiling before us. "The projector," he said, "is not cooperating. Why don't you all go out to the bus now. We'll have it fixed up by the time you get back from the site."

We filed into the jitney and our cheerful guide took us away, out past the sailboats and cabin cruisers moored at Avila, and up the seaward shoulder of the San Luis Range. As we climbed, I looked across the great crescent of Avila Bay to the white dunes at Nipomo, where PG&E had originally planned to locate its powerplant, where persuasive arguments had been advanced against doing so, and where defenders of the dunes even now were caught up in another struggle to restrict proliferating abuse by off-road vehicles. In Santa Maria, I had heard that as many as 50,000 people were expected in the dunes over the coming Memorial Day weekend. Fifty thousand people—and God only knows how many trail-bikes, motorcycles, beach buggies, Winnebagoes. O, for another George Jones at the *Santa Maria Times*, conjuring up rhinoceros-like monsters from the turgid depths of Oso Flaco Lake. Punitive monsters to fit the crime. Monsters especially partial to high-traction tires, crash helmets and leather jackets. *Bon appetit.* And on to Diablo.

A lusty wind was blowing off the ocean when we arrived at the powerplant. Our guide parked the jitney at an overlook some 300 feet up the slope of Green Peak. Directly below us an escarpment covered with wild mustard plunged to the mouth of the canyon, or, rather, to what used to be the mouth of the canyon. The guide explained everything. That big brown structure, he said, housed the turbines. It was 740 feet long. Nearly two and a half football fields. And those two great domes? Those were the reactor containments, three and a half feet thick, reinforced concrete with vapor-proof steel liners underneath. The domes were 216 feet high. The switchyards would be located up the canyon. The outflow for the cooling waters would be aimed toward Diablo Rock, an eighth of a mile offshore, where the sea lions like to sun themselves. The first generator would be in operation in 1975. The second in 1976. Right now, this was the largest private construction project in the whole state of California. The fuel? Uranium-235. No, not fusion. That was still in the future. This was fission. Safe? Absolutely. Not a chance in the world. Any other questions? *Please, someone. Ask him a question? Ask him why the reactor at San Onofre had to be shut down. Ask him about the fish slaughter at the Indian Point reactor in New York. Stop staring at those concrete basketballs and ask him . . . .* No questions.

In the jitney, on our return, the woman across the aisle turned to the man she was with and said, "And you chose *this* over Hearst Castle?"

I am sorry to say that I missed the film. The projector was repaired when we arrived back at the Nuclear Information Center, and another showing was scheduled. But it was late and I had far to go. So I settled instead for a quick verbal summary of what Eeyore had been up to when, on the faltering sound track, he exclaimed: "It won't work!"

Eeyore, it turned out, had been up to no good. I might have suspected as much. Eeyore was one of those negative thinkers, the kind who say it can never be done. The kind who told Columbus that the earth was flat. The kind who laughed at Einstein. The kind who predicted that man would never travel faster than twenty-five miles per hour. The kind who say, or so I gather by implication, that PG&E cannot safely and in harmony with nature generate 2.2 million kilowatts of nuclear energy at Diablo Canyon. These are the pestiferous Eeyores of the world. Ah, but there are *Do-ores*, too. Like Columbus. Like Einstein. Like Neil Armstrong, who traveled 25,000 m.p.h. to walk on the moon. Like the nuclear engineers at PG&E, who know how to generate power in a neighborly way. Damn. I am really sorry I missed that film. The synopsis was fascinating.

Yet with all due respect to Columbus and Einstein and Neil Armstrong, each of whom I greatly admire, I am beginning to think now that Eeyore was miscast in PG&E's movie. Eeyore, if you recall your *Pooh*, was a donkey, and a discombobulated one at that. In short, Eeyore was an oaf. Well, now. Those who poohed Columbus and Einstein were oafs as well. I concede that. But what does one make of howdydoodies who promise environmental harmony in one breath and in the next boast of being responsible for the largest private construction project in the state of California—not to mention what is to come when the generators are in full operation? Me, I make Eeyores of them. Oafs. The kind who, as they fumble with the sprockets of their broken projectors, say with certainty that their reactors are foolproof and failure-free. Eeyore. Yes, I can hear him now. He is braying at Neil Armstrong's moon. Echoes are reverberating in my ear. I hear echoes that sound like *it can't happen here.* Eeyore? Is that really you?

Months later. It is Sunday in New York. I am sitting here with the *Times*. I am looking at the front page and my eye stops at this story by David Burnham:

> WASHINGTON, Sept. 21—The Atomic Energy Commission has ordered 21 of 50 nuclear reactors producing commercial electric power in the United States to close down within the next 60 days to determine whether cracks are developing in the pipes of their cooling systems.
>
> Meanwhile, a leading nuclear safety expert announced he was quitting his job with the commission "in order to be free to tell the American people about the potentially dangerous conditions in the nation's nuclear power plants."
>
> Carl J. Hocevar . . . said in his letter of resignation . . . "In spite of the soothing reassurances that the A.E.C. gives to the uninformed, misled public, unresolved questions about nuclear power safety are so grave that the

United States should consider a complete halt to nuclear power plant construction while we see if these serious questions can, somehow, be resolved . . . .

And I see here, in the small type at the end of the story, that among the public utilities ordered to close down one or more of their reactors is the Pacific Gas and Electric Company of California.

Middens

I saw it first from the air. We were following the coastline north, heading for redwood country in a small plane under charter to *Newsweek*, when the pilot brought us in under low clouds. We made one circling pass, saw the village at the edge of the bay, the fleet of fishing boats, the access road crossing the mudflats on rock fill, the soft green slope of the headland rising, and then, at last, the great white crater itself, yawning like an open grave. "There's your *Hole in the Head*," the pilot shouted over full throttle as we pulled away. "How do you like it?" We said we liked it fine: empty. "I hope they don't fill it in," said the photographer aboard. "Having it there sort of gives you a sense of history."

That was the first time. I had no expectation, then, that I might ever return to Bodega—I mean to be *there* and not over it—for the story of the Hole in the Head had already been told. And when you mentioned Bodega in faraway places, people conversant with current events would know you were talking not only about a location where Alfred Hitchcock filmed *The Birds*, but also of the place where Pacific Gas and Electric Company blew $4 million trying to anchor a nuclear powerplant to the quake zone of the San Andreas Fault.

My work brought me to California frequently after that, and since Bodega is only fifty miles from San Francisco, I did return. The right way. It may have happened that I returned too often for my own good, for I became obsessed with the place. At first, Bodega was where I retreated, intending to accomplish Great Things, to read the galley proofs overdue at the printer's, to finish the draft I had not yet begun, to answer the mail that remained unopened. The attaché case always bulged with the weight of *important* projects. But I rarely unburdened it in Bodega. With its window on the sea and its back to the stark chameleon hills of the Sonoma County coast, Bodega refused to inspire conventional productivity. I found no garret there, no cell in which to work off my debts and obligations. I found only the wind and the headlands plunging to the wild surf, and the changing light on the hills, and the ryegrass growing at the crater's edge, and the pelicans flying. I am not so sure I discovered a sense of history in Bodega. I may have done better than that. I may have discovered something that is closer to a sense of truth.

The name Bodega is used loosely, as it should be. That is, in referring to *Bodega* I do not mean the town of Bodega, which is inland some four miles from the sea. I mean the town of Bodega Bay, Bodega Head (where the Hole is), and that ragged stretch of shore running north through Salmon Creek and Portuguese Beach and Shell Beach almost to Jenner, at the mouth of the Russian River. To me, this is Bodega. My apologies to those who interpret maps more precisely.

The town is the least of it. The houses are strung out along the highway and they are without distinction. There are a couple of motels, three restaurants, two gas stations, a fire house, a post office, a fish market, a supermarket, and a real estate office or two. Not to mention the sales emporium of Bodega Harbour, where 1,630 half-acre lots are being peddled on the promise that this is "California's Cape Cod." Cape Cod? Who needs Cape Cod in Northern California? Cape Cod Go Home. There is also Sereno del Mar, another subdivision. The last I heard, sales had slowed down at Bodega Harbour and Sereno del Mar: tight money, septic tank problems, and an uncompromising Coastal Commission, bless them one and all. There is hope for the real Bodega yet. The real Bodega does very nicely with a population of 700. It needs 5,000 like it needs a Hole in its Head. Like PG&E needs the San Andreas Fault.

The bay at Bodega, protected by the Head on the west and

by the slender sandspit of Doran Park on the south, is said to be the safest harbor of refuge between San Francisco and Coos Bay, Oregon. It is also one of the last resorts of a dying American industry, commercial fishing. One way or another, about a quarter of Bodega's able-bodied men (and a few salty women now and then) go down to the sea in ships—little ships, about thirty or forty feet long, barely of a size to brave the stern and heavy Pacific swells offshore. The boats go out after Dungeness crab, when they are available, which is not as often as it once was. The fleet also pursues the King salmon, cruising about five to six miles offshore, running up as far as Ft. Bragg or all the way down to Half Moon Bay; two, maybe three, men to each boat, with about six lines running deep, about six leaders to the line, and a herring on every hook. The salmon unlucky enough to be deceived by this arrangement are packed in ice at the fishermen's cooperative, then trucked to the processing plants in Santa Rosa and Sacramento. The fishermen do not earn a great deal of money; in fact, some earn barely enough to keep up their boats. But you know how some men are about the sea. They can't get enough of it.

Unfortunately for the salmon, and for the men of Bodega, there are people all over the world who cannot get enough of the sea. This is especially true of the Russians and the Japanese, who take their commercial fisheries more seriously than we Americans do, and who, in order to get as much of and from the sea as they possibly can, go down to it not in little boats but in huge floating factories. Twelve miles off the coast of Northern California, the Russians and Japanese lower their nets to harvest anchovy. In the process, because of the nature of nets, they also harvest salmon. The fishermen of Bodega Bay are unhappy about this. It isn't that they are prejudiced against Russians and Japanese; it would be the same if the crews of the factory ships were Patagonian or Lapp. The fishermen of Bodega are unhappy because other people are now catching their fish. And they remember what happened to the long-gone sardine industry at Monterey, the Cannery Row of the John Steinbeck novel. Cannery Row today is like a maritime Milham City, with tourists. The fishermen don't want that for Bodega Bay.

People have been digging holes at Bodega for a long time, and for a variety of purposes. For example, the Russians, ancestors of those solemn trawlermen who are lowering their nets out at the edge of the twelve-mile limit. Captain Ivan Kuskoff and a party of Aleut hunters arrived here in 1808, down from the north in search of sea otter and a place to grow crops for the starving colony at Sitka. Fearing the Spanish, the Russians promptly dug a pit for their cannon at the top of Bodega Head. Next, they launched their kayaks and proceeded to extirpate the sea otter. And on the hills behind the harbor, they planted buckwheat and maize, but the crops came to ruin. In 1841, the Russians packed up and sailed away, abandoning a small tannery, a brick kiln, and other assorted artifacts of their brief visit, including the hole at the top of Bodega Head, which soon disappeared under a carpet of fiddleneck and lupine and the guano of seabirds. And all of this was before man split the atom and discovered the San Andreas Fault.

A hundred years or so later came the next significant excavation. This hole was not in the Head. This was an archeological dig, sponsored by the University of California, down near the sandspit where the Olamentko People, a tribe of Miwok Indians, had tended to their own business for some 3,000 years. The business of the Olamentko was survival.

Anthropologists believe the Olamentko had seven villages at one time or another and that five of these were at the edge of Bodega Bay. They tell us the Olamentko were shrewd exploiters of the marine environment. Not only did these people manage to survive very handsomely on "all creatures that swim in the water, all that fly through the air, and all that creep, crawl or walk upon the earth, with perhaps a dozen exceptions," as one researcher noted; they also enhanced their capital worth by recycling to the Pomo Indians, inland, the shells of the Washington clams which they dug from the mudflats of their bay. Clamshells were after-dinner garbage to the Olamentko, but in the villages of the Pomo, clamshells were considered hard cash to the trade. So the Miwok entrepreneurs flourished for three millennia, growing fat by the seashore one season, then walking it off in the next on the overland trek to the Pomo cashiers.

Anthropologists believe the Olamentko flourished for another reason. When one group got angry at another, the dispute was traditionally settled by negotiation and a subsequent exchange of goods. Clamshells, perhaps. Of course, negotiation and reparation did not always succeed, in which case the adversaries went to war with their bows and arrows. The Olamentko made great sport of war. The two sides would confront each other across a considerable distance and, after some foot-stamping and fist-shaking, let fly their arrows. It was a group effort and snipers were not allowed. In other words, it was not fair to aim at anyone. In fact, if you were an Olamentko and wanted to aim at an individual on the other side, you couldn't have hit him in any event—he was too far away. But sometimes one side or another might have a tail wind, and occasionally someone *would* get hit by an arrow. Sometimes, by accident, someone would actually get killed by an arrow. If this happened, even if someone was badly nicked, the warriors on both sides would put away their weapons and go home to dinner. And that would be the end of it. Thus did the Olamentko succeed at the tricky business of survival for 3,000 years, or longer. Who knows? We only know they ceased to survive as a people shortly after the Russian hunters were replaced by American settlers. The Americans finished a job that had begun with the Christian missionaries, who were Spanish and who pitied the Ancient People for their savage and uncivilized ways. The Spanish had syphilis. So did the Americans. And this, too, was before man split the atom.

The hole. Part of what we know about the Olamentko comes from the hole University of California scientists excavated in 1949 near Doran Park. The scientists were trying to discover what the Ancient People ate for supper. They were digging in a good place, straight down through the center of a refuse heap—a midden—that had been used for hundreds of years, as the City of San Francisco once used the wetlands of Brisbane, but for a considerably shorter period of time. Everyone has middens. There is even a midden or two on the moon. However—the hole. It went down thirteen feet. Each one-foot layer came out as a section and was carefully placed on a large tarp, where the scientists sifted the loose material for bits of bone and shell and the like. M.G. Barbour, R.B. Craig, F.R. Drysdale, and M.T. Ghiselin, in an excellent work called *Coastal Ecology: Bodega Head* (Berkeley: University of California Press), report that about a third of the total identifiable material, as one might expect, was shell, and that about one-half of this shell material at every depth sampled was California mussel, which would make that species the hamburger of the Olamentko. In addition, there was evidence of Olympia oyster, bent-nosed clam, Washington clam, turban snail, black chiton, and basket cockle. Other midden digs, the authors report, indicate that the Ancient People also feasted on deer, dolphin, sea otter, double-breasted cormorants, loons, scoters, and Canada geese. Fish bones could not be identified as to species. But it is safe to assume that the keepers of these middens dined on salmon as well. It is also assumed that they balanced this high-protein diet with boiled lupine and roasted bracken. And for some curious reason, all of these harvested species flourished. In the villages of the Olamentko, there were no crop failures or Cannery Rows. And those who said "it can't happen here" were absolutely right. That is, they were right until just about two hundred years ago, until strangers arrived with syphilis and promises of eternal salvation. After that the Olamentko discovered that almost anything could happen, and almost anything did.

To the best of my knowledge, the most ambitious excavation ever undertaken at Bodega was the dig sponsored by the Pacific Gas and Electric Company in the early 1960s. This hole is seventy-two feet deep. The spoil, mainly quartz diorite, came out in giant scoops and was carefully deposited on the mudflats of Bodega Bay, on the ancient clam beds, to facilitate construction of an access road to the site of the powerplant. In this endeavor, PG&E had the support of the Sonoma County Board of Supervisors and a handful of residents who believed the powerplant would improve the area's tax structure and in general be good for business. Many of the fishermen, however, were not convinced that the plant would be good for *their* business, inasmuch as it would suck 250,000 gallons per minute from the Bay and then dump the water, heated some eighteen degrees warmer, into the ocean. Considerable doubts about the plant were also raised by scientists from the University of California, who were then in the process of establishing a marine laboratory at Bodega Head, with the intention of studying a diversity of undisturbed biological habitats. And finally there were those who questioned the powerplant's safety. In a memorable ditty composed for the occasion, one anonymous skeptic asked:

> *The Indians lived on Bodega*
> *Their middens are there by the sea—*
> *The Indians are gone, remembered by song,*
> *Will this happen to you and me?*

> *What will become of Bodega,*
> *Dillon Beach and Tomales Bay,*
> *When PG&E puts their stuff out to sea—*
> *What will happen to you and me?*

The key issue was the San Andreas Fault. PG&E engineers said the plant would be located a mile and a quarter from the fault, and that the reactor would be anchored so firmly in bedrock that it could withstand any earthquake. Seismologists retained by the Northern California Association to Preserve Bodega Head and Harbor arrived at some different conclusions. They found that the reactor would be within a quarter mile of the main fault zone, that as a matter of fact the reactor would sit squarely over a subsidiary fault, and that the bedrock was actually fragmented diorite, not the firm granite that PG&E had claimed for the site. These findings were confirmed later by investigators from the U.S. Geological Survey. And in October 1964, the Atomic Energy

Commission's Division of Reactor Licensing, citing "unproven design measures to cope with forces as great as would be several feet of ground movement . . . in a severe earthquake," concluded that "Bodega Head is not a suitable location for the proposed nuclear powerplant. . . ." With great reluctance, PG&E thereupon retired from the field of battle, leaving the Hole in the Head to mend as best it can under nature's direction. Under nature's direction, the Hole is slowly filling with water. It is a splendid place for scoters and geese.

One cannot do justice to the battle of Bodega without a word or two about Rose Gaffney, who was one of the first to raise the issue of the San Andreas Fault. People in the village who are happy that the Hole in the Head is splendid for fowl instead of Uranium-235 refer to Mrs. Gaffney as a grand old lady. At PG&E, she is remembered as "the witch of Bodega Head."

We were sitting one afternoon in the livingroom of her home at Salmon Creek, and once again she was boiling her enemies in the kettle of logic. "There's been talk of more dredging," she said. "Our bay's already overcrowded and now there's pressure for a new marina. They say the people at Bodega Harbour will want to have boats. I say any more boats and there won't be a bay left to put them in."

Rose Gaffney sat by the window. The afternoon light and interior shadow accentuated the lines in her face. I said I supposed she had seen a lot of change in her time at Bodega.

"Everything changes sooner or later," she said. "Trouble is, it's usually sooner. And not always for the better."

"Has Bodega changed for the worse?"

"If we aren't careful it could go that way."

"Even without PG&E?"

"Oh, that would have been the end," she said. "That would have finished it."

Rose Gaffney, when I called on her, had been a Bodegan for sixty years. At the age of nineteen she had come west with her first husband to work as a milker at a ranch on the Head. Sometime later, her first husband died. Her second

husband was Gaffney, the rancher whose father had pur-
chased the Head in the 1880s, and put the first cows there
to graze. Then Gaffney died, too. Mrs. Gaffney lived at the
ranch on the Head for more than two decades, without neighbors. Then she sold the dairy herd and moved to the mainland. When PG&E began to put its holdings together in the
late 1950s, it discovered that sixty-five of the acres it would
have to acquire belonged to Rose Gaffney; and Rose Gaffney
said, in effect, that she'd be damned if she'd sell them to an
outfit that planned to dig a hole in her Head. Under the laws
of eminent domain, the courts ruled otherwise. Rose Gaffney
got a fair price.

We had been talking for a long time. The light began to
soften in the livingroom. The lines began to soften in her
face. "Do you have time to see my warehouse?" she asked.

"Your warehouse?"

"Of Indian artifacts," she said. "I've got quite a few."

We crossed the room to a large antique bureau with shallow drawers, like a map cabinet with trays. Mrs. Gaffney
started at the top. "These are some of the best," she said.
In the opened drawer, each fastened in place by its own elas-
tic loop, were perhaps a hundred obsidian arrowheads, small
and dark and delicate. The kind of arrowheads one could
imagine the Olamentko using under their curious rules of
warfare, or in quest of scoters and geese and the efficient kill
that would not ruffle feathers.

"That's a remarkable collection," I said. "Where did you
find them?"

"On Bodega Head," said Rose Gaffney, proceeding to the
second drawer. More arrowheads, another hundred or so,
slightly larger. Then the third drawer, and the fourth and the
fifth and the sixth. And then into an adjoining room where
the artifacts were stored in cardboard boxes. More arrowheads. Stone hand tools and bone awls and fragments of pot-
tery and chips. Then on into the garage where there were
more boxes. I suspect some hint of skepticism may have
shown in my face, or perhaps Rose Gaffney had encountered
disbelief in others, for suddenly she seized my hand and

forced it to clutch a large rock from one of the boxes.

"What is that?" she asked.

"I suppose it's some kind of tool."

"What does it feel like?"

"A rock," I said.

Rose Gaffney laughed. "Turn it around," she said, "and lay your thumb across the groove in the top."

I did as she instructed, and there indeed was a groove for the thumb. Below the groove, the rock tapered to a hacking edge. "They're all like that in this box," she said. "Try another." I did.

"And all of this is from Bodega Head?"

"I found my first in July of 1914," said Rose Gaffney. "I had a lot of time out there."

"Did you dig? Were there middens?"

"No," she said. "On the surface. Most of it isn't very old. Maybe four, five hundred years."

I asked her how many pieces altogether she had in her collection, and she said, "I guess there must be a million, if you count the chips."

We walked from the last stack of boxes to the gate and stood there admiring the day's waning brilliance. "You must come back soon and see more of my warehouse," she said. "When you have more time."

As I turned to go, Rose Gaffney looked at the sky. I followed the direction of her gaze, expecting to see some rare bird or unusual cloud formation. I saw neither. Except for the thin chalky contrail of a jetliner, the blue skies of Bodega were empty.

After the Kings River, Hanford, Kettleman City, Santa Maria, and Diablo Canyon, I suppose it was inevitable that I should return for one more look at Bodega, thinking it would be a good place to unscramble my notes. But the wind and the waves were there first, and the pelicans were flying. So I checked into a motel, changed into some rough clothes, and drove out across the mudflats on PG&E's road, past the Hole in the Head, to a small unimproved park overlooking the sea.

On the southwest side of the Head, a sandy cove about 150 yards wide has been carved by the surf from the crumbling diorite cliffs. The trail to the cove is treacherous and steep. The beach is wide and sloping. At the mouth of the cove, several rock outcrops—remnants of eroded cliffs—stand like stubborn sentinels against the fury of the sea. The surf explodes against the rock, and in the afternoon the salt spray turns pink in the sunlight. It is a splendid place for people. But only for a few at a time.

I was in luck. Except for a picnicking couple, the beach was deserted. As I crossed the sand in front of them, trying to keep a considerate distance between us, I smiled my apologies. The woman brushed her straight black hair away from her face and smiled back. The man stared at me with the pained expression of one whose privacy has been rudely invaded. Right on, Charlie Brown. I don't blame you one bit. The trouble is, this world's getting smaller.

I crossed to the far side of the cove and sat in the sun with my back to a rock. The sun was hot. The rock was hot. Beyond the surf, the sea was the color of turquoise. Five brown pelicans passed on a thermal, heading north, with fixed wings and bodies like heavy bombers. A squadron of sleek cormorants flashed beneath them, heading south. A shorebird sidestepped a spent wave, then skittered down the wet sand probing for amphipods. The tide went out, tugging the sand. Ebb and flow. Erosion and accretion. Life and death. Everything under the radiant sun going about its business, taking a little energy from here and passing it on there, up the down staircase of biological magnification, and everything changing later than sooner, and so little waste, and so much logic. I slept.

When I awoke, the couple was gone from the cove. I could see them at the top of the cliff, silhouetted against the sky. They were facing the sea, taking that last look before returning to their car. The man's arm was around the woman's shoulder. She turned. As she came around to face him, the black of her hair turned auburn in the sunlight, like the spray off the rocks turning pink. They embraced. And it occurred

to me then that locked in that embrace between the territo-
rial man and the radiant woman, whatever the thermal value
of their heat exchange, was a flow of energy more powerful
than falling water, more combustible than oil, more logical
than fission.

Now the sun was going down behind Bodega Head. I stood
at the balcony of my room, looking down to the tidelands
and the slender arm of Doran Park curving out to the bay. A
great wall of chalky-blue clouds was moving across the orange
sky. The wind from the sea was cold, and the air smelled of
places I had never been and things I would never see. As the
clouds came closer they tumbled like surf in slow motion.
The surf-clouds beat against the sands of my mind until I saw
something that I should not have seen, that I should never
see again. In the clouds at sunset I saw a midden. It was the
greatest midden in the world, a vast repository of possibilities, a refuse heap of promises and shattered dreams. I began
to dig a hole into the middle of this midden, lifting each layer
carefully in my trowel. I found the ruins of a dam. Behind
the ruins I found a canyon filled with silt. Behind the canyon
filled with silt I found a cavern filled with rusty wheels and
corroded pipes and wall-to-wall stalactites. Then I dug deeper
and found a layer of salt, and under the salt were the fossil
traces of cotton and barley and olives and beans. And the
skeletons of cows and chickens. And couplings from garden
hoses and empty wells. And deeper yet I found the rubble of
a highway, two gasoline pumps, the twisted wreckage of an
oil rig (in marine deposits), the scorched lining of a missile
pod and a nuclear reactor with cracks in its cooling system.
At that point, I figured I had seen enough. I came down from
my hole in the clouds, closed the balcony door against the
cold wind, and packed my suitcase for the flight to New
York in the morning.

    It was almost dark when I left. The sky was somewhere
between purple and black, so that you could barely make out
the shape of Bodega Head across the bay. One thing that
helped was the light. A red light was flashing from the top

of the Head. And down near Tomales Bay, the Point Reyes lighthouse flashed back in green. The two lights were a second apart. The synch was almost perfect. Red from Bodega. Green from Point Reyes. Red and green. Red, green. Redgreen. Watching the lights, I had the illusion of approaching an intersection where the signals were telling me to STOP and GO at the same time.

JUNCTION POOL

Spring comes slowly to the Catskills. On the eastern slopes of the rounded hills, snow lies heavy in the shade of the beech and the hemlock, and in the bottoms there is morning fog. Almost always this time of year there is morning fog in the valley of the Willowemoc, which breaks through the hills a few miles north from the austere eminence of Grossinger's kosher resort. Grossinger's is world-famous. The Willowemoc used to be. Still, it is a charming valley even in dour weather, narrow and twisting in most places, broad and flat in others. It is precisely the kind of valley in which one would expect to find what is now called, however wistfully, a trout stream. And so it is, the Willowemoc, if only in the memory of those who knew the stream before it was bridged.

Spring comes slowly until that first April day of warmth and sunshine, and then the snowpacks slump and the freshets spill down the hillsides as the Willowemoc gathers the runoff and dashes swollen and surly toward the larger flow of the Delaware. Along the way, at the edge of the village of Roscoe, New York, the Willowemoc receives the waters of the Beaverkill, loosed from the wilder hills of Ulster County. At the confluence of these two streams is Junction Pool. And when the snow at last is gone and the air is sweet with the scent of new grass, any lingering doubts about spring's authenticity are dispelled as you come from Roscoe across the Beaverkill on an ancient iron bridge and see the cars parked bumper-to-bumper where the river road curves close to the shimmering confluence. From the side of the road you can see the anglers. They are out on the shoals in chest-high waders. Sunlight sparkles on the ferrules of their flyrods, on the tracery of lines flicking back and forth across the pool with the tiniest bundles of feather and hackle and hook. The anglers are silent. There is only the sound of rushing water and the occasional call of a crow. That, in any event, is how it used to be. Now, from time to time, there are other sounds, such as the backfire of a diesel truck on the New York State Quickway, which spans the Willowemoc on a steel truss two hundred yards upstream from Junction Pool.

Even now, Roscoe in the spring is a fisherman's town. In November it is a deer hunter's town. In between it is not much of anyone's town, except for the people who live there. The main drag is one block long, with an arts-and-crafts shop at one end and a gasoline pump at the other. There is a diner and a lumber yard. The population is said to be 1,200, a figure inflated in recent years by outlanders who have built summer homes on the hillsides. Most of the natives are of Irish descent. Most of the names they have given their places are Irish, too. Off the main street is the Antrim Lodge, named for the county in Northern Ireland. The lodge is a rambling frame structure with small comfortable rooms and a first-class restaurant in the cellar. At the height of the trout season, anglers belly up to the bar, elbow to elbow (which is how they belly up to the Willowemoc on opening day), to quench the chronic thirst and tell, as fishermen everywhere are so inclined, of the ones that got away. A 36-inch Willowemoc brown trout, stuffed and shellacked on a plaque above the cash register, fixes the celebrants with a glass eye. One visitor returns the stare and asks, "Where exactly was he hooked?"

"In the mouth," says the bartender. And the men at the bar whoop and laugh until a wise oldtimer interrupts them with dour news. "You fellas won't ever be hooking that kind of fish," he says. "Not around here anyhow."

One oldtimer who doesn't come so often to the Antrim anymore is Harry Darbee. Hunkered down south of Roscoe in a farmhouse on Route 17, the old twisty two-lane 17, Darbee raises chickens and ties trout flies and remembers the Willowemoc before three-foot Browns and two-lane roads became fossils. Then, he would walk with his flyrod out the back door of the farmhouse, straight down the hill and across an open field to the edge of the creek. And there Harry

Darbee would catch and release big trout to his heart's content. But now, when Darbee is out back feeding his chickens, he looks down the old path and the field is gone, his view of the Willowemoc is gone. Now twin ribbons of concrete cross the floor of the valley, and Darbee leaves what fishing is left to those who still want it. "With that highway down there," he told me one day, "you can have the damn river."

In the beginning, I wanted no more of the Willowemoc than anyone, except for the highway engineers, who hadn't arrived yet. I wanted trout. As many as I could hook and net and legally stash away in my creel. It was impudence, of course, to carry a creel in those days, for I had only begun to learn the basic skills of the fly fisher. To more seasoned streamside companions, my casting was not only an embarrassment but a source of great irritation each time my line snapped the surface of a quiet pool; and I recollect I spent more time in the water untangling gut leaders than laying them out easy and straight at the end of a perfect cast. So in the closing days of my first season, I decided to seek improvement in the presence of another rank amateur, one whose experience, I knew, was limited to cane poles and catfish. But where to go? Not the Esopus, for I had already been skunked on that Catskill stream, nor the Neversink, where the water was said to be low. In the tackle shops of New York City there were good reports from the Willowemoc, and that is where we went, to test beginner's luck against the rumored wary lunkers of Junction Pool.

It was a perfect September day, perhaps not so perfect for trout but fine for humans—blue sky rubbing down against the conifer-green hills, and the hardwoods turning gold in the daytime warmth and evening chill of Indian summer. There was an unimproved campsite for fishermen around a bend from the pool, and we left the car and waded, fishing wet, below the confluence. As soon as the sun was down behind the hills across the river, I signaled my friend and together we moved upstream toward the lower end of the pool. At the time, it did not matter that our creels were empty, for we had saved the best place to end our day; and when we got there we were delighted to find only two other fishermen. They were working the pool from the opposite side.

We re-entered the stream just below the lip of the pool, where a glassy glide over deep water suddenly spills into riffles. We changed from wet to dry flies and cast upstream into the glide, and the light was still adequate to follow the drift of a fly on the water. For twenty minutes or more we cast over the lip of the pool. No fish were rising. We changed to lighter-colored flies and waded closer to work the casts into deeper water. My arm began to ache from the casting. My friend lost a fly on a backcast, said, "That's it," and retired to the shore. It was getting dark now. The water was black. And then I heard the first rise, not a splash but a sucking, rolling sound at the center of the pool. And then another, and the next was so close I could see white-rimmed bubbles where the trout had rolled. The dark pool was awake now, filled with concentric rings and the sound of big fish feeding on an evening hatch. I trembled in waist-deep water, trying hard and unsuccessfully to keep the casts clean, to concentrate on the fly I could no longer see in the darkness. I don't know how many times I cast over the pool before the first strike. The fly went under and then came up smackingly through the surface as I set the hook into nothing more substantial than H_2O. "A hit!" I called joyously to my friend ashore, and with half a dozen false casts to dry the hackles of the fly, presented it once more. And another hit. And another empty *smack*. But on the next cast I was lucky. In the microsecond that I sensed—*guessed* is more like it—the fly touching the water, I jerked the rod tip up and my line was tight at last to a fish; not a very large one, I could tell from its struggle, but a fish nonetheless. I played it out of the deep water and netted it in the shallows below the pool.

"What is it?" she asked.

"A brookie," I said, "Or a rainbow. Where's the flashlight?"

It was back in the car. I killed the fish and cleaned it at the edge of the stream. Its sides were slightly rough and scaly to the touch, not smooth and slippery like the trout I had taken that summer in the Adirondacks. Well, I thought, Catskill trout must be different. I placed the fish in my creel and we stumbled up the dark bank to our car at the campsite.

Another car had arrived in the afternoon, and a man was beside it, folding his waders in the glow from a dashboard map light. "Fishin' the pool?" he inquired. We confessed we had done that. He said, "How'd you make out?"

"A small one," I said. "Only eight inches, I guess. And you?"

"Real good," said the man. He turned his own flashlight on the open wicker creel at his feet. It was filled with fat brown trout, five of them altogether, each running to a foot or longer. Suddenly I detested him. And then he asked to see ours.

I reached into my creel and withdrew the solitary fish. As the beam of the flashlight came up to meet it, I explained that it probably wasn't a Brown. "Sure isn't," the man said as we stared at the scaly corpse in my hand. "Nor a brook or a rainbow either."

If it wasn't a trout, asked my friend in a hostile accusing voice, then what was it?

"That?" said the man with ill-concealed disdain. "That is a shit-eating chubb."

In time, the agony of that discovery did not haunt me quite so much as the remembered sight of those five fat Browns and the sound of lunkers dining in Junction Pool. Circumstance and humility kept some distance between me and the Willowemoc for four years; and when I finally returned in the spring of 1965, it was not to do battle with trout but to write the obituary of a classic trout stream. The Quickway, opposed on its chosen alignment by Harry Darbee and others for nearly a decade, was under construction in the valley of the Willowemoc, and in one six-mile stretch it would span the stream with thirteen bridges. The spans alone did not trouble Darbee. What worried him were the concrete pylons they planned to sink in the streambed to support some of the bridges, and how the resulting displacement might cause the water at flood to squirt between the pylons as if from a fire-hose, and what this might do to the silt beds that nurtured the nymphs that hatched into flies that furnished the food where trout dined.

Harry Darbee had worked long and hard to keep the Quickway from his valley, but when I first met him he had already lost. Some say he came close to turning it the other way; and in Roscoe even his former bitter adversaries still speak in admiration of the 15,000 signatures he managed to obtain on petitions to Nelson Rockefeller, then governor. This was indeed an impressive accomplishment, but it was not enough to turn the head of the governor, who listened instead to such ichthyological experts as Public Works Commissioner Burch McMorran. It was McMorran who proclaimed that inasmuch as trout are loafers, they should be thankful for the opportunity to loiter in the shade of bridges and pylons. And another Rockefeller aide was quoted at the time as allowing how "one good highway is more important than any river in America." In view of the former governor's own zealous intervention on behalf of other riparian expressways in New York, one can only conclude that Nelson Rockefeller probably agreed.

Feelings were running high in Roscoe when I talked with Darbee. For one thing, opening day of the season was just a week away; and despite promises by the State of New York that its work would in no way interfere with the joys of angling, huge machines still rumbled along the banks of the Willowemoc and its waters ran to the color of coffee laced heavily with cream. The town itself looked bombed-out, strewn with rubble where the right-of-way struck down the full length of Broad Street as if a cyclone had passed. And there were insidious rumors of deals and payoffs—the code words you hear almost anywhere in America when government gets into the business of taking private property by eminent domain.

"The thing that gets me," said Harry Darbee, "is that they never really listened to us. They just went right ahead and did what they set out to do ten years ago." What the state had set out to do was to build a fast modern highway from Harriman on the New York Thruway to Binghamton in the Southern Tier, and, in the process, divert traffic from the Willowemoc stretch of old Route 17, the corkscrew curves of which had given local tow-truck operators and ambulance drivers insomnia for years. "Hell, we never denied the need for a new highway," said Darbee. "They tried to accuse us of that, but the fact is I drive a car, too." Darbee's proposed alternate route would have avoided the Willowemoc. He had urged the state to shelve it across the hills behind Roscoe. The state replied that such a route would cost too much. Case closed. And at the bar of the Antrim Lodge, the anglers from out of town held Irish wakes for the Willowemoc that spring, though more than a few, one suspects, were secretly pleased at the prospect of halving the travel time to Roscoe when the Quickway was finished.

Doug Bury, the proprietor of the Antrim, did not share his guests' sense of tragedy. "This town's been going down for years," he said. "And just maybe the highway will save it." When one guest, who had long been impressed by the arguments of Harry Darbee, heard this, he said, "That may be, but what about the fishing?"

"Listen," Doug Bury replied. "If there's a problem, it's not the highway. It's you and me and all the others who have been taking the fish."

Fish have been taken from the streams of the Catskills since people got smart enough to catch them. The Indians used spears and nets. The settlers used wire hooks. They chased the Indians out of the valley of the Willowemoc, logged it, then turned to raising dairy herds. Under the manure the worms grew fat and juicy. Eventually some worms turned up on wire hooks in the mouth of *Salvelinus fontinalis*, the native American brook trout. For a hundred years men took trout from the Willowemoc not because it was fun but because it was food. Then one Theodore Gordon came to the Catskills from Pennsylvania to devote his life to the theory and practice of fly fishing as it had been perfected by the gentlemen anglers of the British Isles. Legend has it that Gordon floated the first dry fly in North America on the gin-clear waters of Junction Pool.

Soon the Willowemoc and the Beaverkill, and the Neversink nearby, became legends themselves. Equipped with the latest and most expensive rods of split Tonkin cane, with lines of silk, leaders of gut, and large felt envelopes festooned with colorful Cahills and Royal Coachmen, the disciples of Theodore Gordon rode north in the parlor cars of the New York, Ontario, and Western to test their skills against fontinalis, not to mention the transplanted rainbow and wily German brown. In Roscoe, the anglers were greeted by Frank Keener, founder of the Antrim Lodge, and taken by cab to their favorite pools. And in the evening, in the glow from the great stone hearth in Keener's cellar, they debated the mysteries of entomology and hydrochemistry and spoke of the trout with awe and affection. It was boom time in the spring of those years. Doug Bury, who married Keener's daughter, Anna Mae, recalls there was never a vacant room during trout season; the regular without a reservation would be trundled off, when the bar closed, to some nearby boardinghouse.

The good times lasted through World War II to the mid-Fifties, when democracy at last caught up with the gentleman angler. Then, with the development of fiberglass for rods and nylon for lines and leaders, and reels that went for the price of a theater ticket instead of one month's rent, one no longer was constrained to count himself among the leisure class in order to acquire the suitable tackle for trout. There was yet another development: the spinning rod and spinning reel, which were also inexpensive and brought the barefoot boys with cheek in range at last of those lunkers in the deepest pools. And as the pressure mounted, as more and more fishermen of every kind bellied up to the Willowemoc and the Beaverkill, as more and more of the lunkers were dredged from their lairs, the fabled streams began to lose a kind of magic—a kind of wildness—that no amount of hatchery restocking would ever restore, that special feats of engineering could never replace.

I understood these things the next time I returned to Roscoe. It had been nine years, and the Quickway was already showing its age with frost cracks on the pavement and patches of rust where paint had peeled from the steel of its bridges. What's more, it was not so quick, that highway, not with a 55 m.p.h. speed limit enforced in tribute to the conservation of energy. At noon we hit the Willowemoc Valley and crossed the several bridges into Roscoe. The town looked the same— no richer, no poorer. The Antrim had a new sign, but otherwise the lodge, too, seemed unchanged—still friendly and relaxed, though the lunch crowd looked thin for a Saturday.

"It's the gasoline crunch," said Doug Bury. "And if it continues into the trout season it could hurt us badly."

"How's the fishing been?" I asked.

"Not bad," Bury said. "Considering."

After lunch I drove up the hill to Harry Darbee's place with Pat Smith, whom I had first met in the cellar of the Antrim when he was breaking in as outdoors editor of the old *New York World-Telegram and Sun*, and both of us were writing obits on a river. Smith was now in television, still poking around the outdoors a good deal and still getting paid for it; and he had come back again, as I had, to see if the corpse was really dead. "If Bury says the fishing's been good," Smith said, "Darbee will tell us it's downright lousy." And he was right. On the side of Darbee's front porch was a large sign visible from the road. *SOS*, it read in heavy Gothic letters. *Save Our Streams*. Darbee said the fishing was lousy.

For all the years, he hadn't changed much either. The hair was whiter. The lines in his face were a little deeper, as one might expect of a man who had lived some time with personal defeat. But the eyes were too bright to be bitter, and the handshake was strong. We sat in his study with two dachshunds, one cat, a tank of tropical fish, and a rolltop desk cluttered with books and papers and scraps of hackle from his fly-tying trade.

We talked about Darbee's creek, the Willowemoc. Had the

Quickway truly destroyed it, as he had predicted nine years ago? "Well," he said, "I'll admit the quality of the water has held up better than I expected. But that doesn't account for other things, like the gravel that's getting into the stream. It's filling up with gravel. There are pools I couldn't wade across, once. And today they're only knee deep. And the hatches have changed. Since the bridges came in, we haven't been growing the large nymphs. Burrowing nymphs need silt beds. But the gravel moving off the highway shoulder has scoured the silt away. So the fish aren't getting as much to eat. They're not growing. Used to be you could hook and release four hundred fish each season over fourteen inches. Now, you're lucky to hook one. Oh, sure the spinning has taken a lot of the big ones. But the bridges did their part, too. They've kept the little fish from becoming big fish."

There were other problems that worried Darbee. The herbicides used in highway brush control. The town's sewage treatment system, which, after a brief holding period, dumps primary effluent into the Beaverkill. The new campsites along the Willowemoc, with the litter and their own outflow of occasional pollution. The salt. "They keep the highway salted against ice all winter long," he said. "Now what do you suppose that does to the life of the stream when it runs off?"

We asked Darbee if he felt the Quickway had lived up to its expectations, apart from damaging a stream. "I hear gripes that the town didn't get all the business it had hoped for," he said. "And safety. Why, some nights there's nothing but fog or ice on these bridges. One bridge, I think, has killed nine people already, including a highway safety engineer. You can look it up in the records. I'll bet there have been more deaths between Hancock and Harriman on *this* road than there ever were before on the old one."

Darbee shooed one of the dachshunds off his lap and took us to the door. We shook hands on the porch. *SOS* stood out bold behind his shoulder. And he said, "The Willowemoc will never be the same. But for all its woes, I guess it's still the best damn resource we have left."

In the late afternoon I went down to the lower end of

Junction Pool. The season was not open yet and I was alone
in the grass where the glide breaks out of the pool into riffles.
I sat down on a log and stared at the water. And I remembered then what another Roscoe fly-tier had told me about
nostalgia. He said to beware of it. He said that what Darbee
wanted to do was to turn back to something that was no
longer there. He said, "We all want to do that. Me, I'd like
to go out to St. Louis and watch the Indians sitting around
on the banks of the Missouri. But I'll never see that. The
Indians are gone."

And I was going myself now, back toward the river road
to the Antrim Lodge. As I left through the dry winter grass
I heard the sound of a large fish breaking the water. I think
I heard it. I can't be sure, for when I turned to look, the
slick black surface of the pool told me nothing.

THE TRASHING OF STATEN ISLAND

Once there was a plan. It was a bold and imaginative plan indeed, and in the beginning almost everyone who heard of it thought that it was not only good but necessary. There were even a few who thought it was possible. The plan was to make a perfect community. Not from scratch, of course, for that would be too easy. This plan was to take an established community, old enough to have a few scruffy edges, and, with God's grace and the wisdom of experts, transform it into a showcase of order and beauty, with parks and gardens and birds in the trees and healthy people in happy houses and clean air and sparkling water and exquisite arts and fine public buildings and even trains and ferryboats that would always run clickety-click on time. Over the years, a number of very smart people worked on the plan. In fact there were several plans, each succeeding the one before, so that nothing ever got rusty or obsolete or, for that matter, accomplished. And all of this was to achieve the perfection of Staten Island, the county and borough of Richmond, in the city and state of New York.

Now certainly Staten Island never was, is not now, and never will be, truly perfect. But it might have come closer if people had paid some attention to the dreamers instead of shouting them down with ridicule. One by one, the plans were shouted down as well. Shot down is more to the point— eviscerated, mutilated, stomped and spiked, one after another. People stopped dreaming. Now, the only plan for Staten Island is to let scruffy events run their course, so that no one will feel uncomfortable in the presence of perfection. This is one plan that cannot miss.

For better or worse, Staten Island is a land of opportunity. In the 1960s, especially during the early days of the administration of Mayor John V. Lindsay, it was fashionable for urban affairs writers to be hopeful for the island, and they referred to it affectionately as New York City's "Last Frontier." And it was frontier in more ways than one. What the city's other four boroughs lacked, the island had in spades—undeveloped land, acres and acres of it spilling across wooded hills and sandy flats around the villages of Travis and Greenridge and Rossville and Annadale and Pleasant Plains. It was fertile territory for planners all right. But the territory was infected with certain blights that have afflicted every frontier this nation has known. Social root-rot. Political cowardice. Provincialism. Meanness. Myopia. Greed. The planners couldn't see all this from their ivory towers. And so the spoils have fallen to the spoilers, who even now are busy turning Staten Island into a dump.

"Staten Island," a resident acquaintance of mine once remarked, "is where you put the things that no one will have anywhere else." That was in 1958, I believe, shortly after I had moved to the island because it was green and uncrowded, with birds in the trees, and because it was cheap. At that moment, I didn't know exactly what insight my friend had captured in his remark, so I dismissed it as the ranting of an unreformed cynic whose time had come to move elsewhere. Yet in my own time, I soon discovered that the island was indeed a receptacle for the unwanted—for the sulfurous fumes of neighboring New Jersey industries, for the fecal backwash of the Hudson and Raritan rivers, for a third of the garbage generated every day in New York City, for the storage of volatile fuels, for the incarceration of narcotics addicts, and for the proliferation of tacky subdivisions tossed together to shelter middle-income masses pouring across the newly-opened Narrows Bridge in full retreat from the urban horrors of Brooklyn.

The trashing of Staten Island led me to other discoveries, for, in the course of observing what had gone wrong, I also was privileged to witness a few of the things that still remained right. I mean the way water tumbled over polished stones in the brook that came down through Goodhue Woods into Sailor's Snug Harbor. I mean how the sweetgums grew tall and straight like pillars on the ridge overlooking Stump Pond; and the smell of sassafrass in Buck's Hollow, and how the wild grasses of Latourette glowed in the golden light of an October afternoon, and the sight of a muskrat leaving its wake on a pool, and a great blue heron rising, and how the spears of skunk cabbage parted old snow, and what it was like to be in Reed's Valley when the willows were coming to leaf and the bullfrogs were croaking.

I knew even then that such things could not be forever, no matter how perfect the plan. But there were a few of us who felt we could buy the natural elements some extra time on Staten Island. So we organized. One of the organizers discovered that Henry David Thoreau had written: "A town is saved, not more by the righteous men in it than by the woods and swamps that surround it." And with this for its motto, the group set out to take an inventory of all the woods and swamps and open fields remaining on Staten Island. Aerial photographs were obtained, as well as a list of vacant lots. "My God," said one nature lover. "There's so much to cover, it'll take us a year." Unfortunately, we never learned how large a task it might have been. Before the inventory could get underway, the group was locked in combat with the State Department of Transportation, which wanted to cut down the sweetgums and fill in Stump Pond to make way for a highway. That was in 1966. Eight years later, with the highway battle at a stalemate, the swamp-savers had no stomach for making lists of natural areas. It wasn't that they were weary from the fray or too busy earning a living. It was because, after eight years, it had become possible for one to take an inventory of Staten Island's natural areas in the course of a single Saturday afternoon.

Over the years, for reasons no longer so obvious, the island has been the haunt of nature-loving people. Thoreau himself was a visitor here in 1843, and stayed a year as tutor to the nephews of his Concord friend, Ralph Waldo Emerson. From "The Snuggery," a low brown farmhouse at the foot of the hill which now bears Emerson's name, Thoreau rambled forth to explore woods and swamps as wild as any he would ever encounter near his beloved Walden. Once, he crossed the island to the great salt marsh at Fresh Kills and watched waterfowl darken the sky as he nosed a skiff down meandering channels in the cord grass. Where the channels converged to join the Arthur Kill, at Lake's Island, Thoreau went ashore. It is recorded that he spent a pleasant day there collecting arrowheads. It is also recorded that for all its raw nature, Thoreau did not much care for Staten Island, although he was kind enough to write later that the place "affords very fine scenery."

The scenery likewise impressed Frederick Law Olmsted, who, at the age of twenty-six, came to farm a 130-acre tract in the Woods of Arden overlooking Raritan Bay. "I do exceedingly enjoy the view," Olmsted wrote to a friend, adding, "sometimes it is wondrous beautiful." Perhaps the future architect of Central Park enjoyed the scenery too much, for the farm was a failure. In any event, Olmsted returned to the island briefly in the 1870s to author a report for the local Improvement Commission. Among the several improvements proposed was a plan for a "public common" extending along the high central ridge of the island. It was a bold and imaginative plan. But inasmuch as The Possible fared no better in the last century than it has so far in this one, the central ridge was soon forgotten as parkland and would not be planned for again—at least not until a certain road-builder decided that Olmsted's linear common would be an excellent place for a highway. Excellent, that is, as soon as the sweetgums could be logged off the right-of-way.

Unlike Thoreau and Olmsted, the last of the memorable resident naturalists was a native son. William T. Davis was his name, and for three-quarters of a century he roamed the backcountry of the island as no one ever had before, has since, or will again. Davis had a large nose and an extravagant moustache, and because of his appearance and a preoccupation with entomology—with special attention to the habits of the cicada, or seventeen-year locust—his friends, with affection and respect, liked to call him Professor Bugs. There were

more than a few islanders, however, who would gladly have
called him that for other reasons. When the new electric light
station burned to the ground in 1891, Davis was ecstatic.
Asked why, he replied that now he would not have to go
outside the village limits "to see the night." He also worried
about other changes, about the way the village limits were
pushing harder against his natural haunts. "Only a few human beings should grow to the square mile," he wrote in one
of his voluminous journals. "They commonly are planted too
close." On parks, his tastes were closer to Thoreau's than to
Olmsted's: "The best park," he liked to say, "is certainly a
piece of woodland left as Nature arranged it, with a few paths
cut through." One of his favorite haunts was Fresh Kills,
where brooks came out of the sweetgum forest to blend
sweet water with the brackish tides. Here, with more than
3,000 acres left as nature had arranged it, Davis studied the
dragonfly, watched the great migrations of birds along the
Atlantic Flyway, and sometimes, like Thoreau, turned up an
arrowhead or two on Lake's Island. Those who remember
William T. Davis say he was a happy and cheerful man. And
yet some dark hint of sadness, of unaccountable loss, crept
occasionally into his writing, as in a poem which concludes
with this stanza:

> *The wise they will not own it,*
> *For Nature's charms have fled—*
> *Who would live where the grass is brown*
> *And the trees that were, are dead.*

Davis died in 1945, at eighty-three. In his memory, a modest sign was posted at the entrance to a small bird sanctuary
he had been instrumental in establishing on the edge of the
Fresh Kills marsh. Three years later, in 1948, Davis's colleagues could walk past that sign, down a path smelling of
honeysuckle, and emerge at a point where the vast wet
prairie was spread out before them. In the distance, across
the marsh, they could see drag-lines and bulldozers in the
cord grass. It was the year of reclamation in New York
City, and the machines were there to turn Fresh Kills into

the largest garbage landfill on the face of the earth.

A ride on the Staten Island Ferry, believe it or not, still costs but a nickel. Actually it costs a dime if you board at Whitehall Street in Manhattan, but the return trip is free, as well it should be. People who have braved the environment of Staten Island are entitled to such largesse. The ride across the bay is one of the seven wonders of New York, and from the orange deck of the *John F. Kennedy*, for example, one can gaze upon the full splendor of the World Trade Center, the Bayonne Naval Shipyards and the Verrazzano-Narrows Bridge. If the timing and tides are right, one might also catch sight of the Statue of Liberty rising, as if newborn, from a huge mound of garbage. A closer look will reveal that the scene is only temporary, for a garbage scow is passing now in direct line of sight between the ferry and Miss Liberty. The scow is pursued by herring gulls, which wheel and dive about the cargo. Colorful festoons of paper and plastic flutter behind like pennants in the breeze. "Are they taking it to sea?" inquires a tourist pacing the deck. "No ma'am," one is obliged to explain. "They are taking it to Staten Island."

The disposal of solid wastes is a grim business, particularly in New York, which produces more of it than any other city in the world, including London and Tokyo. Constantly, the Department of Sanitation is hard-pressed to make the vast scope of its task understandable to the man in the street, whose personal contribution must seem inconsequential. And so departmental clerks good with numbers are regularly on call to update and refine statistical comparisons calculated to stagger the public imagination. The latest calculations go something like this: in a year, New Yorkers produce 11 million tons of solid waste—enough to fill the two 110-story, block-square towers of the World Trade Center, and then some. In a day, the refuse collected totals 31,500 tons— enough to fill a football field to the height of a four-story building, and then some. Approximately one-third of this daily waste, collected at marine transfer stations scattered throughout the city from West Harlem to Gravesend Bay, is

loaded into scows and transported to the city's sanitary landfill at Fresh Kills. Which means, in effect, that Staten Island
takes it all up to the 33-yard line.

Since 1948, more than 60 million tons have been ploughed
into the Fresh Kills marsh, sprayed with disinfectant, terraced, contoured, and covered with a final two-foot layer of
earth. The clerks in Sanitation figure the city can continue
filling up four-story football fields, at least to the 33-yard
line, until 1984; maybe 1985 if they should decide to start
filling at Lake's Island, where the scows swing in from the
Arthur Kill. Where Thoreau and William T. Davis searched
for arrowheads.

North a mile from the sanitary landfill is the village of
Travis. Its main street is lined with frame houses and with-
ered shade trees, and there is a cannon caked with rust to
commemorate the ones who went away and never returned.
In Travis I am reminded of Kansas. Apparently the place
strikes other people that way, because Travis is where they
filmed parts of *Splendor in the Grass*, a Kansas story by
William Inge. With a title like that, the camera crew was very
careful to keep its lenses trained away from the grass at Fresh
Kills.

Travis is also known, though not as well as it should be,
to the contractors and home-builders of Staten Island, for it
is here, in another landfill area not far from the village center,
that they are permitted to unload construction wastes. There
is only one catch: it costs them $1.50 the cubic yard, the
value of a full six-pack of beer. As a result, the woods and
swamps surrounding Travis do not save the town so much as
they spare the contractor the expense of a dumping permit.
Along all the lonely roads, tire ruts trail off through the
bushes to small and criminal mountains of solid waste. At
one point, some Sanitation officials feared that Travis might
someday be cut off from the outside world by a Berlin Wall
of discarded lumber and mortar, but fortunately, with the
slump in housing starts, the accretion has leveled off.

South of Travis, below Lake's Island, the Arthur Kill narrows into an industrial waterway that, for meanness, must surely rival such bilious streams as the Cuyahoga River and the Houston Ship Canal. Rotting piers and outfall pipes protrude from the shore, and on the west bank, which is claimed by New Jersey, the discharge stacks of smelters, refineries, and paint processors rise like the scorched battlements of hell itself. As luck and the elements would have it, the prevailing winds pass over these stacks on their way to Staten Island. This circumstance makes the east bank of the Arthur Kill, or, more precisely, the west shore of Staten Island, an ideal place to locate some of the things that no one will have anywhere else.

Though it is hard to believe, I am told that the area was once quite desirable for farming. The fine sandy loam around Rossville at one time yielded one of the largest strawberry crops in the country, and its vegetables were in great demand at the produce markets of Manhattan. Later, as the number of farms declined, some islanders turned to growing flowers. Pansies did especially well. That is, they did well until a factory with a very large discharge stack began reclaiming copper from insulated wires across the Arthur Kill. And the next thing anyone knew, the farmers could get up in the morning, and walk out between rows of pansies and primroses, and look straight through strange holes in the blossoms. At first they thought their flowers had been attacked by some exotic blight. But they were soon disabused of this notion when a sanitary engineer from the U.S. Public Health Service showed up with an air-monitoring device and explained to them the corrosive nature of sulfur dioxide.

Understandably, the farmers became very upset. So did the people of Rossville. They held meetings. They wrote angry letters describing not only the holes in their flowers but the disintegration of their flyscreens and the flaky gray stains on the windward walls of their homes. They demanded action from every level of government, but they got very little. This was about 1960. One must remember the spirit of the times. It was fashionable, for example, to be fearful of strontium-90 in your milk. It was not fashionable to fret about sulfur dioxide on your primroses. And in the city, Mayor Robert F. Wagner's adolescent Air Pollution Control Bureau was still chasing smoke, as if the enemy was soot rather than poison.

In time, of course, the Arthur Kill at Rossville was to become one of the great battlefronts in the fight for cleaner air, and some key interstate issues were first decided there. As fashions changed, so did the rules governing what an industry might lawfully bequeath to the ambient air, and before long the hellish stacks were retrofitted with electrostatic precipitators. Now, so I am told, the westerlies from the Garden State, though smelling from time to time of rotten eggs, are far less toxic than before. Many of those who fought the first round with the copper smelter are no longer around to enjoy the difference. Frank Hauber, the flower grower, is dead—done in, say his friends, by aggravation. And Marie Crookall, whose voice haunted the switchboards of official agencies for years, has moved away. Ms. Crookall at least had some choice in the matter. She chose wisely, for today in Rossville there are more ominous things to worry about than sulfur dioxide.

The last time I poked down that way, I did not expect to find any of the original sulfur-fighters, much less a living, breathing, working farmer. It had been more than ten years since my last visit. Rossville, unlike Travis, was no longer an isolated village. Already there were ticky-tacky boxes on the hillsides where the strawberries once grew, and the people in the boxes were busy growing babies. But down past Marie Crookall's old place, I saw a sign beside the roadside. It affirmed that Herbert Gericke, the organic farmer, and perhaps the very last of any kind of farmer thereabouts, was still hanging on.

I remembered Gericke as a tenacious fighting man for principle. He had told me once how he had come out of his house after a heavy fog to find his lettuce and melons covered with beige spots. "Like someone had worked them over with a blowtorch," he had said. Later, his angry complaints brought offers of compensation from New Jersey. "They thought

they could buy me off," he said. "Well, let me tell you something. I never took a penny from them. And I never will."
And he never did.

Remembering him that way, I came up the drive to the
shed where he retails his own produce and such health foods
as honey and granola. He was standing outside the door,
dressed in bib overalls. His trim Van Dyke beard was turning
white now, and when he came forward to greet me I noticed
he walked with the stoop of a man who has been too long in
the fields, with too little help. I asked if he remembered the
old sulfur-fighting days and he smiled and dismissed them because, I suppose, the issue was no longer as relevant as others.
"I'm eighty," he said, "and I'm tired. I'm tired of fighting."

I expect he felt it, being tired, but he did not show it. He
took me inside the shed and proceeded to deliver a truculent
lecture in defense of organic farming. "They used to call us
nuts," he said. "Now we are not nuts. Isn't that strange? We
are the same people, aren't we? We are doing things the way
we always did them. What happened that we are no longer
nuts?" Suddenly Gericke stabbed his finger at a tomato.
"There's your answer," he said. "You can eat that without
being poisoned. It's organic. No tolerances. You know about
tolerances?" From behind the counter he thrust a document
at me, a U.S. Department of Agriculture listing of tolerable
levels of contamination in vegetables. "See what it says about
tomatoes," he said. Under the heading for tomatoes, the document listed tolerances for lead, endrin, aldrin, malathion,
DDT and 2,4,5-T, among two score other poisons. "Do you
believe it?" said Gericke. "That's what you get with your
commercial tomatoes."

Like most Staten Islanders of conservative persuasion,
Herbert Gericke is no fan of government. As we talked that
day, he denounced the tax structure, the welfare system, the
forty-hour week ("If I had that, I'd be on vacation"), and,
in particular, the interference of bureaucrats in the affairs
of the individual citizen. "The city forced me to pay fifty
dollars for a permit to operate this foodstore," he said.
"They have no right. I am a *farmer*. I would have fought

them in the old days. I'd spend a hundred dollars in court if I could save one nickel they weren't entitled to." And then, with obvious relish, Gericke recalled the details of his brief and personal crusade against Prohibition. "They told Gericke he couldn't take a drink," he said. "I got so mad I went out and wound up buying every kind of alcoholic beverage I could find. I had a drop or two of everything, and most of it was awful."

"Do you still drink?" I asked.

"I never did," said Gericke, "but for that one day."

I asked him about the things that had come to Rossville since my last visit, the kinds of things that no one will have anywhere else. "You read the newspapers," he said. "What else is there to say?" And I looked into his eyes and saw at once the sorrow that was in him, and the frustration of knowing that after so many years of fighting he was no better off than he was before the first sulfur mist wafted across the Arthur Kill. And now he was eighty. And tired.

Yes, I had read the newspapers. After the air pollution, the next unwanted thing that came to Rossville was a state-operated narcotic addiction rehabilitation facility. Actually, the word *rehabilitation* is misleading, for under the guidelines legislated by former Governor Nelson Rockefeller and his Republican lawmakers, the idea in New York is not to rehabilitate addicts in the socio-medical sense but to incarcerate them under penal conditions, with mandatory sentences to boot. In any event, not even the erection of a high chain-link fence, topped with sharp points, was about to assuage the doubts and fears of the people of Rossville. With the drug center's population projected at some 600 inmates, the residents of Rossville's older section—that is, the community predating the little boxes on the hillsides—saw themselves virtually outnumbered. What if there should be a break-out? It can't happen here, the apologists replied. But eventually it did happen. It had to happen. And one of the first to see it happen was Herbert Gericke, because, as fate and his own Job-like luck would have it, the narcotic rehabilitation center is situated directly across Arthur Kill Road from his farm. Gericke and his son were working in the fields. They heard shouting from across the road, looked up, and strangers were running through their lettuce beds. "You get out of here," Gericke yelled. Two of the men did just that. They slipped into the front seat of the younger Gericke's automobile and drove away with it.

Next, to Rossville came the prospect of LNG and the *Absolute Kill Zone.* LNG is liquified natural gas, stored under great pressure at a temperature of 270 degrees below zero. The *Absolute Kill Zone* is an area surrounding the storage tanks. It has a radius of some 1,500 feet. It is where everything goes *poof* if one of the tanks blows up. You have about one and a half seconds to get out. Unfortunately, people's legs can't move that fast. From a 93-acre site on the Rossville shore of the Arthur Kill, where tanks with an aggregate storage capacity of 200 million gallons of LNG have been under construction, the *Absolute Kill Zone* extends south to encompass part of the rehabilitation center and, as luck would have it once again, a corner of Herbert Gericke's farm.

So now the people of Rossville, for the third time in a decade, are angry again. And scared. It is not the storage of LNG that worries them so much as its delivery by tanker up the narrow, cluttered Arthur Kill, and its distribution by barge to other points in the city. The Coast Guard is also worried. It considers LNG so hazardous that it requires all harbor traffic stopped within a mile of a moving tanker, within a half mile of a moving barge. People downwind of Rossville have reason to worry, too. In the transfer process, from tanker to tank, from tank to barge, an undetected leak could allow the volatile gas to collect in a cloud, and the prevailing westerlies could carry that cloud across the island. Anything along the way—a spark from a chimney, a short-circuit in an overhead electric line—could turn the cloud of LNG into an instant fireball. There would be a crackle, like the fast overture of a lightning strike. And then, *poof.*

The people of Rossville and neighboring communities have organized to fight the tank farm's operator, the Distrigas of New York Corporation. The macabre name of the citizen's group is BLAST, which is an acronym for Bring Legal Action to Stop the Tanks. But no one is betting that BLAST will prevail. For one thing, New York City's major power suppliers, the Consolidated Edison Company and Brooklyn Union Gas Company, have been clamoring for years for additional supplies of natural gas to satisfy the city's voracious and wasteful energy needs. And the Federal Power Commission at last has authorized the importation of such supplies, mainly from Algeria. What's more, gas is cleaner than oil, and the city's Environmental Protection Administration looks with great favor on its widest possible use. The promoters of LNG acknowledge there are certain hazards, but they promise that every conceivable precaution will be taken. No one, of course, has been foolish enough to predict that "it can't happen here." Four miles from Rossville, at a tank farm near Travis, it did happen in February, 1973. Forty workmen were killed in the explosion.

"I think Marie Crookall had the right idea," said Herbert Gericke.

"You mean about moving out?"

"That's exactly what I mean," he said. "A person can't spend a lifetime fighting."

"But suppose the gas tanks don't go through. Suppose BLAST stops them."

"Then it'll be something else," Gericke said. "There's always something else."

"Like what?" I asked.

"Like people living wall-to-wall," he said. "I read somewhere it's sure to happen. Even here. Why, pretty soon there won't be space enough to grow a flower. I don't want to be around to see *that* happen."

"Well," I said, "whatever you decide, good luck."

And Herbert Gericke smiled and said, "I'll need some."

Some of the best fiction writers in America today are selling houses on Staten Island. There has been a good deal of plagiarism, to be sure, for in the process of giving his new subdivision an attractive identity, the developer occasionally must borrow the name of a place that is exotic and faraway. More often, he will consider the gross physical inadequacies of his site and then proceed to correct them semantically. Thus, on the edge of a certain south shore swamp, the Staten Island house-hunter encounters *Malibu Estates*. High and dry—and in an architectural style wholly unworthy of old Cape Cod's—is *Provincetown*. And *Hunter's Ridge*, defoliated by bulldozers, where the biggest game is an emaciated sparrow perched on top of a nursery seedling. So it goes, up one side of the island and down the other. And the tragedy is to be found not so much in the billboard fictions as in the fact that, with all the planning, it should never have happened here.

In the eyes of many people who came to the island before completion of the Narrows Bridge in 1964, and who had the good fortune to select a home not yet within some kind of kill zone, the ultimate affront, the most pervasive annoyance, is the proliferation of subdivisions with exotic names and fossilized amenities. Laid out for the most part on rectilinear street grids, as if the builder had cribbed his site plan from a sheet of graph paper, the Malibus and Provincetowns of Staten Island have already obliterated many of the values that had attracted people to come here in the first place. I mean, specifically, the natural features that one can no longer find anywhere else in the city, the woods and ponds and streams that give pleasure to people and true identity to a community.

It could be argued that the open lands of Staten Island were bitched from the start—the start being some time back in the 1920s when an official in Manhattan announced that a tunnel would be dug beneath the Narrows to connect Staten Island to the rest of the city. Land speculators had been waiting for something like this. With great expectations of profits to be reaped, they acquired vast tracts throughout the southern half of the island, laid in a few unpaved streets and unconnected fire hydrants for cosmetic purposes, and waited for the tunnel to spew the suckers into their waiting arms.

As things worked out, the tunnel was abandoned. In the years following the Crash, the speculators had a fine time trying to dodge the men from the tax collector's office; but by 1947 the city had seized, as payment in lieu of back taxes, almost a third of the island's undeveloped land.

Owning idle land, however, did not appeal to the city as much as using that land to generate needed revenues. So in the Fifties, the Wagner administration plunged into the real estate business, auctioning off parcel after parcel until a quarter-billion dollars had been gaveled off the block—with a Narrows bridge as bait. And to assure that the auctioned land would soon have improvements to assess, the city obligingly waived all kinds of land-use and zoning restrictions, which was very good news for quickie subdivisions, little boxes, lost landscapes, and billboard fiction writers.

In his own time as mayor, John V. Lindsay tried to put a brake on all of this. But he failed. He failed because he was too sophisticated, too liberal, perhaps too much the WASP for the Old World Catholic constituency of Staten Island, which, with rare exception, has long favored politicians of a different cast—the kind whose heads are filled with goose down and whose feet are made of lead. Lindsay also failed because his planning people—and there were some good ones —consistently underestimated the power of negative thinking and the political strength of those who would benefit from the unrestrained, unplanned, and piecemeal development of this last frontier.

There were three major casualties in Lindsay's abortive crusade to save Staten Island from itself. The first was the Annadale-Huguenot Plan, which was conceived before Lindsay's time as an "urban" renewal scheme for some 1,000 acres on the island's south shore. Actually, there was nothing urban about Annadale-Huguenot. It was a wooded tract, with few existing homes, many small ponds, and a stand of rare silver beech trees. To preserve these features, Lindsay's people came up with a design concept featuring single-family houses in cluster development, attached town houses with common open spaces for recreation, a few scattered 11-story apartment towers, parks, esplanades, and a marina. The city, which already owned about a third of the land, proposed to purchase the undeveloped private holdings and then resell them to developers willing to work within the guidelines of the plan. Predictably, the plan was shot down by borough politicians and local realtors. The design did not conform to their graph-paper interpretation of the American Dream.

Next to be carried from the field of battle was the City Planning Department's "fenways" project, which was to have preserved several mid-island watercourses as linear parks. Fenways had been advocated for years by the disciples of William T. Davis, and the Lindsay people, liking the nice, crisp Anglo-Saxon flavor of the word, advanced a plan that would secure the streams by conservation easement. But first, there had to be a feasibility study. The contract for that study bounced around a number of city agencies for two years. By the time it was finally authorized, fenways were no longer feasible along all but one of the selected streams. Home-builders, conducting their own studies overnight, had decided that the streams would serve a higher purpose channeled into culverts and covered with blacktop roads.

The last Lindsay project to go down the drain was an ambitious plan to create a public corporation that would oversee the staged development of South Richmond, an area covering thousands of acres. The initial planning was placed in the hands of James Rouse, creator of New Towns, such as Columbia, Maryland. And eventually one of the island's rare progressives, State Senator John Marchi, was enlisted to shepherd the plan through the legislature in Albany. But in the end, Marchi found himself hung up in a silly jurisdictional dispute with the sponsors of the new Gateway National Recreational Area (both South Richmond and Gateway sought to include the same shorefront park). And with the crowd that had crushed Annadale-Huguenot twisting political screws again, the final effort by the Lindsay team to do right by Staten Island collapsed.

Now the reins of municipal government have been passed along to Abraham Beame, who knows Staten Island well. As budget director and comptroller in the Wagner administration, Beame had been the one to mastermind the auction-block sale of city-owned land. He is a practical city boy, this new mayor. His interests are with the coin of the realm. If someone in his presence were to mention silver beech, I suspect Abe Beame would think it some kind of foreign currency and promptly inquire as to its rate of exchange.

In the days when Beame was at the auction block, another city boy named Robert Moses was busy planning and building the highways of New York City. Moses liked to plan ahead. As each new road was completed, it invariably would come equipped with an interchange to plug it into the next new road on the master builder's list, which was endless. Even if the next new road was not yet funded or authorized by public hearing, Moses would build his interchange anyway. And when the time came at last to build the next road, and people said, "O please don't build it *there*," Moses would simply reply that he *had* to build it there because of the interchange and the money already invested. And it worked every time until, about halfway between his new Narrows Bridge and the Arthur Kill crossing, Moses erected an interchange that was aimed at the heart of the Staten Island Greenbelt.

I want to say for the record that I admire Robert Moses. In his day he was responsible for many splendid public works and recreation facilities, including a string of state parks that rank among the finest in the nation. And he did always plan ahead with the best of intentions, as some men will when they think they are right. But the trouble with Moses was that, in planning ahead, he frequently operated on the fragile assumptions of the past. I suspect he believed that if something worked once, it would work again and again. In the 1930s he had made the Bronx River Parkway work, and it soon became the model for planners elsewhere who wanted to provide both transportation and recreation service within a single corridor. But the Thirties and Forties were long gone when Robert Moses built his interchange on Staten Island, believing that trees were somehow compatible with tetraethyl and that people could still enjoy, in the choking environs of New York, that ancient amenity known as the Sunday Drive.

The area that Moses proposed to skewer with his Richmond Parkway is not a *greenbelt* in the classic sense of that word. It encircles nothing, but rather is a green belly itself encircled by a belt of residential development. It has no official identity, no absolute boundaries. It is simply a big woods, about 1,000 acres, with a few secondary roads winding through, a blessedly undeveloped park, a nature center, a scout camp, a day camp operated by the Federation of Jewish Philanthropies, two golf courses, the overgrown grounds of a moth-balled municipal tuberculosis hospital, a landmarked lighthouse, a chain of spring-fed kettle holes left behind by the last visiting glacier, and a hill that is said to be the highest point on the Atlantic coast south of Mount Desert, Maine. The area was logged more than a century ago, so that some of the second-growth trees, mainly white oak and sweetgum and beech, are now of spectacular size. The fauna are somewhat less spectacular, though occasionally one finds herons and muskrats at the ponds, hawks in the hollows, and I am told there are those who have witnessed the tracks of raccoons. By wilderness standards, of course, the Greenbelt is a bust. But it is the best that Staten Island has to offer. In all of New York City you will come no closer to wildness anywhere. And yet, for all of its values and all the borrowed time its defenders have won in their battle with the disciples of Robert Moses, the future of the Greenbelt remains uncertain. You drive across the Staten Island Expressway to Sunnyside, at the foot of Todt Hill, and the barricaded interchange is still there, like an event waiting to happen.

The event almost happened in 1965 when Mayor Wagner, *two days* before leaving office, bestowed his official blessing on the Richmond Parkway and thereby authorized the letting of bids for the highway's construction. It was that close. In fact, it could not have been any closer when, from out of nowhere, an obscure organization called the Staten Island Citizen's Planning Committee appeared with an implausible plan to reroute the highway around the Greenbelt. "Ridiculous," said Moses, who had not yet retired from public life. "Impossible," said the State Department of Public Works, anxious to award its contract to the lowest bidder. Wagner said nothing because he was gone. But Lindsay listened. And though it was later ruled in court that the new mayor had exceeded his authority, Lindsay liked what he heard and promptly rescinded Wagner's approval.

That the Staten Island Citizens Planning Committee could accomplish so much with so little so late in the game was, at the time, considered something of a local miracle. The group had no real standing, legal or otherwise. It had no professional expertise in the planning of highways, though one of its leaders, Bradford Greene, is a respected landscape architect of nationwide repute. It lacked grassroots political clout, being comprised largely of liberals and Unitarians, people of dubious midwestern ancestry and such unorthodox habits as walking in the woods. In short, the leaders of the Staten Island Citizens Planning Committee were almost wholly deficient for the task. Except for two things. They had vision. And they displayed it with class.

I will have a hard time forgetting the first highway hearing I attended at Borough Hall. All the island politicians were there, looking grim behind their elevated desks as, one by one, they warned of disastrous consequences if Lindsay and the Planning Committee should have their way. The hall was packed with ringers. People who had barely heard of the parkway or the Greenbelt, much less seen the land through which the right-of-way would pass, rose to denounce the "tree lovers" and "daisy sniffers" and then sat down to thunderous applause. Greene was there, and the late ebullient lawyer, Frank Duffy; and Bob Hagenhofer, the graphic designer and dream merchant who, because he happened to hail from Chicago, was long suspected by the opposition to be a front man for the Syndicate; and Terry Benbow, the Wall Street attorney whose public intonations always ring with just the proper tone of righteous indignation. And when these few got up to speak of the Greenbelt through the boos and the catcalls, I thought it was all over. I thought we were finished. I thought the Greenbelt was finished.

"Looks bad," I said to Benbow outside the hall that night.

"That's only round one," he replied. "What the hell are you worried about?"

Round two opened in the summer of 1966, and the Greenbelt crowd came out swinging. While city, state, and federal transportation officials had been debating the pros and cons of a half dozen possible alternate routes, the Planning Committee had been busy pulling in some reinforcements, among them such heavyweights as the National Audubon Society, the Sierra Club, the Scenic Hudson Preservation Conference, and the prestigious Municipal Art Society of New York. Also, there was a new militant group called SIGNAL (Staten Island Greenbelt-Natural Areas League), the same group which had set out to discover that there was nothing much outside the Greenbelt left to inventory. But the priority *was* the Greenbelt, and Messrs. Greene et al. had been doing their homework. Greene was a great admirer of the works of Frederick Law Olmsted. With a bit of research, he discovered in Olmsted's 1871 report to the Staten Island Improvement Commission a reference to the same green belly of land that was now so hotly contested. As Olmsted had seen it:

> In the case of Staten Island, it would be a simple plan to form a park . . . four miles in length. It would . . . turn to good use a large extent of land. . . . This ridge extends from the Fresh Kills near Richmond to Stapleton, but while its altitude is melted away in gentle slopes to the northward, permitting in that quarter the greatest freedom in the location of roads, it descends toward the sea on the south in steep and broken declivities, totally unsuited, not to say impracticable, for roads for rapid travel.

Greene was quick to note that the steep and broken declivities were precisely where Robert Moses wanted to build the Richmond Parkway.

Punchy position papers and slick publications had been hallmarks of the Planning Committee and SIGNAL strategy almost from the very beginning. And now their presses were rolling again. This time it was a sixteen-page brochure in which the new coalition of civic and conservation groups proposed development of a 4.7-mile linear park that would be named the Olmsted Trailway, in honor of the original visionary. Paths for hikers and bikers would wind up the long ridge, past the camps and High Rock Park Nature Conservation Center, to the historic restoration site at Richmondtown. There would be picnicking on Ketchum's Hill and canoeing on Richmond Creek. But no Sunday driving. No tetraethyl in the sweetgums. The idea was to have the trailway occupy—indeed, preempt—the acquired right-of-way of the original route of the Richmond Parkway. City Parks Commissioner Thomas P.F. Hoving and U.S. Interior Secretary Stewart L. Udall both hailed the plan as a milestone in the advancement of outdoor recreation and urban conservation.

And I think this is where the tide began to turn. With a new and positive mission outlined for the Greenbelt, the coalition pressed more effectively for a Greenbelt bypass, designated Alternate Four, that would connect with the Staten Island Expressway several miles west of the Moses interchange. The city's own data, in fact, showed that of all the alternate routes under consideration, Four was the shortest and least costly to build. At the time, it would have required condemnation of only seven buildings and the relocation of no more than two families. A study by landscape architect Ian McHarg, the ecological determinist with a Scottish burr, further confirmed the superiority of Four. Using a method in which social processes (such as residential and institutional values), physiographic features (such as slope and soil), and natural values (such as forest, water, and scenic resources) are superimposed one upon another, McHarg came up with a unique composite picture of the Greenbelt. Where the shading of natural/social values was darkest, with good land values, steep slopes, high-quality forest and superior scenery, there was the corridor of maximum social cost—and the original route of the Richmond Parkway. Where the shading was lightest, there was the corridor of least social cost—and, not surprisingly, the alignment of Alternate Four. Of the original route, McHarg noted:

> *It would destroy important institutional, scenic, recreation and wildlife resources—glacial ponds, high quality forests and ecological diversity. Dramatic physiographic features would be obliterated. In addition to all of these losses, the intrusion of noise, dust, hydrocarbons, lead and carbon monoxide would constitute further offense to man, plants and animals alike.*

And of Alternate Four, McHarg's study explained:

> *As social values are at a maximum to the east, in the area of the Greenbelt, any corridor west of this will produce less social costs. Consequently route #4 represents a dramatic reduction in social costs.*

The Lindsay administration embraced McHarg's findings and promptly announced in favor of Four. Governor Rockefeller conceded that the original route was a "disaster" and, with some reluctance, agreed that a western alternate might be preferable. And the Tri-State Transportation Commission, having once approved the original route, now shifted its official sanction to the Greenbelt bypass.

In the early evening of March 25, 1969, Irving Scheinbart of the New York State Department of Transportation arrived on Staten Island to preside over a public hearing on the social, economic, and environmental effects of the proposed parkway. Scheinbart appeared to be a gentle and patient man. I imagined him thinking how lucky he was to have pulled this particular assignment, instead of some free-for-all over a cross-town expressway through Greenwich Village or a confrontation with angry blacks about to be dispossessed by a highway through Ossining. I imagined Scheinbart was figuring to catch the midnight ferry back to Manhattan. He kept looking from his wrist watch to a pile of index cards bearing the names of those who were waiting to present their views. The pile was very high. The audience was very rude. People were booing and hissing and clapping and shouting "Bravo!" On numerous occasions, Scheinbart had to gavel for order. The midnight ferry pulled from its slip in St. George, and still there were people waiting to be heard. In fact, there were people waiting to be heard until 4:48 the next morning, at which time the hearing was adjourned. Later, after a good day's sleep, Scheinbart is said to have told friends he would rather accept transfer to the boondocks than return to Staten Island ever again on official business.

The arguments Scheinbart heard were long and repetitious. For the most part, the backers of the original route denounced any further delay in construction. They spoke to the issue of traffic congestion. They said the Greenbelt was a myth, that it was inaccessible, that the original route would not destroy anything. Frederick Zurmuhlen, an engineer, invited the "*suede-o* conservationists" (Mr. Zurmuhlen's pronunciation) to "get off the backs of the road-builders," and then went on to explain how roads never destroy natural beauty; they simply take people to it and in some cases even "enhance" it. Near the end, a most unusual solution was advanced by a woman who said her name was Sarah Haley, but gave no address. Ms. Haley explained that in karate, one starts with a green belt and engages in matches with other contestants, advancing from one level to the next, the highest being black belt. "Well," said Ms. Haley, "the same thing is true for Staten Island. There is a Greenbelt, but it only takes a match to make it into a black belt." And, holding up a thin splinter of wood with a bulbous blue head, she added: "*This* kind of match."

For its part, the Greenbelt coalition argued that the original route would gouge ninety-eight acres out of Latourette Park in violation of the Federal Highway Act of 1966, that Alternate Four would provide superior traffic service, and that the real myth of the evening was the opposition's claim that the Greenbelt, without a parkway through it, was inaccessible. Said one environmentalist:

The borough president (Robert T. Connor) has said of the Greenbelt, and I quote from The Staten Island Advance, *"This area cannot be used. You can't get to it. . . ." I don't know why you can't get to it. One hundred and fifty thousand children get to it and into it every year, and most arrive, I might add, not in cars but in buses (which most city parkways exclude). . . . The engineers who sought to dam the Grand Canyon argued that a reservoir would enable visitors to glimpse the canyon's geologic record from boats. The Sierra Club's response to that, and it is applicable here tonight, was: "Should we also flood the Sistine Chapel so tourists can get nearer the ceiling?"*

As the evening wore on, the Greenbelt supporters managed to deflate another myth—that the overwhelming majority of island residents favored the original route. This claim had first been made by borough president Robert Connor, who put the favorable percentage at ninety-eight. When challenged as to how he had arrived at such a figure, Connor instructed his staff to conduct a survey. The survey, by telephone and applied to a small, unscientifically selected sample, turned up 77 percent in favor of the original route. Whereupon Connor reduced his own mythic majority to 95 percent, a figure brazenly reiterated at the hearing by City Councilman Edward Curry. Congressman John Murphy (of the trucking Murphys of Staten Island) was more cautious. In his statement, he claimed only 90 percent. Yet just a few hours later, Anna J. Meyer came to the podium (and what follows is from the hearing transcript) to present Scheinbart with a petition:

> MRS. MEYER: . . . signed at this hearing by those who attended and express support of Alternate Four of the Richmond Parkway. It contains 551 signatures.
> VOICE: Bravo!
> MRS. MEYER: There are 950 seats in the auditorium so I think we have a majority.
> VOICE: May I sign that and I'll make it 552.
> VOICE: 553.

It wasn't a knockout, not by a long-shot, but at last the Greenbelt crowd was ahead on points. And this time around, when Messrs. Greene, Duffy, Hagenhofer, and Benbow completed their statements, they sat down to cheers.

I would like to say that this is how it ended, with cheers. With the Olmsted Trailway and Alternate Four. But it was not the end. There were still some fossils lingering in the cellars of the state and federal highway establishments, friends of Bob Moses, obdurate and grim, angry that a whippersnapper mayor and his *suede-o* conservationists could hit them with so formidable a monkey wrench as the Olmsted Trailway *cum* Alternative Four. So they played the waiting game, knowing that Rockefeller's heart wasn't really with Lindsay and that if they waited long enough Lindsay would be gone. The federals thrashed around for logic to find Four unacceptable, which they did, citing the loss of Robert Moses's one-million-dollar interchange. And while the city waited on the state, and the state waited on Washington, some enterprising developers moved their bulldozers to the west flank of the Staten Island Greenbelt and proceeded to build, within and across the proposed Alternate Four right-of-way, a solid wall of brand-new homes. And now, for all intents and purposes, Four is dead. The state and the Beame administration are pressing for Six, which is a minor variation on the original theme. And the Greenbelt? The Greenbelt remains as vulnerable as ever it was the day the first slab of cloverleaf concrete was poured for Bob Moses at the foot of Todt Hill.

It was spring on Staten Island when I last walked the Olmsted Trailway. I should say the *de facto* Olmsted Trailway; it is still the mapped right-of-way of the Richmond Parkway. I started at the interchange, where graffiti artists have inscribed their barbaric yawps on the exposed serpentine rock of the southbound exit. At the end of the concrete I followed a wide ravine strewn with tires and kitchen appliances, and then slabbed up the side of Todt Hill into a forest of beech. Near the top of the hill is a burned-over place choked with bullbriar, and you are well-advised to go through it with your collar turned up and your hands in your pockets, for the trail is narrow and the briars are sharp. And I remembered the hike with Lindsay and Hoving in the winter of '67, after the ice storm, when the tops of the briars tinkled like glass as you brushed them. Everyone called it a crazy but wonderful day to be off in the woods, because Lindsay was there, and Lindsay was hope.

Beyond the briar patch I crossed Ocean Terrace and went into the woods again past the old St. Francis Seminary and the pavilion shelters of Henry Kaufmann Campgrounds. It was a weekday. The shelters were empty, quiet now, and shadows of trees fell diagonally across their low-pitched roofs. I picked up the Water Glade Trail and followed it to the first of the glacial ponds within the right-of-way. At the far end of the pond a blue heron was feeding in the shallows. It took to the air on heavy wings, wheeled over the pond with soaring grace, and disappeared through the treetops at the crest of the ridge. There are several clearings at the top of the ridge, and from one of them, on a day as clear as mine was, you can look down across all the rows of houses marching through Dongan Hills and New Dorp to the water; across the great curve of the Hudson Trench reaching out through the Narrows, to the parachute jump at Coney Island and the distant dunes of Sandy Hook across Raritan Bay. Moses had planned to put a filling station here off the northbound lanes, so that people could park, drink pop, and enjoy the view through their windshields. Lindsay had planned an overnight bivouac with Tom Hoving, to dramatize the natural values of an urban trail. For some reason as logical as the fact that overnight camping is not permitted in New York City parks, the mayoral safari never materialized. For that matter, neither did the filling station. Not yet, anyway.

I pushed on. Through the cathedral-like grove of sweet-gums at Stump Pond. Down into the valley of Hour-Glass Pond, which the original route would drain and fill. To High Rock Park and Bucks Hollow, with their loosestrife and skunk cabbage. To Lighthouse Hill and Latourette Park. Except where I had crossed a road or two, I saw no one in that whole distance. No one in more than three miles. But I have walked it in the summer and on weekends and I have seen hundreds. I have seen families fishing for calico bass in the ponds. I have seen them afoot and on horseback. I have seen scouts by the score on land where overnight camping *is* permitted, and schoolchildren out on the footpaths of High Rock, getting the kind of education you can't find in books or absorb through the windshield of an automobile. And either way, in solitude or in a surfeit of company, you begin to wonder how all of this could possibly be sacrificed in order to preserve the integrity of an obsolete concept and the investment of $1 million in steel and concrete.

The Olmsted Trailway ends at Ketchum's Hill, below Richmondtown at the southern end of Latourette Park. There was a British fort here briefly in the Revolutionary War, and for a time such artifacts as buckles and bayonets were turned up as readily as Davis and Thoreau had plucked arrowheads from Lake's Island. Once, Ketchum's Hill was covered with cedars, and Thoreau may have wandered across it on his way to the marshes at Fresh Kills, for his journals record that certain parts of the island were "fragrant with cedar." But the fragrance is long gone. The cedars are long gone, not even artifacts, done in by air pollution.

From Ketchum's Hill there is a view that is almost as panoramic as the one from the ridgetop over Raritan Bay. The view from Ketchum's is to the south and west. On the far horizon, across the Arthur Kill in New Jersey, you can see the high discharge stack of a copper smelter. But without binoculars, you cannot see the LNG tanks clearly, much less the organic farm of Herbert Gericke. Next, moving the eyes slightly to the right as you face south, are the stacks of Consolidated Edison's Arthur Kill Station, where a 50-day supply of soft sulfurous coal—mothballed now because there is oil to burn, but available nonetheless for the next energy crisis—lies like a low black mountain against the gray Travis shores behind it. And in between, as if framed by the smelter and the powerhouse, is Fresh Kills—the largest garbage dump on the face of the earth.

The sun was rolling down the sky, and it was late. I had 4.7 miles to go, back across the trailway to the interchange. I descended Ketchum's Hill by a different path that took me into a field scorched by fire. The trees on the edge of the field were blackened to a height of six feet. Some of them were dead. The grass in the field was black, too. In the middle of the field I saw an automobile—a heap, a scorched wreck undoubtedly abandoned there before the fire. One little boy or girl with one little match, I thought, not Sarah Haley of black-belt Karate fame.

The car rested on its axles in the charred grass. It had been stripped so that nothing remained except the frame and chassis. I looked into the empty front well. There in the damp and the shade, I was surprised to see that the burnt grass had regenerated in its own ashes and, in the space designed for an engine, sparked a riot of vigorous green.

THE WINGS OF MAN

In the early winter of each year, about the time the first snow turns the color and texture of mushroom soup in the gutters of northern cities, and even as frost sidles across the higher hills of Dixie, there is an urge among certain large warm-blooded creatures to seek the golden sunshine of South Florida. I do not mean the birds migrating down the ancient flyways, though they undoubtedly experience a similar yearning. I mean that portion of the human species which is airborne, rising above the clouds on the Wings of Man, riding the thermals in Yellowbirds generic to Boeing, strapped in three abreast, a pale face at every window. These people are flying to Florida to fulfill their version of the American Dream. They are dreaming of two weeks in the sun, white sand beaches, fresh orange juice, Royal palms, calypso music, dog races, and a full moon over Miami. For some of the passengers the expectations are greater, transcending the brief delights of tourism. One sees the faces lined with age and guesses that for these it is a one-way trip to the social insecurity of retirement. The old people sit uneasily as the plane dips toward Miami International Airport. Possibly they wonder now if they have made the right decision after all, moving so far from home to take up residence in some trailer court or bungalow village, with inflation waiting to unravel the flesh from the skeleton of their life savings. Well, no matter. It is cold and drear back home. The kids have flown the coop. Old friends are gone. It is better to face death under blue skies than under gray. So the plane descends toward the runway. And at the end of each armrest, loose skin tightens on the knuckles of the old ones who have come to Florida to dream awhile in the sun before dying.

Florida—or, rather, the southern half, which is where most of the tourists and immigrants go—is divided into two parts, one part for people, the other for birds and alligators and cypress and saw grass and similar wild things that function best where humankind functions least. The two parts are more or less mutually exclusive, and there are quite a few of the one kind who still believe that there is no longer any room for the other. Given Florida's rate of growth, they are probably right, or will be soon enough. Of course, a few individuals understand that should the wilder half of South Florida ever disappear, it will be curtains for the tamer half. They understand it and, of late, have been talking bravely of limiting growth. But so far no one has quite figured out how to do that. "It's a nice idea," says one Dade County planner, "except for one thing. Limiting growth keeps coming up against the Bill of Rights."

In the late 1960s it was the fashion for out-of-state journalists to write South Florida down the drain. Only the travel writers dissented, as was to be expected. Jim Dooley, a pitch man for one of the airlines, was constantly on television exhorting his viewers to "come on down." Invariably, Dooley would add: "The water's fine." As it turned out, the water was anything but fine. It was disastrously scarce, low in the aquifers supplying the cities, spread thin over the conservation pools of the Central and Southern Florida Flood Control District, choked with algae in the sloughs and 'gator holes of Everglades National Park and the Big Cypress Swamp in Collier and Monroe counties. Park Service rangers and Audubon wardens, fisheries biologists, apostate poachers, and almost everyone else in a position to know the backcountry well enough to care, all predicted apocalypse.

It had not quite come to that, but it was an effective way to draw some general attention to a local problem—sort of like screaming "Rape!" in response to a raunchy bar-room proposal. In Florida, however, a certain amount of carnal knowledge was already demonstrable. Levees completed in the early 1960s by the Army Corps of Engineers had blocked the historic overland flow of water from Lake Okeechobee to the mangrove wilderness of Florida Bay. What little water did manage to reach Everglades National Park carried pesticides and fertilizers from farmlands upstream. North and west of the park, in Collier County, corporate land hustlers promising "new worlds for a better tomorrow" moved into the cypress swamps with drag-lines and dynamite, opened canals to the Gulf to suck the land dry, and used limestone spoil from the dredging to build access roads to their mail-order lots. Finally, as if this were not enough, the Dade County Port Authority announced the raunchiest proposal of all: a plan to establish the world's largest jetport in the Big Cypress just six miles north of Everglades National Park. And the press, knowing that bad news is good copy, descended on Florida like locusts. The promoters of flood control and jungle jetports couldn't understand what the fuss was about. "What's more important," they asked, "alligators or people?" One Miami transportation official even suggested that it was the responsibility of all men to "exercise dominion over the land, sea and air above us as the higher order of man intends." Hearing such rhetoric, and seeing the environmental havoc such rhetoric had already unleashed, one was hard pressed to remain journalistically objective. For my own part, as time went on, I gave up trying.

I was a stranger to Florida when the first reports of havoc began to percolate through the conservation press into the national prints. My editor had sent me south not to count birds but to cover the countdown and launch of a Gemini mission, manned and orbital, from Cape Kennedy; and as the auspicious event approached, I grew increasingly anxious to be somewhere else, anywhere else, away from the neon of Cocoa Beach, the plastic motel bars named after missiles, and the sterility of the NASA briefing rooms. It was not that I lacked respect for the venture; I was bored by it. I was out of my element in a situation defined by the mysteries of physics, chemistry, metallurgy, and Einsteinian math.

On the eve of the scheduled launch, word was passed down from Mission Control that a defect had been detected in the launch rocket's propulsion system. "O Christ," wailed a bright young science writer at the bar in the Polaris Motel. "Now they'll miss the window and it'll be at least a week."

Someone glumly ordered another round of drinks. The man from Hearst stalked to a telephone to beg permission to fly home. Me, I managed to conceal my own delight, and in the morning NASA made it official. Human error somewhere in the drafting rooms or on an assembly line had given us five days' freedom. I called my editor. "There's a good story in the Everglades," I said. "They're drying up." He was a moon-and-missile man himself, and not much impressed. But he was generous. I went.

I drove out across the Tamiami Trail, U.S. 41, west from Miami under cumulus clouds taller than mountains, along the levee the Corps had built; past the Blacks and Cubans fishing canals with cane poles, the airboat concessions, the thatched shops of the Miccosukees, the billboards offering acreage for almost nothing down. I noticed these things by the side of the road, but what I saw was the country beyond them. As far as the eye could see, the saw grass rolled away yellow-green in the sunlight and gray under cloud, a "river of grass," as Marjorie Stoneman Douglas described it in her epic history of the Everglades, grass rooted in ancient beds of peat and washed by the imperceptible southward flow of water—southward, that is, until it reached the levee and the four huge water gates clamped down over the Shark River and Taylor Slough. I tried not to think much about the gates and the levee, for without them it was strange and wild country, full of mysteries infinitely more awesome than the calculated ones of Cocoa Beach and Cape Kennedy.

Out near Forty Mile Bend, the oceanic horizon of grass slipped away into a tassled gray wilderness of cypress trees, and at the slough crossings now the open-prairie look of things gave way to the tangled appearance of tropical jungle. At a place called Monroe Station, I stopped for gas. Fantastic country, I said to the man at the pump.

"There ain't none better," he said. He was an old man with white hair and furrows like sloughs meandering over his sun-bronzed face.

"Been out here long?"

"Fifty years," he said. "On and off." And for a while we

talked, since there was not much business that afternoon at the pumps, and he told me how it had been before the Tamiami and the tourists and souvenir stands, before the engineers had come in battalions to alter the flow of the water. There had been a simple dirt track west from Miami, he said, and where it ended you parked your car and walked. The old man admitted he didn't know much in the beginning, being soft and green, but soon he learned the swamps from the Indians he met along the way and the oldtimers who had been there when the profit was in plumes. He would be gone for weeks at a time, traveling light with a tin cup, a poncho, a sack of oatmeal and dried fruit, and a sawed-off .22-caliber rifle. "You didn't need for more," he said. "There was plenty of eating out there, and more than enough water." And then his eyes left me and he looked across the Tamiami Trail at the low gray façade of the Big Cypress Swamp. "It's still there," he said. "Most of it, anyway."

I asked him how long he thought it might last.

"Not long enough."

And what was his reason for saying that?

"People," he said. "It's as simple as that."

The Big Cypress Swamp is so named not because of the size of its trees but because of the extent of its territory, which covers just about every available acre south of Lake Okeechobee that isn't already occupied by wet prairie (the true Everglades), pine ridges along the coasts, mangrove estuaries, and assorted human places that no longer qualify as landforms. Strangers who mistakenly interpret "big" as modifying the tree instead of the swamp are invariably disappointed, for most of the trees are of the dwarf pond-cypress variety—short and scraggly. The bald cypress can be something else. It *was* something else, despite intermittent logging, until the tough water-resistent qualities of its wood were discovered by Naval procurement officers early in World War II, after which many of the true bald cypress giants sailed off to the South Pacific in the form of PT boats. Only a few big trees are left, mainly in the Fahkahatchee Strand near

Ochopee and the Corkscrew Swamp northeast of Naples. And Corkscrew was where I was heading.

At the time, the situation at Corkscrew was something of a *cause celébrè*. Its 10,000 acres had recently been designated a National Natural Landmark, in recognition of its fine stand of bald cypress ancients, some of which, it is said, were already one hundred feet tall and festooned with moss when Columbus blundered into the New World. Corkscrew, moreover, was and is a National Audubon Society sanctuary, and its purpose as such is quite specific: the tall trees along the Corkscrew slough provide what is possibly the most significant rookery remaining in North America for the endangered wood stork. Bald cypress and wood storks are especially dependent on water—neither too much water, nor too little, but a cyclical natural flow just sufficient to protect the peat-bedded cypress roots and to concentrate fish in convenient pools for the foraging storks. But now the cycle had been broken by the promoters of new worlds for a better tomorrow. The Gulf-American Land Corporation, boasting that it was "literally changing the face of Florida," had invaded the country downstream from Corkscrew and, with a multimillion-dollar fleet of bulldozers, drag-lines, and 55-ton "Tree Crushers," was draining 200 square miles of the Big Cypress (and, because of the nature of water and gravity, Corkscrew as well) down puckered canals to the Gulf of Mexico. Just a few months before I arrived there in the summer of 1966, Gulf-Am had poked its main 60-foot drainage canal to within a mile of Corkscrew's south boundary. "It was like pulling a plug in a bathtub," said Phillip Owens, the sanctuary director. "We were left with soup."

Copious summer rains had since diluted that soup and raised the water level of the slough, and as I followed Owens along the boardwalk trail into the big trees it was difficult to reconcile the healthy appearance of the place with the director's dour remembrance of things past. It was early evening now; the sun was low. Thin shafts of light, penetrating the green canopy and silver-gray shrouds of Spanish moss, slanted across the strand as if through stained-glass windows, and the broad tapering cypress trunks rose from the dark water like columns in a cathedral. The air was still and heavy. We heard the mournful shriek of a limpkin, the splash of a cooter in the water. We saw an alligator in a bed of water lettuce, a wild turkey on a cypress branch, otter scat on the boardwalk. The storks? "They're up north till December," said Owens. "Then they start drifting in, just a few at first, sort of looking things over. By January, we'll have three to four thousand pairs."

"What about next winter?"

"They'll be back," he said. "But how well they'll do depends on how much rain we get between now and then. That, and on how much goes down those canals to the Gulf. If it keeps getting worse, we'll have to build dikes to slow down the runoff."

For the next three days I moseyed around Collier County looking at canals and ditches and dying pond-cypress, and talking to people in Naples who weren't terribly happy about what was happening up in the boondocks. Not that all of them shared Owens's concern for the wood stork—some of them just didn't fancy submerged cypress logs coming down the canals and into Naples harbor to bust the propellers on their fancy yachts. And I spent one morning at Gulf-Am's sales headquarters, observing the unctuous hustle. Already Gulf-Am's eager salesmen, buoyed by a nationwide advertising campaign, had committed 20,000 buyers to the dotted line. Thus, for a pittance down and so-much a month, could one exchange his good judgment for the privilege of someday owning a modest piece of the Sunshine State, complete with resident water moccasins and no utilities.

On the fourth day I returned to Cocoa Beach. Gemini was patched, reprimed with liquid oxygen, ready on its pad at the Cape. The launch was set for the next afternoon. A-Okay and all that sort of thing. In the morning I dragged myself to the press observation area in the dunes behind the launch pad and sat in a canvas chair in the sun, watching the crew from CBS set up their cameras. Cables were spilling from the network's trailer like spaghetti. Directly in front of me, in line of sight with the Atlas-Agena rocket that was to propel a pair of astronauts into an orbital docking exercise with some hardware from a second rocket, I saw two of the network men setting up chicken wire around a patch of beach grass through which, from time to time since my arrival, various heavy-footed people had been tromping. I had no idea why they were doing this, nor did I particularly care. I assumed that chicken wire must have some technical relevance to the business of broadcasting from a sand dune, and that whatever its purpose, the whole thing was undoubtedly beyond my comprehension. Or so I thought until the men went away and I saw that inside the corral of chicken wire, protected now from the careless feet of cable stringers and other such technicians, was a bird nest with young in it, camouflaged against the dun landscape of sand and grass.

The countdown was into its last minute when the parent bird returned, saw the wire, circled it, and came down for a landing in the beach grass nearby. I am no birder, and was even less of one then, so I cannot cite the species. A bittern perhaps. It doesn't matter. What mattered was that here was this wild bird bewildered by the wire strung around its nest to spare the fledglings a ghastly stomping, and here were two brawny men who, in the midst of this vastly complex and anthropocentric adventure, had concluded that birds did matter after all. And then the cables of the distant gantry cranes fell from the poised rocket, and we saw the flash of ignition at the rocket's tail, and the puff, and the slow grudging lift, and with the sound of it came the first waves of shock, like gusts of hot wind, and tremors from the ground rattling the inside of your belly. *"Go!"* somebody yelled close behind my ear, and *"Ride 'em, cowboy!"* And as the gleaming rocket vaulted on an orange plume to the sky, I watched the other bird fly in terror and haste across the dunes toward the ocean, and wondered then how the storks would fare next winter in the cypress strand at Corkscrew Swamp.

I wonder still. Not only about Corkscrew and its birds, but about Florida and its people and how well or badly they are relating to the land and the water and the wild things they need to have around if they want to go on living there with some prospect of a decent environment. I wonder because nothing seems to get resolved in Florida, not that things generally get resolved anywhere else. But for Florida one keeps hoping. I mean if men can go out of their way to string chicken wire around a vulnerable bird nest, if Phil Owens can raise dikes to save a slough and others can open dikes to spare a national park from the crushing burden of artificial drought, if good and courageous people can stand up and say what ought to be done, if ill-sited jetports can be blocked—well, then. There is hope. There is the promise of something better coming. Or is there? Since that first visit, I have been back to South Florida four or five times looking into such things, and each time there is the promise of something better coming, a solution to this, or a halt to that. Yet the very next time I am down that way, something better isn't happening. Something bad is getting worse.

Like water. Historically, since people began living there in sizable numbers and mucking around with the hydrosystem, water has been such a great and vexing problem in South Florida that from afar one might think the region at times was totally arid, a misplaced Mojave appended to the underbelly of the U.S. of A. Actually, South Florida is among the wettest regions in the Lower Forty-Eight, second only, I believe, to Western Washington. South of Orlando the average annual rainfall is figured at about sixty inches. That is five feet of water, and if it all fell at once you could drown in it. As a matter of fact, quite a few people did drown in it back in the days of the great Okeechobee floods; which is why all the dikes, levees, and canals were built to pool the water and send it safely to the sea. Well, not all of it—a quarter of it, about sixteen inches, about three billion gallons a day down the drain to the Gulf of Mexico and the Atlantic Ocean. This still leaves forty-four inches, figuring annual rainfall. But now comes the tropical sun, and green plants with their roots in the spongy peats and soils; and evapotranspiration soon takes its cut, which is the largest by far—some forty-two inches right off the top. And what's left? Two inches. Two inches of rain to percolate into the wells and aquifers that are supposed to sustain the human herd of South Florida for better or for worse, in sickness and in health, from this day forward. Two inches on a sustained-yield basis might do just fine for the present population of South Florida. The trouble is you can't count on it (the taps of Miami almost ran dry in the spring drought of 1971), and the herd keeps growing. Despite recession, inflation, and the energy pinch, the so-called Gold Coast from Coral Gables north to Palm Beach is growing at the rate of 3,000 new residents a week. And until tight money put the squeeze to housing starts, Florida as a whole was accounting for more than a quarter of the national increase in building permits.

From time to time in recent years, schemes have been trotted out by people determined to deprive the sky and the ocean of their full share of the water, thereby making more of it available for increasing urban and agricultural growth. One ambitious, if not altogether brilliant, plan called for coating parts of Lake Okeechobee with a paraffin-like emulsion to suppress evaporation. The hope was that this might cut the losses from the surface of the lake—and substantial losses at that, up to an inch or more a week in the hottest weather. But experimenters soon discovered that their suppressant was inhibiting something else besides evaporation, namely the emergence of insect larvae essential as food to the lake's commercially valuable catfish and bream. At the same time, another plan was advanced to reduce the profligate waste of water pouring down canals to the sea. Here, the idea was to install pumping stations that would intercept and backpump the water into the conservation pools of the Flood Control District in Dade and Broward counties. But this plan was flawed as well, for the water coming down many of the canals was spiced with the runoff from citrus groves and melon fields and cow pastures, a witch's brew heavy on such things as nitrogen fertilizers and, until recently, chlorinated-hydrocarbon pesticides. Now this might have been acceptable to the farmers. Like the penurious character in a contemporary novel who refused to rinse his toothbrush after brushing, on the theory that the residue saved him the equivalent of one tube of toothpaste every two years, the backpumped farmers might have calculated certain savings on their chemical bills. But urban consumers were not overly delighted with the plan, and neither were the administrators of Everglades National Park, which depends on the conservation pools for much of its overland flow of water.

Since its dedication in 1947, the park has figured prominently in the water woes of South Florida, usually as the reluctant—and innocent—adversary of such other consumers as commerce and industry. In the horrid droughts of the 1960s, some worm-brained Floridians were incredulous that the Park Service should expect any water at all from the Flood District. And while most of these critics were content to pit rhetorical alligators against people, others were carried a step beyond, even to claiming that wetting the park would be tantamount to condemning the children of Palm Beach to the agonies of death by dehydration. Fortunately, wiser heads prevailed. By law, the park is now guaranteed a minimum annual release of 315,000 acre-feet of water from the Flood District, through the gates under the Tamiami Trail to the Shark River and Taylor Slough. So the park is sitting pretty again, at least by most official accounts. But there are rangers who say otherwise; who, knowing the 'glades and how they work moving water to the mangrove estuaries, say the guaranteed release is not properly distributed; who say more culverts under the Trail are needed to correct this situation; and who report that in recent years the west side of the park, the side watered not by the Flood District but by the Big Cypress Swamp, has begun to dry up.

But now there is the promise of something better coming: The Big Cypress National Preserve authorized by Congress in 1974. Conceived as a deterrent to the kind of drainage and development pioneered by the Gulf-American Land Corporation, among others, the Cypress Preserve covers some 570,000 acres—or will, when and if the federal government appropriates its share of the acquisition funds (the State of

Florida already having put aside $40 million as its contribution). One property in the Big Cypress, however, is not for sale. This is the forty-square-mile site of the proposed Everglades Jetport, which everyone thought had been laid to rest in 1969 when former Governor Reuben Askew and the Nixon Administration ordered a halt to its construction. By agreement between Dade County aviation officials and loftier levels of government, one completed runway and some support structures were allowed to remain, to be used by airlines as a training facility. Aye, the chink in the armor, the foot in the door. Meanwhile, Dade officials went through the motions of searching for an alternate site for their super jetport. And what did they find after more than four years of weighing options? Why, they found that the alternate sites are unacceptable. And now, friends in Florida tell me, the Everglades Jetport is back again on the front burner, stewing away under a lid that is likely to blow at any moment.

To some officials, including many of the original promoters, it seems to make no difference that time and events have greatly altered the rationale for another major jetport in South Florida. It seems not to matter that the need for another jetport is already anachronistic, since air traffic at Miami International Airport has been declining, as it has everywhere else, because of recessionary incomes and inflationary fares. Or that training flights are now so few and far between at the Everglades site, because of fuel costs and a need for fewer pilots, that the Federal Aviation Administration no longer has much heart for staffing the control tower there. Nor does it seem to matter much that the original arguments against development of this site still prevail, including all the logic assembled by the National Academies of Science and Engineering and the U.S. Geological Survey to show that a jetport of this magnitude, at this location, would surely accelerate the collapse of natural systems in Everglades National Park. It is, of course, foolish to condemn the absence of logic on the other side of the argument. Logic has no place in the pork-barrel ethic.

One encounters curious attitudes in South Florida. I suppose they are no more peculiar than the attitudes of some people almost everywhere in America today, but they are distressing nonetheless. And they drag one screaming to the conclusion, if I may articulate an unabashedly snooty bias, that for all the environmental and cultural awareness we the people are supposed to have acquired in the past decade, we the people are still largely Visigoth at heart. We suffer yet from arrested sensitivity. I mean what can one expect of a society in which a Disney World attracts nearly fifty times more visitors than an Everglades National Park; in which "Monkey Jungles" and "Love Stories in Stone" and caged bears and stuffed serpents and cock fights and 'gator 'rassles draw *ooo*'s and *ahhh*'s from the gullible throngs, while the glorious backcountry at best provokes a disdainful yawn? At Everglades Park headquarters in the winter of 1974, a Park Service official told me that the way he figured it, the gasoline shortage could only *help* attendance. "I know it sounds crazy," he said, "and maybe we won't be getting as many visitors from out-of-state. But the locals from Miami will be pouring in here by the droves. You see, most of them have never been here—and now they'll come because it's so close."

I was then heading through the park to Flamingo, and on the way I stopped at the Pahayokee overlook, where the Park Service maintains an elevated observation platform at the edge of a vast saw grass prairie. There was only one car in the parking lot, and it bore Florida plates. The owners of that car were on the platform, a man with a camera and a woman with flaming red hair.

"Harold," the woman was saying, "what in heaven's name are you doing?"

"I'm taking a picture," said the man.

"There's nothing to take a picture of," said the woman.

"There's grass," he said.

The woman laughed. "Oh brother," she said. "*Big* deal."

The wood stork, *Mycteria americana*, is a large white wading bird with a baldish black head and a passion for maximizing mileage on a minimum of fuel. The stork is an energy conserver. By soaring on thermal air currents, it can travel great distances with hardly a flap of its wings. Contrary to archaic opinion in some quarters, the stork is not where human babies come from. The stork is where stork babies come from, and this great bird's struggle to keep enough of them coming out of its nests each year to sustain the species is a matter of some public concern; especially to those who not only appreciate wild diversity for its own sake, but who see the bird as a kind of living barometer of the natural pressures on everything else in South Florida, including *Homo sapiens americanus.*

Though other stork species hang on here and there throughout the world, this is the only one that is native to North America. It breeds almost exclusively in South Florida, where thermals stack up quickly under the hot sun and the fishing is easy, or was, before drainage. For some time now, great numbers of nesting wood storks have convened in the cypress at Corkscrew Swamp, clearly because the large trees provide excellent shelter and, more importantly, one suspects, because Corkscrew is strategically located within striking distance of good fishing holes, such as Catherine Isle, the Fahkahatchee, and the Okaloacooche Slough. The wood stork is an unusual fisher. Unlike its distant cousin, the heron, the stork locates its prey not by sight but by touch; it gropes with its beak in the water, using a sideways raking motion. Thus, to fish successfully, the stork must have its food concentrated in shallow pools. And though I have boasted of its frugal use of energy, it nevertheless requires a great deal of protein. During the breeding season, with young on the way or in the nest, an adult stork must rake up some five to fifteen pounds of fish each day.

In the nearly twenty years since men began counting storks and nests in the cypress at Corkscrew Swamp, the number of nesting adult birds and fledglings produced there has declined. Not steadily, year by year, but in a sort of oscillating downward curve, from a peak of 12,000 adults and 17,000 young in the winter-spring breeding season of 1960-61, to 2,000 adults and about 4,000 young in 1973-74.

To be sure, one cannot pin the entire blame on the Gulf-American Land Corporation, which is blessedly defunct, or on its successors in the drainage racket, for the record shows that nature, too, can be ruthless with storks. Cold snaps, freak pre-season hurricanes, high water from heavy rains (instead of low water concentrating the fish during the October-to-May dry-down period) have taken their toll in the rookery, so that as many as three straight years have come and gone with the great flocks producing no young, or worse, with the nests deserted and the young abandoned to crows and vultures. So it goes out there in the screaming wild; and so it has always gone. Nature has its own reasons for mucking around, perhaps reasons that become very logical in human terms as we begin to understand a little about the dynamics of population and food supply, among other things. The wood stork has been confronting such logic for millions of years. Somehow it has coped. But now the stork must confront an additional and unnatural interference from humankind, with its drag-lines and tree crushers and artificial droughts. And somehow, the stork is no longer coping.

Not that it isn't trying to cope. I have before me now a report by Joan Browder of the University of Florida's Center for Wetlands in Gainesville. Ms. Browder is a bright young environmental scientist I first met wading through a cypress swamp at the height of the jetport controversy in 1969. More recently she has been up in the air in a small plane, monitoring the feeding areas of wood storks nesting at Corkscrew Swamp. Ms. Browder's research is part of a larger project called the South Florida Environmental Study. Her part was undertaken on the assumption that the wood stork is an indicator of wetland productivity. In other words, as the stork goes, so goes the land's ability to capture, store, and process energy.

Ms. Browder started monitoring the storks' fishing holes in December of 1973, right after the birds began to convene at Corkscrew Swamp (and right after my last visit there). Flying out of Ft. Myers in a Cessna chartered by the National Audubon Society, Ms. Browder and her pilot crisscrossed the skies of Southwest Florida at intervals over a six-month period. Feeding birds were spotted from altitudes of up to 1,500 feet, and occasionally soaring storks were followed on thermals up to 5,000 feet. As nesting activity progressed at Corkscrew through the winter, the birds gradually shifted their feeding from scattered sites throughout the region to the major sloughs, where the dry-down had not yet affected the level of the pools and fish were still plentiful. Rainfall was far below average during this time, and soon even the sloughs and marshes that normally held water until June were running dry. Yet despite the accelerated dry-down, the storks produced. Eggs began hatching in late February, and by May young birds were testing their wings above the rookery.

By May something else was happening. South Florida was drying down to its marl underpinnings, and the Weather Bureau at Ft. Myers was calling it the most severe drought in eighty years. Now the storks in their rookery were facing a critical time, for there were 4,000 fast-growing fledglings to feed. But in the Fahkahatchee Strand and the Okaloacooche Slough, the old reliable cupboards were bare.

Until May, it had commonly been assumed by those familiar with the habits of wood storks that the bird's effective range—that is, the maximum distance it will travel out from the rookery to its feeding areas—is about forty miles. And forty miles more or less from Corkscrew covered just about all the sloughs and marshes in which Joan Browder had sighted wood storks before the final bone-dry stages of dry-down. On May 2, 3, and 5, Ms. Browder and her pilot flew sorties south and west from Ft. Myers over the old feeding areas. In her log, she noted: ". . . dry everywhere . . . nothing but mud puddles . . . fires burning in scattered spots over entire area . . . dense haze of smoke over Southwest Florida." And no storks at the traditional fishing holes. But there were storks in the sky, riding the thermals on a coordinate from Corkscrew toward Lake Okeechobee. When the Cessna banked over the northwest shore of Okeechobee, Joan Browder looked down at the vast wet marshes spreading back from the lake along the Kissimmee River and counted two hundred wood storks (and thousands of other waders) feeding there. And this was *sixty* miles from Corkscrew Swamp.

I am awed to think of it—these tenacious birds, brooding like black-cowled monks in the treetops, knowing the fish are dead and rotting in the Fahkahatchee, waiting for the sun to get up and for thermals to rise, then rising themselves and soaring sixty miles to the only place in South Florida where food is still concentrated in shallow pools, and fishing all day and storing the catch in the stomach, to be regurgitated at sunset for the fledglings after sixty more miles on heavy homeward wings. It is inspiring as well as awesome, and one comes away from Joan Browder's report with a new sense of hope, with a vision of wet marshes hunkering forever along the shores of Lake Okeechobee as a fail-safe for foraging wood storks in times of drought. Yes, if the Okeechobee wetlands can permit the storks to conclude a successful year of reproduction, as they did in the season of 1973-74, there is hope all right. And the promise of something better coming. Right? Wrong. We should have known better. For here comes the Army Corps of Engineers again with a scheme to increase the storage capacity of Okeechobee by raising the levees around it several feet, and no one knows what effect this endeavor might have on the Okeechobee marshes. The best educated guess is that elevated levees will probably muck up the area's hydrological rhythm and turn the marshes into dehydrated flats, fine for sugar cane maybe, but not for storks.

So Florida continues to grow by metes and bounds and breakwaters and canals. And levees. Someday, at the rate it is growing, Florida may be right up there at the top, behind New York and California. It will be a curious sort of place, all patched and emulsified and planted with exotic palms from the Caribbean. And along with the Disney Worlds and the Monkey Jungles and the moon missiles replacing the howitzers in front of city halls, there will be roadside museums filled with plastic animals. Among the specimens, surely, will be the replica of a large white wading bird with a baldish black head. And glass eyes. And a little boy with a pasty face—tans no longer being as prevalent as they once were in the Sunshine State—will point at the big bird and say, "Daddy, what were *those* for?" And Daddy, knowing perfectly well where babies come from, won't have the foggiest idea.

SO SMALL A CITY, SO LARGE A JAIL

Gallup is the eleventh largest city in New Mexico, following Albuquerque, Santa Fe, Las Cruces, Roswell, Clovis, Hobbs, Alamagordo, Farmington, Carlsbad, and Los Alamos, in that order. Its population, according to the last census, is 14,596. The statistic is appropriate from Monday through Friday only. On weekends, if one counts the transients, Gallup at the very least replaces Clovis in fifth place and often edges past Santa Fe (41,000) to second. It is a distinction some residents of the city—that is to say, those whose livelihoods are not dependent on retail sales or services—would just as soon do without. But in Gallup, as elsewhere, the majority rules. And while the city sustains a few industries processing onion rings, piñon nuts, infant furniture, air-conditioning pads, sheet metal, oil, natural gas, and uranium, the greater share of individual and community wealth flows directly from the city's 75 gasoline stations, 47 restaurants, 45 motels, 33 handicraft shops, and 38 assorted establishments licensed by the State of New Mexico to sell alcoholic beverages over the counter to persons twenty-one years of age or older.

Gallup is situated in high plateau country at an elevation of 6,000 feet. The mean annual temperature is 47.6° F., and the winter nights are bitter cold—a circumstance of no small significance to the county coroner, whose knowledge of frozen corpses may possibly qualify him as one of the nation's leading authorities on death from exposure. The cold is exacerbated by strong winds which gust through the surrounding sandstone hills and scour the town's windowpanes with grit from the Rio Puerco arroyo. The riverbed itself runs east to west through the city, separating the largely Mexican-American community of the north side from the Anglo population to the south. The river and hills together are responsible for the city's linear configuration, which is

110

further defined by three parallel arteries of commerce and transportation. First is Coal Avenue, the main street named for the fossil fuel that was discovered and mined here in the days when trains were powered by steam. One block to the north is 66 Avenue, after old U.S. Highway 66, now made obsolete by Interstate 40 outside of town but still the kind of thoroughfare in town where one can get his kicks, as the song once promised. And finally there is the mainline of the Atcheson, Topeka and Santa Fe Railroad. This is where the coroner who is knowledgable about exposure also learned a great deal about the effect of locomotives on the human body—that is, until it was decided to erect a chain-link fence to prevent semiconscious loiterers from bedding down between the rails on Saturday nights.

For so small a city, comparatively speaking, Gallup is extraordinarily well-endowed with public works. Across the street from the adobe county courthouse is a modern, block-sized federal building, put there by the General Services Administration at a cost of $4 million. In the sere hills of the south side are new parks and schools for the Anglos and, for others who have some past or present affiliation with Uncle Sam, a huge, highrise Public Health Service Hospital which appears, from a distance, like the floating mirage of a Hilton hotel. And down near Route 66, where the highway comes in from Albuquerque past the Red Rocks and the hogback ridge at the edge of town, is Gallup's grand investment in criminal justice—a $950,000 structure housing the city's 56-member police department, the McKinley County Sheriff's Office, a municipal court, and a jail whose capacity, at 500 prisoners, exceeds that of any other detention facility in New Mexico, including the State's own penitentiaries.

Until Interstate 40 came along to clear some 200 homes from its right-of-way through the run-down north side, across the river from the railroad tracks Gallup had another grand investment: the Indian Ceremonial Grounds. As any good student of municipal claim-staking knows, Gallup is "The Indian Capital of the World." Signs proclaim this title along the highway, and so it must be, despite rumors to the contrary from such diverse places as New Delhi and Wounded Knee. Wounded Knee has had its showdowns—two, so far—but so far it has never had a ceremonial the likes of which Gallup has been putting on for twenty-five years. Personally I have never seen the Indian Ceremonial in Gallup, but those who have tell me that for all the grease-paint and whooping and war-bonnets it puts the memory of Barnum and Bailey and Buffalo Bill to shame.

"What do the Indians get out of it?" I once inquired of a non-Indian member of the chamber of commerce.

"They get to put on their old clothes," he replied.

As for Gallup, it gets the retail business of some 40,000 tourists who drop by for the four-day ceremonial each August. But now the old stadium has been lost to the right-of-way of the interstate highway, and as I write this, plans are moving ahead to relocate the arena in a new five-million-dollar multipurpose park carved into the majestic Red Rocks east of town. A brochure describing the proposal promises that the park will produce over its first twelve years $34.5 million in off-site spending for the Gallup area. And the Indians will still be able to put on their old clothes.

All of this—the weekend population boom, the Indian Ceremonial, the Anglo prosperity, the new public works, the jail for 500, the thirty-eight liquor licenses, even the senseless deaths on the snow or rails—all of this is largely the result of Gallup's unique location. It is not so important that Gallup lies athwart major east-west rail and highway arteries, midway between Albuquerque and Flagstaff, Arizona. That certainly helps. But what is more important, what truly makes the city tick, is its proximity to the fourteen-million-acre Navajo Indian Reservation and to the 136,000 people who count themselves as members of that tribe. Gallup, of course, cannot expect to serve as trade center for the entire Navajo nation. The distances in this part of the country are too great; so while some Navajos find it more convenient to sample the white man's world in Flagstaff or Winslow or Farmington, others rely for their needs on the one-stop traders scattered across the wild reservation backcountry.

Still, most Navajos with access to a motor vehicle head, at one time or another, for Gallup. The city has had a reputation for treating the Indian reasonably well. And the Indian is eager, as always, to reciprocate. For thousands of Navajos, going to Gallup on weekends is the thing to do, as long as the money lasts. Once, before Kit Carson and the blue-eyed generals, the people came on ponies to the forts to do business with traders. Now they come in pickup trucks to Gallup to exchange United States currency for groceries and appliances and dry goods and pharmaceuticals. There is something else in Gallup—something one cannot purchase legally anywhere on the reservation. There is alcohol. So the city, already favored by geography, is rewarded as well by legislation which forces a person to travel eighty miles to buy a drink.

I saw the place, that first time out, from the window of a Greyhound bus. We came in from Albuquerque, past the buried ammunition bunkers of Ft. Wingate and the Red Rocks and the fork where the highway swings down along the tracks of the Santa Fe Railroad. There had been patches of snow on the desert, and now, behind the cafés and motels and taco parlors, the chimneys of Gallup were trailing thin streamers of piñon smoke across a slate-colored sky. I saw what makes the town the way it is, though I could not even begin to understand that at the time. I saw its past and present, and possibly its apocalyptic future, beside the road as we came in. I saw a Navajo woman wrapped in a bright red blanket. She was sitting cross-legged, and her long flowing skirt was tucked around her feet. There was a Navajo man beside her. He was lying on his back, his face hidden beneath a battered Stetson. His knees, in thin denim, were aimed at the sky. One hand clutched a brown paper sack. The Navajo woman was rocking back and forth, like a child in a crib, and she stared across the highway at the desert beyond the smoking chimneys. It was a Sunday morning, still early, and very cold outside the bus. I remember wondering as we passed the couple how, on such a day, anyone could possibly sleep outdoors. It did not occur to me until later, after I left the bus at the depot and began to explore the streets of the city, that the trick to sleeping outdoors in Gallup in the winter is easy. The only prerequisite is to be a Navajo without a ride back home to the reservation, and to have spent your last dollar the night before on a head-splitting shot of Southern Comfort in some Anglo saloon.

I lived in Gallup for four months that winter, working as a reporter for the daily *Independent*. I did not take much to the town itself, though I found the people I encountered warm and friendly. The town depressed me with its gray shabbiness, and I longed to move on to some greener place where I would not have to spend Friday nights covering high school basketball games and the after-dinner antics of Rotarians. Most of the staff—and there weren't many of us— worked a six-day week. This was especially painful because it precluded any extended forays out of town into the magnificent country roundabout. An occasional Sunday saw me only as far as the Petrified Forest, or Zuni, or Sheep Springs, or the McCaffrey Mountains, where an advertising salesman and I negligently conspired to scorch the floor of a pine forest by turning our backs on a briquet fire. In the blue distance, it seemed, I could always see mesas and escarpments I would never reach by nightfall. And in the city room I listened with envy as seasoned explorers, sufficiently tenured to have earned days off two-in-a-row, told of trips to the volcanic slopes of Mt. Taylor, to the holy mesas of the Hopi, to Canyon de Chelly and Monument Valley, to Shiprock and the Chuskas and Moccasin Arch, to Ear of the Wind and Sun's Eye and Navajo Mountain and Rainbow Bridge. And so I never got beyond the tamest fringes of the Navajo country. What I saw instead were the people themselves, the *Dineh*, always coming from the other direction, from some of the very places I wanted to be, congregating on the sidewalks of Gallup. And the winter sleepers in the back alleys, and the men shivering in the morning with blood-shot eyes, and the women in shawls and blankets waiting outside the door of the municipal jail.

It was a small jail, then, about the right size for a town

such as Gallup, if Gallup had been somewhere else. There were bunks for twenty-five prisoners, but in a pinch the facility could take fifty for short periods. Like overnight, Saturday night. But some Saturday nights the Gallup jail slept— *held* is more accurate—seventy-five people, and most of these, the overnighters, were Navajos. God only knows how awful it was, Saturday night in that place. I never inquired. I simply looked at the police blotter, recorded the number of bookings for public drunkenness and disorderly conduct, and dropped the statistic into my Monday-morning summary of crime and punishment, somewhere between the knife fight on Coal Avenue and the alleged rape on the north side. This was about two years after the repeal of Prohibition for American Indians off the reservation. Opinions in the community regarding the possible duration of the problem, not to mention the adequacy of the Gallup jail, were about evenly divided between the generous naïve and the malicious uninformed. The former held that everything would be all right once the novelty of legal alcohol no longer lured the Navajo to overindulgence. They predicted it would be like the early Thirties had been for the law-abiding non-Indian: after repeal, one prolonged fling with the bottle and then— moderation. The others, the uninformed, citing the dubious precedent of history, identified the Navajo drinker as an hereditary alcoholic, physiologically incapable of taking any amount of spirits without becoming intoxicated. Word soon got around the country that Navajos were lying unconscious in the gutters of Gallup, and, before long, dozens of sociologists, missionaries, and assorted doctors of this and that were in town to study the problem. Meanwhile, the problem grew worse. In the reservation schools of the Bureau of Indian Affairs, where Navajo children at the time were trained to be "white," two conflicting commandments remained in vogue. *Thou Shalt Not Resist Assimilation* was the first. The second was *Thou Shalt Not Drink*. In Gallup, a post-graduate generation was obeying the first dictum while disregarding the second; and on Saturday night there was standing-room-only in the municipal jail.

I am not quite sure, as I look back on that Gallup of some twenty years ago, exactly how the business community re- acted to this legacy of open saloons and overcrowded cells. I believe there was some show of Anglo consternation. But it was mild when I was there. It was mild because even then the most concerned retailer understood to what extent he was dependent on Indian trade. Once, long after I had left the place, I read or heard somewhere that the Indian ac- counted for 72 percent of retail sales in Gallup. More recent- ly, city officials have estimated that the Indian is responsible for about 60-65 percent of the retail dollar. This is the *direct* contribution. It does not account for the influence of the Indian, drunk or sober, on revenues derived through tourism. Barring periodic gasoline shortages, the Indian Capital of the World attracts thousands of tourists. It is handy to Grand Canyon, Mesa Verde, Arches, Canyonlands, and Capitol Reef national parks, as well as to a dozen or so national monu- ments. When the tourists get tired of looking at rocks, they come to Gallup to look at Indians.

Before I got there, tourists also came to Gallup to look at cowboys. The cowboys were ringers from Los Angeles. They came as extras and stunt men for the motion pictures that were then filmed in the red sandstone formations east of town. I like old Westerns. I see a lot of them on television, without remembering their names. From time to time, I see a lot of the Red Rocks, jutting out from the side of the screen to backdrop horsemen who, according to the scenario, are galloping for their lives through the sage of Wyoming or Utah or Arizona. But if you know the Red Rocks, you under- stand that in reality the horsemen are galloping on the out- skirts of Gallup, New Mexico. For all its hospitality to the visitors from Hollywood, Gallup acquired no residual rights in these films. It did, however, manage to stake a claim on the Red Rocks; and having done that, the city proceeded to seek some new way to exploit their wild beauty in the in- terest of tourism.

The first idea for the Red Rocks sounded as if it might have come straight out of a movie itself. It was a big story, to be sure, and it occasioned the only special edition I worked on during those four months at the *Independent.* The edition was printed with ink the color of rust, and the headline announced in 72-point Bodoni type:

Indian Colossus Comes to Red Rocks!

That the colossus never arrived is no fault of the editor who wrote the headline. In the exuberance of that time, it seemed like a sure bet.

The colossus, conceived by an Ann Arbor sculptor, was to be the largest figure ever erected by man—250 feet tall, head and shoulders over the Statue of Liberty. The materials were to be granite and steel, which would be hoisted by giant cranes to the site atop one of the sandstone mesas. The cost, including ancillary museum and amphitheater facilities, would be $9 million. "Never in the history of man," the lead story began, "has one civilization created a great memorial to another. . . . For the state with the vision to create such a memorial to the First Americans, the rewards will be indeed rich and lasting." The story then went on to explain how the statue would rise above "the last great home of the Indian in America"; how an eternal flame (undoubtedly fueled with waste natural gas from a nearby refinery) would—and here the story quotes one of the sculptor's entrepreneurial associates—"commemorate the Indian's firm belief in everlasting life . . . forever symbolic of his eternal campfire, once flecking this great continent as a rash of stars punctuates the night." Finally, almost as an afterthought, the story mentioned that the project would be financed by charter memberships, contributions by industry, and public subscription "reaching into every level of American life."

About a month later I gave notice to my editor and left Gallup. As I drove east from town, I looked at the Red Rocks and tried to picture a great figure of steel and granite with its left arm extended toward Navajo country. I could not guess that the whole scheme would be down the drain within two years—no funds to speak of, and the entrepreneurs not answering long-distance calls in their Ann Arbor offices. I

looked at the rocks but I could see no colossus. In my mind
I saw something else. I saw a Navajo woman in a red blanket, waiting for her man to pick himself up from the frozen
ground.

Through the rest of the Fifties and Sixties, from the greener
pastures of California to the big rotten apple of New York,
the memory of Gallup and of what I had seen and felt there
was always with me, like the aftertaste of something hard
and indigestible lodged in the gut. And I knew I would have
to go back, if only to purge myself of the blurred and dreary
visions.

On the pretext of having pressing business in Albuquerque,
I returned to Gallup for another look in 1971. It was January, appropriately, with patches of snow on the desert. And
it was Saturday. I rented a car at the airport and cruised
down 66 Avenue to where U.S. 666 comes in from the north,
from Navajo country. There was a traffic jam at the light.
Pickup trucks were backed up a quarter mile across the railroad tracks on the north side, their fenders powdered with
the ocher dust of the reservation. I could see that Women's
Liberation had not yet come to the Navajo, for the women
still sat with the dogs in the open backs of the trucks, bun-
dled in blankets against the cold and the dust, while the men
sat three abreast in the cabs with the heaters going. On Coal
Avenue, now a one-way street, the trucks jerked slowly along
in low gear. Groups of Indians were everywhere—at street
corners, in front of store windows, standing around their
trucks in the parking lots and the new shopping plaza. I had
never seen so many at one time in the old days, never imagined the city could contain so great a crowd. I asked the
waitress in a coffee shop if something special was going on
that day. "Not that I know of," she said. "It's just *their* day
in town."

In the afternoon I called on City Manager Jim Fleming at
his office in the municipal building. He was two years into
the job, a seasoned professional with more than a decade of
management behind him in Tucumcari. We talked for a while

about the Gallup I remembered, which led inevitably to the
Navajo and alcoholism. Fleming said the city was hoping for
help from the U.S. Department of Health, Education and
Welfare. "It's a problem and it's getting worse," he said.
"We're dealing with three to four hundred hardcore drinkers.
We've got to have some rehabilitation facilities in here."

"They were saying that back in 1955," I said. "What happened?" Fleming said he didn't know.

He took me then on a tour of the south side. "This just
might be the richest little city in the whole Southwest," he
said as we drove up into the hills. "You won't see many signs
of a recession here. Almost four million dollars in building
permits last year. Two hundred new housing units." We
passed a park with ballfields, tennis courts, and picnic tables.
"That's new, too," said Fleming. "Cost four hundred thousand dollars. And that water tank up there." He pointed
toward a huge green cylinder sunk into the top of a hill.
"That's just in, and it adds four million gallons to the city's
capacity." Now we were at the top and I could see the new
highrise Public Health hospital straight ahead, and, off to our
left, the expensive-looking homes of the country club section. Fleming parked the car.

"Where's the money coming from?" I asked.

"A lot of it's coming from our city sales tax," he said.
"And most of that's coming from over there." We were looking north now, across the city to where Highway 666 comes
down from Gamerco and the Navajo Indian Reservation.
Fleming waved his hand in blessing on the scene. "You've
seen what it's like in town today," he said. "Well, it begins
over there on Friday afternoons and doesn't let up till Sunday morning. All those people. All those vehicles bumper to
bumper. Everything heading for Gallup like a river of gold."

On Sunday morning I drove alone against the spent current
of that river, north on 666 and west to the real Indian Capital
at Window Rock, Arizona, where the Navajo Tribal Council
presides over its 25,000-square-mile domain. But the highway
wasn't paved with gold. It glittered instead with the shards of
broken wine bottles and beer cans jettisoned from pickup

trucks bearing the liver-wounded home from Gallup. And spaced out along the road were the stragglers, the ones who had shot their last dollars last night at Dan's or Eddie's or the Rendezvous Nite Club on Route 66, the ones who were too proud to turn toward the traffic and stick out a thumb. It is a long walk from Gallup to Window Rock, about twenty-five miles, but Navajos are used to such things. Not even the Spanish, with horses so easy to steal, could break them of walking. Navajos like to walk. The United States government recognized that in 1868 when it sent Kit Carson to scorch their cornfields, corraled them into Canyon de Chelly, and then—at gunpoint—invited the Navajos to walk 300 miles across New Mexico to a concentration camp called Bosque Rondondo, where the tribe dwindled down to a precious few. But now, despite short life expectancy and a high rate of infant mortality, the Navajos number 136,000 and still walk. Home from Gallup on Sunday morning.

Dinebeiina Nahiilna Be Agaditahe, or DNA for short, is a legal services program with headquarters at Window Rock and field offices in Crownpoint, Chinle, Tuba City, and Shiprock. The words are Navajo for "attorneys who contribute to the economic revitalization of the people"; the people being, of course, the Navajo nation, in which nearly half the employable are unemployed, the median annual income of the working-age is less than $3,000, and the overall average income per capita is barely $1,000. So the attorneys, some two dozen in all, have much to which they can contribute, and they do. DNA was founded in 1967 and funded by the Office of Economic Opportunity until Richard Nixon decided to dismantle the poverty programs initiated by Lyndon Johnson before him. Now the funds come to DNA from the Department of Health, Education and Welfare, and, as long as this continues, there will be a number of unhappy businessmen and politicians in the states of New Mexico, Utah, and Arizona, which are overlapped by the Indian nation the DNA attorneys seek to revitalize.

The reason for DNA's unpopularity is quite simple: in the

process of revitalizing the Navajo, the attorneys have found it necessary on occasion to sue the bastards who have devitalized the Indians for decades. For example, there have been certain reservation traders from time to time who abused their roles as merchant and pawnbroker and postmaster and buyer of Navajo wool and jewelry. According to one DNA report issued in the early Seventies, a few traders were known to have forced Navajo clients to sign welfare checks over to them, to have engaged in questionable pawn practices, and to have purposefully wrapped the Navajo in debt, to the point of total dependence on the trader. And car dealers who sold Navajos over-priced vehicles that could barely make it out of the lot, and then followed up with high-pressure collection tactics or illegal repossession. And peddlers of appliances who stumped the backcountry with gobbledygook fine-print contracts, sometimes even making the sales pitch to illiterate families remote from any source of electricity. And law enforcement officers in border towns, who, until recently, were said to have booked on charges of driving while drunk any Navajo with the slightest trace of liquor on his breath.

Peterson Zah, a young man of thirty-two when I first met him that Sunday at Window Rock in 1971, is the deputy director of DNA. He is a Navajo and a graduate of Arizona State, where he played basketball because he is strong and athletic and six feet tall, an uncommon height for an Indian of the American Southwest. Zah learned a great deal at Arizona State. Among other things, he learned to forget a lot of the nonsense drummed into him at a Bureau of Indian Affairs boarding school. He also learned how to drink whiskey without getting drunk. "My father and his father," said Zah when I talked with him at Window Rock, "they had no opportunity to learn. They couldn't buy liquor. They couldn't even go into a bar. If you cannot be seen with a bottle, then you put what's in the bottle in your stomach and carry it that way. At boarding school in Phoenix they taught me it was bad to drink, that alcohol was evil. I don't think it is. I learned how to cope with it. I think our educators have to be educated. They shouldn't be saying 'do not drink.' They should be teaching *how* to drink if you want to." I asked Zah if he felt the problem might be eased by permitting liquor sales on the reservation. "No," he said. "The reservation is not ready for that yet. It is still politically touchy to speak of liquor on the reservation."

"Then the alternative is Gallup," I said.

"Yes," said Peterson Zah. "Gallup. But where is the promised rehabilitation? The city has three times the number of liquor licenses it should have by law. Because it claims the reservation is an extension of the city. That's not right. Gallup has a moral responsibility. It should not just stand there waiting for the Indian with its hands out. The hands should give as well as receive."

Leaving Window Rock, I passed a slow pickup truck turning off the highway onto a dirt track. A large sticker was pasted across the rear bumper. The message was short: *Indian Power.*

On the front page of the *New York Times* one morning in March of 1973, a familiar dateline attracted my eye. I mean familiar to me, for I do not suspect it had been seen too often on the front page of any eastern newspaper, or of any newspaper outside New Mexico for that matter. The dateline was Gallup, and the story, displayed as a sidebar to the running account of the second battle of Wounded Knee in South Dakota, told of the abduction of Mayor Emmett Garcia—at gunpoint in the Gallup municipal building—by two young Indian activists, of their subsequent retreat to, and seizure of, a local sporting goods store, and of the shoot-out in which one of the abductors was slain by police after Garcia dived through a plate-glass door, taking most of the glass with him, not to mention a charge of shotgun pellets in his buttocks. Garcia, an amiable man who lost his bid for re-election the following month and moved a safe distance from Gallup to Pinetop, Arizona, believes he was the victim of a conspiracy. "The incident was planned," he told me when I spoke with him by phone some time later. "I just happened to be more convenient than the governor." But under questioning, Garcia freely admitted he was not the most popular public official among members of the Indian community. There were some grievances against the business establishment, for example, and it was said that Garcia had not moved fast enough to redress them. There had been demands for a new Indian community center, and again it was said that the mayor had been unresponsive. And finally, there was the Navajo Inn near Window Rock, on the very edge of the reservation. The inn held a license to serve liquor, and its owner was Emmett Garcia.

One detail most of the stories did not mention at the time, perhaps because it did not seem important, was the business to which Garcia had been attending when the two Indian militants ordered him out of the municipal building. Ironically, the mayor was attending to the city's liquor problems. In fact, he was in conference with the Gallup Alcoholism Coordinator, and the two men were reviewing data for a community development masterplan to be published in April. Among the observations and statistics which would find their way into the plan were admissions that "a city of 14,596 is required to maintain a police force of 50-60 officers because of the problem of public inebriates"; that the police had been making eight to ten thousand arrests yearly for public drunkenness; that another 48,000 people, "primarily public inebriates," were utilizing a free sleeping shelter over the course of a year; that "the visibility of the problem adversely affects the main industry of the area—tourism"; and that rehabilitation efforts, "while improving, remain inadequate." It is also likely that, at some point before they were so rudely interrupted, Emmett Garcia and his alcoholism coordinator discussed the recent submission of a grant request to the National Institute of Alcohol Abuse and Alcoholism in Washington, D.C. Prepared by the Gallup Inter-Agency Coordinating Committee, an affiliation of forty-two private and official agencies (churches, courts, schools, hospitals, tribal councils, social welfare organizations, and law enforcement offices), the application to Washington requested $11 million over eleven years to fund a program that would once and for all identify, treat, cure, counsel, and employ the scourge of Gallup—the public inebriate. Against this $11 million, should it be forthcoming, the State of New Mexico, McKinley County, the City of Gallup, and the nonprofit Southwest Indian Foundation had pledged a total of $339,000 toward capital financing of the complex such a rehabilitation program would require. Of this, Gallup's share would be $50,000, about the same amount of money the city spent to install tennis courts at the new park I had seen in 1971, in the hills of the south side.

Whatever may have been under discussion when the Indian men appeared with guns in the municipal building, the conference was never resumed. And more than one full year after the incident, the rehabilitation grant request still sat without approval on some desk in Washington, D.C., where, as far as I can tell, it may well sit forever.

On July 1, 1973, by an act of the state legislature, public drunkenness was stricken from the statute books as a criminal offense in New Mexico. Under the new law, police officers were authorized to pursue three courses of action when confronting an inebriate. The preferred action was to take the subject home, or, if he or she appeared to be in particularly bad shape, to a rehabilitation center for alcoholics. The third alternative, the last resort, was to place the non-offender in jail for his own personal safety and to hold him there until he sobered up—for as long as twelve hours if necessary, but without booking or fingerprinting. As might be expected, the new statute was hailed as a humanitarian victory, especially by the forty-two federal, state, county, municipal, and private agencies which, in one way or another, were purporting to deal with the problem of the Navajo inebriate in Gallup, New Mexico. The options in Gallup, however, were limited. Police officers, for example, were not about to transport their prototypical weekend drunkard to the threshold of his own home, which was likely to be anywhere from twenty-five to a hundred and twenty-five miles away, up some dusty arroyo in Navajo country. What's more, after years of small talk about establishing a meaningful program for alcoholics, with in-patient services and facilities, after analyzing and cataloging the need, after submitting, albeit belatedly, its $11 million request, Gallup still lacked both program and facilities to help the Navajo alcoholic back on his feet. And so, by default, the last resort—the drunk tank—became the only option for Gallup under the new law.

The law had been on the books for half a year when I returned to Gallup my last time. It was winter again. It was always winter for me in Gallup. Another weekend was approaching, the "river of gold" would soon be flowing, and the saloon stewards were requisitioning large supplies of beer and port and tokay and muscatel. Mannie Gonzales, a tough, knowledgable police sergeant when I had worked at the *Independent*, was now director of public safety, and he was telling me how, with the new law, some hardcore drinkers were getting picked up fifteen to twenty times a month, not even recuperating from one binge to the next. Gonzales explained the system. The drunks picked up by city police officers and county sheriff's deputies are taken to the drunk tanks at the new jail, the one I had seen under construction in 1971, the one that can hold 500, the largest one in the state. In addition, there are four public safety officers, non-uniformed Navajos, who take turns driving an unmarked white Ford delivery van around the city picking up other drunks. The drunks in the van are taken to a different place, a low green concrete building at the west end of town near the railroad tracks. The place is called Sleep-in, or Turquoise Club by those who have never spent a night on the floor there. It is the same hostel which, as mentioned in Emmett Garcia's 1973 masterplan, accommodates 48,000 a year and is operated by the Southwest Indian Foundation with a night watchman assigned from the sheriff's office to oust unmanageable belligerents. And when all the space on the floor of the Sleep-in is taken, as it often is on a cold winter night, by two or three hundred people, then the Ford van takes the left-overs to the new jail, where, under the circumstances, there is always room for one more.

Because of the Sleep-in, there is some doubt now that the new jail will ever be filled to capacity, unless public drunkenness is made a crime again in New Mexico. In February, 1974, when I was shown through the jail by Police Chief Robert Leyba, four cellblocks containing 150 bunks had been unused since the change in the law the previous July. The other four cellblocks held a total of forty-six prisoners booked on a variety of felony and misdemeanor charges. The occupied cellblocks were filled with the sound of Muzak and inscribed with graffiti. One inscription, scratched into the wall above a seatless toilet bowl, read: *AIM was here.* AIM is the American Indian Movement. Around the corner from the cellblocks were the drunk tanks, one for a hundred males, another for fifty females. Each tank was equipped with narrow benches hung from its walls and drain-holes in a stark concrete floor. Half a dozen men were lying on the benches in the larger tank. They had made the mistake of getting drunk before the Sleep-in opened at 8 P.M. So had the three Navajo women in the tank next-door. Chief Leyba said the two tanks would be holding one hundred Indians between them within ten hours. It was then five o'clock, Friday afternoon. "It's a revolving door," Leyba said. "Unless we get a decent rehabilitation program going in Gallup, the law sooner or later will have to get changed back to what it used to be. As it is, all we're doing here is running a taxi and hotel service for the intoxicated."

On our way back to the chief's office, we paused in front of a small one-man cell. "This is a holding cell," Leyba explained. "The violent ones go in here until they cool off. And the ones with the DTs." A Navajo man of indeterminate age, toothless and wrinkled, his clothes soiled, his hair matted, stared between the bars with wide and wild eyes. His knees were rubbery, and only his hands clenched tight on the bars, so tight that the knuckles were blue, stopped him from falling backwards into the dark interior of the cell. A deep guttural sound rose in the man's throat and the eyes rolled back in his head until only the bloodshot whites showed, and the body snapped and quivered as if it had been struck by lightning. "He's hallucinating," Leyba said. "He believes he is being chased by animals."

Animals loom large in the Navajo mind, as they do in the minds of all Indian peoples who have managed to save the old legends from assimilation, Christianization, and other cultural obfuscations of one sort or another. It was explained long ago, for example, that the Red Rocks got their color from Coyote. It was said in the hogans of the Navajo that Coyote wished to pluck a star from the sky. "How will you get there?" asked Rabbit. And Coyote replied, "You shall see." Then Coyote summoned all the small animals that lived in the ground and asked them to build a giant slingshot. The animals worked hard until one day the slingshot was finished. And Coyote said to them, "Tonight when the skies are clear and bright from the light of the crescent moon, I shall pluck a star from the sky." And Coyote climbed into the pouch of the slingshot and said to Badger, "Cut the rope." And Badger did, with his sharp claws. And Coyote was flung into the sky. But on his way to the stars, Coyote hit the sharp edge of the crescent moon, and he began to bleed. And the drops of blood fell to the earth and became rock. And that, it was said then and is yet repeated in some hogans of the Navajo, is why the rocks are red.

There is another legend they tell in Navajo country. It is the story of the Thunderbird which causes lightning by the opening and closing of its eyes, thunder by the beating of its wings, and rain from the tilting of the lake on its back. To the Indian, the coming of the Thunderbird means rich grass for his sheep, abundant crops, enduring peace and good fortune. It is a benevolent symbol, the Thunderbird, and white men throughout the West and elsewhere have embraced it as their own, applying the name to their cars, beverages, ranches, restaurants, theaters, and especially their motels, including the one on Route 66 which is situated almost directly across the railroad tracks from the Gallup Sleep-in. This Thunderbird, with its neon escutcheon, promises no enduring good fortune. It simply offers color television in every room and a manual thermostat which allows one to forget that on this particular Friday night the temperature outside will plummet, under Coyote's clear skies, to five degrees above zero.

At 9 P.M. Thomas Yazzie arrived at the radio room of the Gallup jail. He was a short, thin, wiry young Indian with worried eyes, and he was wearing a heavy sheepskin jacket. The sergeant at the desk explained that I wanted to ride with Yazzie in the white Ford delivery van. The Indian looked at me with curiosity. "Be thankful for the company," the sergeant said to him. "There's a dance tonight at Cathedral High." Yazzie nodded his head and we went outside to the van and got in, and while we waited for the engine to warm up, I turned to examine the interior. Directly behind us was a heavy wire screen and beyond that the floor of the van ran straight back, without seats of any kind, to double doors which could be opened only from the outside. When I turned back, Yazzie had his sheepskin jacket open and was unbuckling a cartridge belt with a holstered 38-caliber revolver. He placed the belt and the weapon on the dashboard.

"Do you really need that?" I asked.

Yazzie did not reply at first. He put the van in gear and we pulled out of the parking lot beside the jail and headed west toward the saloons of Coal Avenue. And suddenly he said, "I am a full-blooded Navajo," as if a clarification of his ancestry might somehow explain the presence of his gun. He took one hand off the steering wheel to turn up the heat. "Out there," he said, "is cold, huh?"

We cruised down Coal Avenue, past the window-shoppers and the lines outside the movie theaters, on past Dan's Café and the laundromat which is so popular with Indians who have no place in particular to go after dark. Yazzie turned right one short block and then came back along 66 Avenue. At the corner of Second Street two men and a woman were leaning together for mutual support. The woman saw the van first and stepped off the curb waving her hands. Yazzie pulled over and stopped. I waited for him to get out, but he stayed at the wheel. He turned in his seat and watched the back of the van, and then the double doors opened and the three

Indians helped each other in, pulling the doors shut behind them. When the lock snapped Yazzie again put the van in gear and pulled away from the curb.

"They seemed to be waiting for you," I said.

"Yes."

"They come voluntarily then? Like these?"

"Some do," said Yazzie. "When it is cold."

"How do they know how to find you?"

"They see where I go," said Yazzie. "They know."

We were cruising Coal again when a radio call came through from police headquarters requesting a pickup at Eddie's Café on the north side. "Uh-oh," said Yazzie. "That's trouble." Yazzie didn't like Eddie's place. Once, on a call there, six men had attacked him in the parking lot. They tried to take his gun. They gave him a drubbing with their fists, and one of them, he discovered later, had put a hole in his sheepskin jacket, apparently with a knife. But Yazzie hung on to the gun. He was very frightened. Just before the men ran away, he had pulled the gun free and his finger was ready on the trigger. But he didn't shoot, because the men had been drinking and would be sorry the next day. And besides, they were Navajos.

"Were you hurt?" I asked.

"Only a little," said Yazzie. "They missed a lot with their hands."

At Eddie's, we circled the parking lot until our headlights picked out the men who were waiting for Yazzie to take them to the Sleep-in. There were eight. They shuffled alongside the van and as they passed I could see there had been fighting. One of the men was bleeding from the mouth while another held part of a bloody shirt against the side of his head. The last one into the van shut the doors, and when the lock snapped Yazzie gave the engine plenty of gas. "Goodbye Eddie's," he said. Now there were eleven people behind the wire screen, sitting on the floor with their backs against the steel insides of the van. Someone cursed softly in English. Then it was quiet as we drove toward the Sleep-in, and the van began to smell of stale beer.

Unless he was responding to a radio call, Yazzie did not drive anywhere directly. There was always another empty lot or back alley to search out with the headlights, looking for the ones who had passed out and might be dead from exposure by morning. Yazzie knew what alcohol does to the body temperature. He had heard that in January alone eleven Navajos had been found in the mornings, stiff as boards and gone forever. "We try to find them," said Yazzie, "but sometimes they crawl into places where you can't see."

The radio crackled in the dashboard under Yazzie's holster, and the voice of the dispatcher requested a pickup at Cathedral High School. Yazzie stopped cruising and turned south across the railroad tracks. When we got to the school, two patrol cars from the McKinley County Sheriff's Office were parked outside the auditorium with their engines running. The parking lot was littered with empty quart beer bottles. In the glare of our headlights, we saw two deputies struggling with a young Indian woman. "These dances are trouble," Yazzie said. "They'll come a hundred miles just to dance, all the way from Chinle. There must be a thousand in there, I'll betcha." Suddenly one of the deputies seized the girl's ankles while the other lifted her in a full-nelson. They carried her to the back of the van, opened the doors, and dropped her across the legs of the Indians already inside. The woman began to scream, pounding the floor of the van with her fists.

"Ssssh," said one of the men from Eddie's. "We go Sleep-in."

We arrived at the Sleep-in at 9:45. Yazzie opened the doors at the back of the van and the Indians came out one at a time, blinking with the lights in their eyes, their breath turning to vapor in the cold air. The young woman from Cathedral High was unconscious. Yazzie and the watchman carried her inside. The watchman wore a deputy's blue uniform. His name was Hoskie. He said he was Thomas Yazzie's brother.

The Sleep-in reminded me of the drunk tanks at the Gallup jail—two rooms with drain-holes in a concrete floor, and long green mats instead of benches against the wall. Already there were fifty or sixty people inside. Some had been waiting in line when the door of the Sleep-in was opened at 8 P.M. Now they were sleeping on the green mats or sitting with their backs to the wall. The temperature was about sixty degrees. There were no bars in the windows, no lock on the door. A person was free to leave at any time. But most of the people chose to wait until morning. In the morning, at 6:30, a mess truck from the Gallup jail would bring coffee and oatmeal. At 7 A.M., everyone would be turned out. "Daylight savings time is not so good," said Hoskie. "It is still pretty dark then, and cold, but those are the rules."

"How many will you have tonight?" I asked.

"Two hundred," said Thomas Yazzie. "Maybe more, after the cafés close."

"Where will they go in the morning?"

"Home," he said. "The ones who can. The others we will see again tomorrow night."

In the morning I scraped the ice from the windshield of my rented car and pulled out on 66 Avenue, heading east. Ahead of me, out past the Continental Divide toward Mt. Taylor, the purple sky showed hints of orange. But as Hoskie had said, daylight savings time was no good in Gallup at 7 A.M., so I followed my headlights through town, past the turnoff to Window Rock and the sporting goods store with the one-year-old plate-glass door. The streets were deserted. They would not be for long. Soon the patrons of Dan's and Eddie's and the auditorium dancers would be coming down from the Sleep-in and the Gallup jail, fortified with oatmeal and black coffee, to wait in the chill dawn for sunup. And after a while the cafés would reopen and clerks in the retail stores would unlock their cash registers and the streets would be crowded with Indians again. And the City of Gallup would continue to do rather well by itself. Especially if everything worked out as planned for the five-million-dollar tourist attraction in the Red Rocks—without a colossus this time, but with the seats of the Indian Ceremonial arena blasted out of the sandstone cliffs where Coyote had hemorrhaged. The Red Rocks were not holy to the Navajo, so there would be no trouble; and besides, there would be plenty of jobs for Indians. This much had already been promised, as it had been once before when the men who made electricity came to Shiprock and told the Navajo of the job he could have, helping to build the largest coal-fired powerplant in the world. And so it was built, this Four Corners generating station that dusted the Navajo's grazing lands with sulfur dioxide. And the Navajo, representing more than 75 percent of the available labor force, got 8 percent of the jobs.

I was past the Red Rocks on Interstate 40 when I turned on the radio in time to catch the end of a news broadcast from one of Gallup's local stations. The announcer was summarizing the events of Friday night, which did not include what had transpired at Eddie's or Cathedral High, but which did take into account the latest basketball scores. Next came a short commercial for used cars, and then a taped interview with Police Chief Robert Leyba. The chief was announcing that the City of Gallup planned to build a Civil Defense facility. The interviewer wanted to know what for. To be used in the event of an emergency, said Leyba, who did not sound very enthusiastic. I thought I knew why. Leyba said the structure would cost the city about $300,000. The interviewer suggested that was an awful lot of money to invest in something that would have no use until the next war or a natural catastrophe. Oh no, Leyba explained. The building would have a large exercise room and it would be open to the public. For handball.

The interview was over. I reached down to turn off the radio, but there was something else now. The announcer was wrapping up the broadcast with a late flash. The frozen body of an Indian from Chambers, Arizona, he said, had just been found in a snowdrift at the city dump. The man had been missing for a month, and police, he said, were investigating the possibility of foul play.

THE ASBESTOS GITCHE GUMEE

There is nothing puny about the Reserve Mining Company of Silver Bay and Babbitt, Minnesota, except, perhaps, for its corporate soul and its good-faith standing in the congregations of the socially responsible. Everything else—what it is and does and causes others to do—is colossal. Other mining corporations in America may be larger and more profitable, but in one special sense this company is unique. In just twenty years, with but two outfalls aimed at the blue expanse of Lake Superior, Reserve has managed to cast its industrial offal over 2,000 square miles of the world's greatest freshwater body and into the water supplies of a quarter-million people in two states. The offal contains trace elements of such minerals as copper, nickel, lead, zinc, and manganese. These, however, are of no significance compared to the trillions of tiny silicate fibers, each no larger than a red blood cell, which are flushed daily from Reserve's ore processing plant at Silver Bay. Many scientists and doctors believe these fibers can cause cancer in humans. But because an accurate understanding of the morbidity of such things takes time—say, twenty-five years—and because there are no corpses yet at the water taps of Superior and Duluth and Two Harbors, and because Reserve employs some 3,200 persons in a region of acute economic depression, with its payroll of $40 million and heavy tax contributions to the two counties in which it operates, silicate fibers may pour into the lake at Silver Bay for years to come. Exactly how *many* years will depend to a great extent on decisions now pending in the federal courts—and on the contrite good sense of Reserve's directors, none of whom, one suspects, could possibly relish the prospect of moral judgment should cancer of the larynx, pleura, gastro-intestinal tract, or peritoneum ever begin to exact an excessive toll in human lives in the cities down-current from the outfalls of Silver Bay.

In taking the measure of a corporation, it is customary to begin with goals. Though small and angry outside factions may voice dissent, the real goal of Reserve Mining is neither to induce cancer in Minnesotans nor to destroy the biomass of Lake Superior, but to produce iron ore pellets and pass them along profitably to its joint owners, the Republic and Armco steel corporations of Ohio. The pellets are dark gray, almost a half inch in diameter, the size of a small-bore musket ball. Reserve produces 30,000 tons of them each day, or about 15 percent of the domestic ore consumed by the U.S. steel industry. The profits, passed on directly to Armco and Republic, are substantial—nearly $60,000 a day, two dollars a ton. Not bad. Understandably not bad at all when you consider that Reserve incurs virtually no operating costs whatsoever in the disposal of its mine tailings, which are likewise substantial. Gravity is cheap.

And so it happens that from the gray shores of Silver Bay one can perceive a parting of the ways. One can see great ore freighters, their holds piled high with pellets, steaming darkly east toward the Sault Ste. Marie and soon turning south to the piers of Cleveland and Toledo; and then the rail cars rolling to the blast furnaces where pellets become pig iron and pig iron becomes steel; then more rails, and assembly lines, and welders' torches, and finally the machines that will sell for two dollars a pound, or more, on the showroom floor at your friendly neighborhood automobile dealer's. Yet this is only half of it, and not even that. Because in the parting of the ways at Silver Bay, for every ton of processed pellets piled on an ore boat sailing east, two tons of tailings come roaring to the outfalls, down the sluiceways of the concentrating plant and lickity-split along the giant "launders" reaching nearly half a mile across the delta of crushed rock. Down it comes like a river of paste, around the clock, 67,000 tons of solids suspended in two million tons of water, each gallon charged with billions of silicate fibers and each fiber honed from the milling to a fine cutting edge. From the lips of the launders, the slurry is vomited across the edge of the delta to the lake. And while the heavier particles sink slowly toward the bottom of the so-called Great Trough offshore, the lighter ones sweep out into the prevailing Superior current, which runs to the west, toward Duluth. On bright dazzling days, from overlooks along the scenic North Shore Drive, you can see the milky green spoor of tailings in the water, writhing with refracted light.

It looks so harmless. What's 67,000 tons of solids a day in a lake whose surface encompasses nearly 32,000 square miles? That is only two tons per section, if you could spread it around, and in some places the lake is 1,000 feet deep. A drop in the bucket? Well, perhaps. But Reserve's drop is estimated to be greater by a factor of five than all the sediments which are deposited naturally in the lake by erosion and streamflow. And still the green waters flow on toward Duluth.

A quarter mile out from Duluth's Lakewood Pumping Station, and sixty feet straight down, the mouth of a huge pipe yawns open and water surges cold at forty degrees into the pumphouse. The system is unfiltered. Chlorine, fluoride, and ammonia are added sparingly to the water. The idea is to kill bacteria. But there is no measurable destructive effect on silicate fibers. Centrifugal pumps force the treated water into four hilltop reservoirs. From the reservoirs, as needed, the water feeds directly through 325 miles of mains to the faucets of Duluth.

The Lakewood Pumping Station is a landmark of sorts. It was built in 1897, and its bold Victorian lines are typical of the style in which that period's architecture was executed with classic heavy hands throughout the American Gothic Midwest. Some of the information in and around the Lakewood Pumping Station appears to be more or less of the same vintage. On a wall inside the pumphouse, for example, is the faded message: "The quality of the water is unsurpassed anywhere, having less than 3 grains per gallon hardness." There is another message outside the pumphouse—a sign on the shoulder of U.S. Highway 61, which soon becomes the scenic drive to Silver Bay. The sign reads: "Pure Cold Drinking Water 500 Feet." And sure enough, in 500 feet is a roadside rest area and a water fountain fed by pipe from the pump-house nearby. The base of the fountain is constructed of fer-rous metal, possibly of Minnesota ore. Turn the handle of the fountain. The water comes up crystal clear. It tastes good. The cold bites the teeth. Down the hatch to the warm beaches of the gastro-intestinal. It seems so harmless, this cold soft soothing water. What's one or five or even ten mil-lion silicate fibers to a bucket as big as the human stomach? You can't see them. You can't taste them. You can't even feel them. Not yet.

The Biwabik formation occupies the eastern end of the Mesabi Iron Range, roughly extending from the vicinity of Eveleth, Minnesota, along a crest of low hills to the spruce bogs of Superior National Forest. The hills are covered with glacial drift, about twenty feet of it, and below the drift lies a flint-hard, dark-veined rock. The rock is very old, formed more than a half-billion years ago by sedimentation on the floor of a shallow Precambrian sea. Each successive layer of sediment put pressure on those underneath, so that as geo-logic time marched on, the rock grew harder. About 200 million years ago, in Mesozoic times, the sea receded. Then volcanic intrusions came to bake the rock harder yet, fusing within it a variety of elements, but mostly silica and magnet-ite, the black oxide of iron. The rock is called taconite. It is the stuff of which automobiles and bridges are made. And water fountains. And possibly, under recent unnecessary cir-cumstances, cancer.

More than half the volume of taconite rock in the upper layers of the Biwabik formation—the layers now being mined by Reserve—is composed of a metamorphic silicate mineral known to geologists as *cummingtonite-grunerite*; or, if one prefers the formula, $(Mg_1 Fe) Si_8 O_{22} (OH)_2$. Cummingtonite-grunerite is an amphibole, which means it belongs to a com-plex group of hydrous silicates generally containing calcium,

magnesium, sodium, iron, and aluminum. Its chemical properties are remarkably similar—if not identical—to those of
asbestos, which is not a mineral *per se* but rather the commercial name for any tiny silicate fiber capable of performing
colossal feats, such as resisting fire, or, with its rapier edges,
perforating human tissue. Cummingtonite-grunerite is not
what the Reserve Mining Company needs for its pellets.
Reserve needs the magnetite, representing about a quarter of
the volume of the crude rock. It is the magnetite, mainly,
which Reserve extracts magnetically from the crushed rock
at Silver Bay. The magnetite is made into pellets and posted
by freighter to Ohio. The cummingtonite-grunerite is posted
by launder to the shining big sea waters of Lake Superior, to
the asbestos Gitche Gumee.

The taconite deposits at Babbitt, from which Reserve now
strips some 30 million tons of rock each year, were discovered in 1871 by a prospector named Peter Mitchell. Wan-
dering cross-country from Knife River north toward Lake
Vermilion, Mitchell noticed one day that his compass and dip
needle were acting strangely. There was only one thing to do,
and he did it. He dug a hole down through the glacial drift.
And ever since then, men have been digging there with such
fierce intensity that Peter Mitchell's pit is now nine miles
long, a mile wide, and nearly a hundred feet deep.

In the early days, the mining of taconite was simple
enough, but converting it into a blast furnace feed—at a cost
and of a quality competitive with the higher-grade hematite
ores of the Mesabi Range—was something else. One company,
organized at Babbitt in 1919, went broke in five years. Soon,
however, the high-grade hematite ores began to give out. And
at the Mines Experiment Station of the University of Minnesota, E.W. Davis, "Mister Taconite" himself, was hard at
work developing a process that would allow Reserve, by the
mid-Forties, to emerge as the pioneer of a new and profitable
industry. The plan envisioned a 47-mile rail spur linking the
company's mine at Babbitt to a huge processing complex at
Silver Bay. And the tailings? The tailings would simply go
into the lake with the blessings of the State of Minnesota.

Dumping permits were officially awarded to Reserve in December of 1947. It was a time before most people in Minnesota, or anywhere else for that matter, had been exposed to either the principles of ecology or the politics of pollution. So when Reserve stated at public hearings that the tailings would be as pure as the driven sands of Superior, that they would be contained within a nine-square-mile area of the lake, that they would have no harmful effect on fish life, much less on human life, these same people—including the state's commissioner of conservation—tended to believe. A few feisty fishermen raised forlorn objections, but their testimony was overwhelmed by Reserve's "expert" witnesses, many of whom then worked for the company or were soon to join the payroll. One state biologist, in an effort to determine the rate at which tailings would settle in the lake, conducted his experiments in room-temperature water bottles. "Lake Superior," a team of environmental reporters noted much later, "is obviously not a bottle of water." Another scientist, retained by Reserve with the understanding that he would testify at the hearings, determined independently that the tailings would indeed have an adverse effect on fish spawning areas near Silver Bay. Reserve's attorney, W.K. Montague, declined to call this scientist to the stand. And so—on condition that the tailings would never discolor the lake beyond the nine-mile area, never adversely affect fish, nor cause unlawful pollution, nor have material adverse effect on public water supplies—the permits were granted. And construction moved apace toward that signal day in 1955 when, with the gates of the launders thrown open, the first gray sleeve of tailings reached out to the lake. One can picture it even now: the sleeve, and the hand coming out, and a slurried middle finger, dripping with cummingtonite-grunerite, going up, straight up and nail-side out, to the face of America.

Armco Steel Corporation of Middletown, Ohio is the fifth largest steel company in the United States. Republic, with headquarters in Cleveland, is the fourth largest. Each company is represented by five of its top executives on the 11-member board of directors of the Reserve Mining Company. The eleventh member, Edward M. Furness, is president of Reserve but not chairman of its board of directors. The chairman is C. William Verity, Jr., top man at Armco and a figure of considerable prominence in Republican Party fund-raising circles.

Though some of his associates have fallen on bad times of late, things in general couldn't be better for C. William Verity, Jr. In one recent report to Armco shareholders, Verity proudly described how all of the company's profit centers combined to achieve a record level of earnings in the face of inflation and price controls. The earnings, for 1973, were $107.5 million, of which more than two-thirds came from the manufacture and shipment of some seven million tons of steel mill products forged, in large part, from Biwabik taconite ore. Elsewhere in the Armco annual report, it is noted that a "Corporate Responsibility Committee" has been established "to assure the Board that the company is responding properly to its social responsibilities and to the public interest," especially in such areas as safety and "environmental improvement." And finally, on the back cover, appears a typical Armco advertisement. It shows an appealing three-year-old child named Jenny, looking out a window into the waning light. The headline: "Pollution is waiting out there. How are we cleaning things up for her?" The answer supplied by the text is that Armco is working hard to recycle wastes in Middletown and to "vacuum" up air pollutants at four other locations. There is, of course, no mention of Armco's half-interest in the Reserve operations at Babbitt and Silver Bay, nor of its resistence over the years to any and all efforts to clean up Armco's own untidy left-overs from the waters of Lake Superior.

For most of the decade after Reserve, in behalf of Armco and Republic, administered to Superior the first of the last rites, only the fishermen and a handful of North Shore environmentalists took more than a passing melancholic interest in the situation at Silver Bay. But before long, melancholy turned to militancy as reports were circulated that a federal biologist, one Louis Williams, had information that dissolved solids from the Reserve outflow were unleashing nutrients in the water, thereby encouraging a bloom of undesirable algae. In Washington, D.C., meanwhile, environmental lobbyist Verna Mize, a native of Michigan's Keweenaw Peninsula (which juts into Lake Superior 130 miles east of Silver Bay), was making the rounds of congressional offices. Ms. Mize minced no words. Reserve, she said, was wrecking the lake; and what she demanded was nothing less than total abatement of the discharge.

The first official response came from the U.S. Department of the Interior. Under the direction of its Great Lakes regional coordinator, Charles Stoddard, a Taconite Study Group proceeded in 1968 to take a long, hard look at the Reserve operation at Silver Bay. The group's findings, released early the following year—*leaked* is more like it, inasmuch as there were mighty attempts in high official places to suppress the information—did not win enthusiastic reviews, especially in the board rooms of Armco and Republic. Among other things, the Stoddard Report found that suspended tailings were causing "green water" for distances at least eighteen miles southwest of the point of discharge, that lake currents were carrying some particles across state boundaries, that water quality standards for lead and copper were being violated, that bottom fauna important as fish food were adversely affected, that the tailings were lethal to the sac fry of rainbow trout, and that eutrophication of the lake was accelerating. In summary, the report recommended that Reserve be given three-years' grace to investigate and construct alternate on-land disposal facilities. This, one should remember, was in 1968. And Reserve, however reluctantly, was still investigating in 1975, presumably in the hope that it could somehow stretch grace into a plenary indulgence.

If anyone at the time doubted the determination of the Armco-Republic-Reserve consortium to obfuscate the issues, such charitable thoughts must surely have been laid to rest at the first of several federal water pollution enforcement conferences convened specifically to examine the situation at Silver Bay. In a crowded Duluth ballroom in May of 1969,

Reserve President Edward Furness coolly repeated to the assembled conferees the same simplistic argument that had been offered at permit hearings more than twenty years earlier. The tailings, he said, are "inert, inorganic, insoluble," like "the material that is washed from sand beaches" and eroded from cliffs by the waves. "From a conservation standpoint," he added, "Reserve's use of Lake Superior is sound. There is no waste of water, no injury to water. . . . No agency, industry, or individual—public or private—is more interested in preserving the high quality of Lake Superior than is Reserve Mining Company." Ignoring the fact that at least half a dozen other mining companies in the Mesabi region dump their tailings at on-land disposal sites, Furness added, "We would have located the processing plants near the mine if that had been possible."

The hearings and conferences continued for another two years, yet despite the accumulating evidence that Reserve's use of Lake Superior was anything but sound, no government pressure was brought to halt the discharge. None, that is, until faint hearts in the old Federal Water Quality Administration were replaced by a new and aggressive team headed by Environmental Protection Administrator William D. Ruckelshaus. In the summer of 1971, Ruckelshaus ordered Reserve to develop a water pollution abatement plan within six months or face the consequences of a battle in court. Reserve responded with an implausible scheme to pump its tailings directly to the bottom of Lake Superior—and Ruckelshaus rejected it.

In retrospect, there is nothing surprising about the arrogance of Reserve and its parent corporations at the time, for who was young Bill Ruckelshaus to kick them around when they could count on such good friends as Maurice Stans, the commerce secretary and Nixon fund-raiser who viewed Ruckelshaus as the figurehead of an eco-freak conspiracy? Stans had set up his own counter-insurgency group, the National Industrial Pollution Advisory Council, among whose esteemed members were none other than Republic Steel Chairman Willis Boyer and Armco's C. William Verity. Boyer was then vice-chairman of the Ohio Republican Finance Committee. And Verity was well-remembered for the $14,000 he had raised for the Nixon campaign of 1968. What's more, there were friends of big business, and enemies of Ruckelshaus, at large in the White House—namely advisor Peter Flanigan and, according to Washington columnists Evans and Novak, one Charles W. Colson. It was Flanigan, for example, who had come to the aid of Armco in another dispute with the EPA, involving Armco's discharge of heavy metals into the Houston barge canal. From press reports and the transcript of hearings before the House Committee on Government Operations, one can trace Flanigan's fine hand in negotiating for Armco a six-month delay in meeting the EPA compliance deadline. But this, of course, is so much turgid water over the dam, for Messrs. Stans, Flanigan, and Colson are no longer with us in government. For a somewhat different reason, neither is William D. Ruckelshaus.

Yet, in his time at the EPA, Ruckelshaus did manage bravely to fend off the intruding executive hands. At his insistence, on February 2, 1972, the U.S. government finally moved against Reserve. Joined eventually by the State of Minnesota as co-plaintiff, by intervenors Wisconsin, Michigan, and by five environmental organizations, including Save Lake Superior Association and Environmental Defense Fund, Inc., U.S. attorneys filed a complaint alleging that Reserve's discharge into Lake Superior violated sections of the Refuse Act of 1899, the Federal Water Pollution Control Act of 1970, and the common law of public nuisance. Reserve, for its part, confidently prepared its defense—*confident* because it had already been to court in a minor skirmish with the State of Minnesota, and had won. But in June of 1973, a month before the federal case was to go to trial in the U.S. district court in St. Paul, the central legal issue suddenly shifted from water pollution to public health. The EPA had discovered asbestiform fibers in the water a hundred thousand people were drinking daily in Duluth.

Babbitt, due south of Ely and the sparkling lakes of the

Boundary Waters Canoe Area, is billed in the local literature as "a new city in the wilderness." A brochure distributed by the Business and Professional Association acknowledges that the town "doesn't have everything yet, but it does have the important ingredients for growth: youthful spirit and vigor!" Such expressions of boosterism lead one to wonder if the town might possibly have been named in honor of J.F. Babbitt, Esq., anti-hero of the Sinclair Lewis novel, who extolled the virtues of the vigorous Regular Guy in his own zestful "zip city" of milk cartons and service clubs. In fact, I put the question myself to a Reserve public relations man last summer, but he promptly dismissed the association as an ugly coincidence. The town, he said, is named after Kurnal Babbitt, a New York state judge. It turns out Judge Babbitt drew up the papers for the original mining company that failed after five years in the taconite business (which was two years after publication of Lewis's *Babbitt*), and for this reason, or possibly others, never set foot near the town that now honors his name.

One has to see Babbitt to believe it. I do not mean the town, which has hardly anything yet except housing for some 3,000 people, half of whom work for Reserve in order to support most of the other half. Driving slowly, one can see all there is to see of the town in five minutes. So it isn't the town, but the mine and machines that are working there; and how the one called the Jet Piercer, screaming like a rocket, its burner head generating a 4,300-degree flame, spalls down through the naked rock; and the ammonium nitrate paste that is pumped into each 40-foot hole; and the sirens before the shot; and how, from a mile away in an August drizzle, you can see sparks following the electric fuses across the top of the mining bench, and then the dust cloud that hovers 40-stories high over a half-million tons of shattered taconite. And next, the giant power shovels and trucks, and rocks the size of refrigerators pouring into the mouth of the gyratory crusher—the "world's largest" mortar and pestle, 3,500 tons per hour reduced to eight-inch pieces. Then four-inch pieces. Grapefruits. And the locomotives going down the rails to

Silver Bay, a departure every three or four hours, 120 to 160 rail cars each trip out, and each car filled with eighty-five gross-weight tons for the concentrating plant. And for the waters of Lake Superior.

The town of Silver Bay itself is much like the town of Babbitt, the only substantial difference being that Silver Bay enjoys a scenic view of Lake Superior, while Babbitt enjoys an airshed that is somewhat less clouded by gray taconite dust, occasional ammonium nitrate explosions nearby notwithstanding. Silver Bay sprawls across the slope of a hill above the lake, inland from the Reserve plant. A wide road winds up through poplar and birch from U.S. Highway 61, and as you approach the development you are greeted by signs of welcome from the community's churches and service clubs. There is a shopping center with two gasoline stations, Big Dollar, Kosy Korner Bakery, Fish's TV Appliances, Minnesota Power & Light, Rexall Drugs, the First Northwestern Bank, Skogmos, Montgomery Ward, a laundromat, a bar, and a fast-order café called The Silver Platter, where rib-sticking fare is served up on roadhouse ceramic antique. The curvilinear streets are lined with post-war ranch-style homes. The lawns are trim and green. The birds are singing in the ornamental trees. The tykes are out on their bikes, and football players are in front of the high school, gulping huge lungfuls of air for the summer scrimmage. In short, the American Dream—as long as you keep your back to the launders, the "green water," and the persistent smudge that lingers over U.S. Highway 61 as it passes Reserve's pelletizing furnaces.

The taconite grapefruits arriving by rail at Silver Bay contain 23.5 percent magnetite ore. The goal is to increase that percentage by separating the magnetite from what Reserve prefers to call "unwanted" and "useless" minerals, such as cummingtonite-grunerite. The process begins uphill from U.S. 61 and progresses, generally by conveyor belt, down through a number of stages to the edge of the lake. In the first stage, the grapefruit are fed through a dump hopper to a cone crusher system. The grapefruit are reduced to pecans. Next, the pecans are conveyed under U.S. 61 to the storage bins of the concentrator plant; and from the bins they are fed to a mill to be tumbled and ground by steel rods to the consistency of coarse sand. Still, each particle is only 23.5 percent magnetite. Then the coarse particles are conveyed to a magnetic separator, which discards a third of the "useless" minerals and sends the useful—now some 40 percent magnetite by volume—to a second milling system. In the second mill, steel balls in a rotating drum grind the particles even finer, to a flour-like consistency. And again magnetic separation, so that now the flour is more than 60 percent magnetite. And through all of this is a constant voluminous flow of Lake Superior water, cooling the grinding rods and balls and carrying off the useless unwanted minerals. But now the water is sucked away, and what remains is a jet black concentrate that is rolled again and again in another drum until the moist particles embrace each other and snowball into pellets. Small-bore musket balls. Finally, the musket balls are conveyed to the furnaces of the pelletizing plant, where they are baked six minutes for hardness and porosity at 2,400 degrees. *Voilà.* Who needs or wants to know more? Except for one thing: where did all the useless unwanted minerals go?

Seriously. I mean here are brochures and throwaways prepared for visiting tourists and the press. They explain everything you ever wanted to know about taconite mining and processing except . . . where did all the rest of it go? Here is a "Photo Clip Sheet" kit from Reserve, detailing every conceivable step of the operation. But aside from the pellets, which are only a third of the volume, where did the rest of it go? And here is "Your Visit to Reserve," eight newsy pages in duotone offset for "up to 2,000 visitors" who are said to stop each vacation day for a "detailed explanation of the process." And detailed it is, from how much Reserve pays in taxes to a functional chart of the whole complex process, crusher to furnace to ship. The cover of this booklet shows the full spread of Silver Bay—everything except for the launders. Why were the launders cropped? O, if only the cover had been an inch wider. And the functional chart? Beyond the furnace it ends with the explanation, "Plant discharge:

2 tons waste, 1 ton pellets." All right. We know about the pellets. But where does the rest of it go? The two tons, hell. The 67,000 tons daily. It was as if the useless unwanted minerals had somehow been vacuumed into the not-so-thin air of Silver Bay, which is something I am sure C. William Verity and his associates would like to pull off, if only there were some way to do it for free.

I was beyond the furnaces and the fantasies. I stood at the lip of a launder with my guide from Reserve. The tailings poured out across the delta to the lake. I asked a question.

"Aren't there any industrial uses for the tailings?"

"Lots," he said. "Get the water out of it, and you can use it for the foundations of highways, the manufacture of glass."

"Why not, then?"

He had been looking at the lake, at the gray-green water curling out across the rich blue roof of the Great Trough. Slowly he turned away. "Nobody could possibly use it all," he said. "There's just too much."

On April 20, 1974—after 139 days of trial, after hearing more than 100 witnesses, examining 1,600 exhibits, and reviewing nearly 20,000 pages of courtroom transcript—U.S. District Court Judge Miles W. Lord issued a terse 13-page memorandum. In his findings of fact, he held that the Reserve Mining Company's "discharge into the air substantially endangers the health of the people of Silver Bay and surrounding communities as far away as the eastern shore in Wisconsin," and that its discharge of asbestos-like fibers into the water likewise "endangers the health of the people who procure their drinking water from the western arm of Lake Superior." Judge Lord further found that testimony and representations by the chief executives of Armco and Republic, heard under oath that very day, and by the defense in general in seeking to place conditions on Reserve's abatement of the discharge (such as obtaining federal and state subsidies), were "unacceptable . . . preposterous . . . absurd" and "shocking." Faced with the defendants' "intransigence," Judge Lord concluded, "the Court must order an immediate curtailment of the discharge." And at one minute after midnight on April 21, Reserve's mills and magnets and drums and conveyors fell silent. The lips of the launders went dry. Yet within forty-eight hours, on the evening of the fourth anniversary of Earth Day, an emergency panel of three judges from the U.S. Court of Appeals for the Eighth Circuit granted Reserve's attorneys a stay of Judge Lord's injunction. So, once more, the tailings poured down the launders at Silver Bay. And sweet dreams for C. William Verity.

In staying the injunction until the merits of the case could be heard and decided by the full appellate court, the circuit judges found that the plaintiffs had failed to prove a demonstrable health hazard; that the assumption of such a hazard was based solely on medical hypothesis and was, therefore, "simply beyond proof." In other words, asbestos fibers might be a murder weapon, but show us the bodies. Moreover, the panel held that Judge Lord's resolution of a reasonable doubt in favor of public health might better have been left to a legislative body. And with the implication that Judge Lord had somehow ruled inequitably in "balancing the health and environmental demands of society at large against the economic well-being of those parties and communities immediately affected," the panel went on to quote from an opinion once rendered by Chief Justice Warren Burger of the U.S. Supreme Court, when he had been sitting as a circuit judge:

> Our society and its governmental instrumentalities, having been less than alert to the needs of our environment for generations, have now taken protective steps. These developments, however praiseworthy, should not lead courts to exercise equitable powers loosely or casually whenever a claim of "environmental damage" is asserted. The world must go on and new environmental legislation must be carefully meshed with more traditional patterns of federal regulation. . . .

The panel further noted its somewhat magnanimous belief

that "there are neither heroes nor villains among the present participants in this lawsuit." But it did condition its stay on Reserve's "good faith" in taking "prompt steps" to abate the discharge and move its disposal of tailings to an acceptable on-land site. Exactly what constitutes *prompt steps* in the eyes of the Eighth Circuit Court was not made clear. After many months and with what seemed to be an indefinite stay keeping its launders open, Reserve was still skipping across the hills of the North Shore, playing pin the tailings on the donkey.

When and if it is ever finished, the United States of America vs. Reserve Mining Company—or 5-72 Civil 19 as it is known to the file clerks of the U.S. district court at St. Paul—may well enter the record books as the longest and most complex environmental litigation since society, as Mr. Justice Burger put it, began taking protective steps. Motions, briefs, opinions, applications, remands, and appeals have been filed and cross-filed, some all the way from Judge Lord's chambers through the Eighth Circuit to the U.S. Supreme Court and back again. And if it were possible to collect all of the original documents, and each single mimeographed copy thereof, I would not be at all surprised to see the accumulation filling a couple dozen of those 85-gross-ton ore cars that run from the mine at Babbitt to the plant at Silver Bay. Then Reserve could dump the entire record, and its own persiflage, into the lake as well. For despite the appellate court's skepticism on the question of endangered public health, it was not the government that emerged battered from its 139 days in court. It was Reserve, which had sought to project for itself and its Ohio profit centers an image as the undisputed Mister Clean of Lake Superior, but which came away instead as a corporate wastrel with failing grades in almost everything from ethics to mineralogy.

Reserve had contended from the beginning, for example, that cummingtonite-grunerite entered the lake from a number of natural sources; indeed, that it was present in the waters of some sixty tributaries feeding the lake. Yet the plaintiffs also sampled sediments from streams, including those between Silver Bay and Duluth, and in only one of fifty, the Montreal River, was cummingtonite-grunerite found by X-ray diffraction. Of the Reserve analysis, Judge Lord noted in a memorandum supplementing his shut-down order of April 20: ". . . when exposed to extensive cross-examination . . . it became clear that the [Reserve] criteria used for identifying cummingtonite-grunerite in this study was highly subjective, with bias entering into the determination." Moreover, Judge Lord pointed out, the government's finding was consistent with testimony that cummingtonite-grunerite is *not* present in core samples of lake-bottom sediments predating the start of Reserve's operations.

It was also Reserve's contention that virtually all of its tailings, rather than sweeping out into the lake, settled safely to the bottom of the Great Trough, at depths of from 600 to 900 feet. The force of gravity, said Reserve's witnesses, simply pulls the heavier fluid downward from the delta. A "density current," they called it. Yet the court found that the density current was not what it was cracked up to be—that, in fact, it *is* cracked up by thermoclines which peel off layers of tailings; and that vertical turbulence and deep mixing spread those tailings around the entire western arm of Lake Superior, not to mention Duluth's municipal water supply. Samples of that supply, taken from the Lakewood Pumping Station during the years 1939-1940, 1949-1950, and 1964-1965, and preserved in vials, showed no traces of cummingtonite-grunerite for the first two periods (before Reserve came to Silver Bay), but did show positive traces for the latter. Reserve then claimed that cummingtonite-grunerite undoubtedly was present in the older samples, but unfortunately dissolved over the years.

All of this was merely prelude to the two main events—the question of asbestos and public health, and the feasibility of shifting the disposal of tailings to an alternate on-land site.

In defending itself on the health count, Reserve contended that the level of exposure to people inhaling or ingesting fibers from its discharge was not sufficient to pose a hazard;

and, therefore, no health problem could logically be associated with the discharge. To support such a claim, Reserve fielded its own medical and scientific witnesses. But later in the trial it embraced the testimony of Dr. Arnold Brown, chairman of the department of pathology and anatomy at the Mayo Clinic and Judge Miles Lord's own court-appointed impartial expert witness. It was Dr. Brown's belief, for example, that asbestos fibers are present in the lungs of most urban adults throughout the country, and that such fibers have been detected as well in beer, wine, and ginger ale at levels greater than the asbestiform count in the Duluth water supply. There was no evidence at present, Dr. Brown testified, that any increased incidence of cancer at Silver Bay or Duluth could be attributed to asbestos fibers in the air or water; that, in fact, it was impossible to predict an increased incidence of cancer simply by virtue of the presence of the fibers in the water. Still, Dr. Brown's testimony did not altogether please the attorneys for Reserve, for he concluded: ". . . the fibers should not be present in the drinking water of the people of the North Shore. . . . the presence of a known human carcinogen (and here he was speaking of fibers in the air) . . . is in my view a cause for concern, and if there are means for removing the human carcinogen from the environment, that should be done."

For its part, the government relied heavily on the testimony of Dr. Irving J. Selikoff, director of the Environmental Sciences Laboratory at the Mount Sinai School of Medicine in New York. Dr. Selikoff said he had conducted epidemiological studies of four separate groups of factory workers exposed to asbestos. Three of these groups, he said, numbering in aggregate more than 18,000 individuals, showed an excessive rate of death from lung cancer, pleural and peritoneal mesothelioma, asbestosis, and cancer of the stomach, colon and rectum. The deaths did not occur until twenty years or more after the first exposure. And in each group, it was reported, the number of excess mortalities was three times greater than the number of expected deaths projected for these diseases and the population as a whole by the U.S.

Office of Vital Statistics. Dr. Selikoff further testified that a distinct public health hazard was posed by the presence of amphibole fibers, morphologically consistent with amosite asbestos, in the Duluth water supply. And amphibole levels in the ambient air at Silver Bay, he added, were ten times greater than those measured near an asbestos insulation spraying site in New York (which measurement subsequently resulted in a ban there on asbestos spraying).

The Selikoff testimony was supported by a number of other government witnesses. Dr. Thomas J. Mason, a statistician with the National Cancer Institute, reported that he had examined cancer mortality statistics for Duluth for the period 1965-1969 and had found fifty-four "excess" deaths as compared to the rate for the entire state of Minnesota. He also testified that rates for cancer of the rectum were increasing in Duluth while national rates have been declining. And while Dr. Mason could not state unequivocally that excess cancer deaths in Duluth were caused specifically by amphibole fibers, neither could he conclude "that there is no risk to the population (of Duluth) . . . as a function of their exposure to water-borne asbestos particles." Dr. William J. Nicholson, biophysicist and associate of Dr. Selikoff at Mount Sinai, added: "If we wait until we see the bodies in the street, we would then be certain that there would be another thirty or forty years of mortality experience that would be before us. And to wait for deaths would in fact be, from public health considerations, irresponsible."

As the trial plodded on in U.S. District Court, the central argument soon shifted to whether or not Reserve could come up with an alternate disposal system that would be acceptable to the government. Reserve maintained there was only one feasible alternative—a so-called "deep water" plan whereby the tailings would be pumped through pipes directly to the Great Trough. Day after day of testimony was heard as Reserve witnesses and attorneys sought to assure the court of the plan's environmental benefits, such as the addition of some 12,000 pounds-per-day of polymers to hasten settling of the tailings on the bottom. The government promptly demonstrated that among the basic building blocks of one of the polymers Reserve proposed to use is a known mutagen and carcinogen called ethyleneimine. Wherever ethyleneimine is found in an occupational setting, the U.S. Department of Labor prohibits drinking fountains, among other things.

The impracticality of the deep-water plan apparently was also known at the time by Reserve executives, even as they continued to hail it in court as the only alternative. As Judge Lord reconstructed it in his supplemental memorandum: "Notwithstanding (Reserve Vice President Kenneth M.) Haley's denials under oath, there was a plan in existence which provided for total on-land disposal of tailings. . . . Records provided during the testimony showed that the 'deep pipe' system presented by Mr. Haley to this court had in fact been rejected by Mr. Haley's Task Force in 1972." Clearly annoyed by such "misrepresentations," Judge Lord found the defendants had acted in "bad faith" by withholding documents "in violation of plaintiffs' discovery requests and this Court's order."

Then began what Judge Lord was later to describe as "the corporate shell game." The on-land disposal plan which had been discovered in Reserve's files proposed that the Palisade Creek Valley, some 1.2 miles inland from the lake and just across a low ridge from Silver Bay, be converted into a vast tailings basin contained by a series of dams. From one configuration advanced by Reserve, it appeared that the main dam would be twice as long and as high as the Grand Coulee. What the Reserve planners had failed to take into account, however, (or, as some cynics have it, what they *did* take into account with malice aforethought) was the Minnesota Department of Natural Resources' interest in this same valley, which had not only been identified in the early 1960s as a potential park site, but as one of the seven most attractive of some 700 sites considered. Moreover, as Judge Lord noted subsequently in his response to the circuit court's order of remand, it became evident that Reserve's plan for the Palisade Valley "was being fashioned before the Court's very eyes." In effect, Judge Lord found that Reserve's plan was "conceptual at best": no tests had been conducted to determine the stability of dam construction material. There had been no test drillings or geological surveys of the area. And Reserve, by its own admission, "had done nothing more than eye-ball the area to determine whether the tailings would be visible from Highway 61." Later the judge toured the area himself, on foot, scrambling across rock ledges to view the valley's lush forest of maple and birch and fir, and the creek winding down past beaver-built pools to the shining waters of Superior. And having seen it, the judge wrote:

The Palisades area provides a place upon which to roam, to be free, to enjoy the opulence of the scenic wonders that have been provided by nature. This Court cannot allow the present greed of a few to deny priceless treasures to many. It cannot allow the immediate problems of some to cheat others of their environmental birthright.

As Reserve defined them, the immediate problems were of course economic. And with the Palisades plan about to be shot down by a hang-tough judge, Reserve was now forced to consider other alternatives for one reason or another unattractive to it—alternatives such as the International Engineering Company's design for a new concentrator plant at the mine site in Babbitt, with on-land disposal nearby and only the pelletizing and ship-loading functions remaining at the end of the rail line in Silver Bay. The relocation, according to International's figures, would cost Reserve $188.7 million in capital expenditures. Reserve promptly factored this estimate up to $391.2 million, a figure the government termed "outrageously high" in view of cost estimates announced by two other taconite processors planning new facilities at Hibbing and Virginia, Minnesota.

The fiscal laments of Reserve were further discredited by the testimony of economist R. Glenn Berryman, who calculated that, rather than sapping Reserve's economic vitality, the International plan would in fact result in increased profitability. Using figures supplied by Reserve, Berryman computed the company's average income after taxes for the years 1970-1972 at $18 million annually, its income per-ton-shipped at $1.88, and its rate of return (to Armco and Republic) on assets at 8.27 percent. Next, Berryman made a forecast of Reserve's potential profitability based on certain assumptions: capital expenditures of about $188 million for on-land disposal and concentrating at Babbitt; increased operating costs as a result thereof; but a decrease in other operating costs as a result of product improvement. (With up-to-date equipment installed in a new concentrator plant, product improvement would come through a reduction in the silica content of the concentrate, a subsequent reduction in the overall cost of blast furnace fuel and maintenance, and enhancement of the iron content—not to mention the market value—of the finished pellets.) With these assumptions, Berryman came up with a forecasted profitability for the years 1973-1975 that could result in an annual after-tax income of $31.6 million, an income per-ton-shipped of $3.17, and a rate of return on assets of 9.68 percent. Even without product improvement, Berryman testified, Reserve could make the move to Babbitt and still pass on a profit to its parent corporations. But of course Reserve does not want to move anything to Babbitt, or anywhere else for that matter. Why should it, with tight money and inflation clouding such forecasts as Berryman's, and when, by most accounts, it has already saved more than $50 million by allowing gravity and a lake to dispose of its tailings?

So the shell game continues. In one of the most recent moves, Reserve (with some encouragement from the Eighth Circuit Court of Appeals) offered yet another on-land disposal plan, this time for Mile Post 7, seven miles up the rail line from Silver Bay, near Lax Lake. Judge Lord characterized the proposal as "shabby and hollow." And once again from Reserve came ominous hints that if it could not have its way, that if it must abate the discharge on anyone's terms other than its own, then perhaps it might pick up its marbles and go home to Middletown, leaving its 3,200 workers to the vicissitudes of unemployment and public assistance. In response to earlier threats, Judge Lord had written:

> . . . *defendants are using the work force at Reserve's plants as hostages. In order to free the work force of Reserve, the Court must permit the continued exposure of known human carcinogens to the citizens of Duluth and other North Shore communities. The Court will have no part of this form of economic blackmail.*

On October 11, 1974, the United States Supreme Court denied without prejudice the government's application for an order vacating the stay granted Reserve by the Eighth Circuit Court—Justice William O. Douglas dissenting. Mr. Justice Douglas noted in his dissent that the circuit court's position seemed to hold that "maximizing profits" was the measure of the public good. He added:

> *If . . . there is doubt, it should be resolved in favor of humanity, lest in the end our judicial system be part and parcel of a regime that makes people . . . the victims of the great God Progress. . . . Our guiding principle should be Mr. Justice Holmes' dictum that our waterways, great and small, are treasures, not garbage dumps or cesspools.*

Ben Boo is the mayor of Duluth. He is a friendly, accessible man, an able administrator, and a shrewd politician. And he does not scare easily. From the windows of Ben Boo's City Hall office, you can look down to the waterfront of what has become, since completion of the St. Lawrence Seaway, one of the busiest ports in North America. The day I was there the harbor was crowded with ships, the docks and storage facilities brimming with lumber and grain. And iron ore. Duluth is filled with magnificent old houses and hard-working people. It is a fine city; and, as far as I can tell, Ben Boo is a fine mayor who doesn't run scared. We talked about water, the kind that you drink.

Mayor Boo said that it had been some year, all right, beginning with the EPA discovery of asbestiform fibers in the city's water supply, and *that* coming right at the start of the tourist season. "It hurt us some, the publicity," he said. "But the people here were wonderful. No one panicked. I guess a lot of them had the feeling it would go away." Despite the prevailing optimistic mood of his constituents, Boo wasted no time. He immediately retained a firm of consultants to draw up plans for a filtration system at the Lakewood Pumping Station; asked for and received pledges of federal aid; put the state's civil defense people on standby with tank trucks to provide 600,000 gallons of well water daily, if such action were deemed necessary (it wasn't); arranged, through the U.S. Army Corps of Engineers, for the installation of portable water filters in public places; and demanded in no uncertain terms that the Reserve Mining Company halt its discharge into the water of Lake Superior.

Later, the City of Duluth moved to intervene as a party plaintiff in the case being tried by Judge Lord, much to the chagrin of the Duluth Area Chamber of Commerce, which had already thrown in its lot with the other side. And so it went, through the summer and into the winter and on to the spring of 1974; until the morning of April 23, to be exact, when the people of Duluth awoke to some reassuring news. The Eighth Circuit Court had reversed Judge Lord on the health issue, and faster than you can say cummingtonite-grunerite, in many people's minds all those amphibole fibers were thereby and forever rendered harmless. In August, the Army Engineers notified the mayor that they would no longer provide and install the portable filters as a public service. Why not? Why, because, according to the Corps' inverted logic, it had been proved that there was no health hazard (which is not quite the same thing as a health hazard not being proved).

"They weren't too successful anyway," said Ben Boo. "The filters. They needed a lot of maintenance. They were gradually plugging up."

"With asbestos?"

"With whatever came with the water."

"But what about the Selikoff testimony?"

"Scare sories," said the mayor.

"So you are not terribly concerned about the health issue."

"Oh, we'll still go ahead with the filtration system at the pumping station."

"Then you *are* concerned."

"No," said Ben Boo, "I am not."

The Pickwick Restaurant on Superior Street in downtown Duluth features fresh lake trout and a splendid view of the harbor, and to get to either, or both, you go in through a door with a sign that reads: *FILTERED WATER.* The filter itself, one of those installed by the Army, is located under and attached to the water tap where the waitresses fill glasses on their way from the kitchen to the room with a view. The filter is a 12-inch jar packed tightly with thin shafts like pipe cleaners—your Maginot Line against a mouthful of amphibole fibers. To partake of water free of asbestiform fibers, of course, a resident of Duluth does not have to go out on the town every night. Ben Boo has made filtered water available at the city's firehouses, and WDIO-TV, the local broadcasting station, generously shares its copious hilltop well with the populace, which carries away about 45,000 gallons each month. Not much, considering that Duluth's total consumption is 25 million gallons a day. Still, the WDIO water is there for anyone who wants it. And those who do, if you bother to ask their opinion, are more than happy to express themselves on the current distressing situation. "How come," said one elderly man emerging from the well shed with a plastic jug in each hand, "how come I have to pay for sewage disposal and everyone I know has to pay for sewage disposal and that outfit up the lake, that Reserve, gets it for nothing? How come is what I'd like to know."

And at the bar of the Pickwick sat a man who worked for twenty-eight years as a brakeman on trains hauling ore from Mesabi. He is retired. I found this out after I mentioned the filtered water. And then he began to speak of Lake Superior. "I love that lake," he said. "I fish it a lot, but mostly just look at it. In the war it was good to be from Minnesota because Minnesota was part of this lake. And you could be proud because all your buddies knew that this was where the fresh air and clean water was. But now these sons-of-bitches in Cleveland and Dayton. . . ."

"Middletown," I said.

"And Middletown—all the way down in Ohio, can you believe it?—are pouring their crap in this lake. And they are killing it." Having said that, the man who loves Lake Superior slammed his fist on the bar and stalked out through the door, the one with the sign that reads: *FILTERED WATER.*

Me, I stalked out, too; and in the morning drove out along U.S. Highway 61, past the Lakewood Pumping Station. The pumphouse, I now understand, is finally to be retrofitted with a filtration system. The project may possibly be complete in time for a Bicentennial Year christening. Possibly but not probably, because Ben Boo is haggling with the United States of America, the State of Minnesota, and the Reserve Mining Company over the delicate question of who will help him pick up the six-million-dollar tab.

And then I was talking with Dr. Donald Mount, a biologist and director of the EPA's National Water Quality Laboratory, not far from the pumphouse off Highway 61. "Every liter of water coming into Duluth right now contains about 35 million asbestiform fibers," Mount was saying. "I can't understand how we can treat so many people as if they were laboratory animals."

A few miles northeast of Silver Bay, the pink porphyritic ledges of Palisade Head rise 350 feet above the lake. Legend has it that Chippewa braves, from their canoes below, made great sport attempting to shoot arrows to the top of the cliff. Very few succeeded; and it is said that occasionally a brave or two perished in the attempt, for what goes up and misses must inevitably and swiftly come back down again. Gravity is not only cheap, it is ruthless.

Behind the cliff, the Head rises another hundred feet or so to a small windswept dome covered with stunted mountain ash and June berries. Standing there, and turning counterclockwise, one can enjoy a most unusual view: the distant shores of Wisconsin, dead ahead at high noon; the lake spreading out as if there were no end to it, and the spruces at nine o'clock, leaning over the water at Baptism River State Park; then the deep forested hills at six; and finally, at three, the shoreline running raggedly back to the institutional sprawl at Silver Bay. And there it is. The gray in the sky and the green in the water, and the silicate fibers without end or beginning flowing on to Duluth. *O, Veritas. O, Verity. Requiescat in cummingtonite-grunerite.*

And goodbye, Superior.

HOME, TO MICHIGAN

The window of the room where I spent the better part of my
first fourteen years—the formative years, as they say nowadays; the better part only insofar as one measures time and
not experience—faced north. The view was pleasant but not
spectacular, although occasionally it could be both with a
deliberate effort of the imagination. Mine was a second-story
window above the kitchen. It overlooked a narrow finger of
backyard which, for a portion of that time, was dedicated to
the cultivation of lettuce and beets and tomatoes and okra
and Swiss chard, as well as to gangling competitive weeds that
often brought ruin to the legitimate crops and grief to me
and my sister, who were supposed to prevent such calamities
by spending more hours than we cared to, in the backyard,
on our hands and knees. We were told a weedless garden
would help speed Victory in Europe and the Pacific; yet
somehow I could never truly appreciate the strategic impor-
tance of it all, especially on certain lugubrious occasions
when my patriotism resulted in a steaming bowl of boiled
okra, the memory of which makes me gag even to this day.
So from my point of view, it was not the garden that particularly enhanced the backyard perspective. It was the surrounding woods: maples and oaks mainly, a few ancient beech, a
scraggly nursery hemlock or two. The canopy of leaves was
dense in summer, and from my window I could see neither
through nor over the tops of the trees, as one could later,
after Halloween, when the wall of foliage fell apart to reveal
a gray web of branches running north toward the unseen
scabrous factory whose whistle screeched each morning ten
minutes to eight.

The fact that my window faced north held no great significance for me until, passing the time with an atlas one
day, I happened to discover that due north was Michigan. I

discovered that if I laid the edge of a ruler against Cincinnati, Ohio, where all this victory gardening was going on, and aligned its axis with true north, the top of the ruler pointed at Emmett County, Michigan, where my family had owned a place in the Twenties and Thirties and where I had spent the first few summers of my life. And with that discovery, a new world of fantasy opened for me at my north-facing window. I would sit there in the oppressive humidity of those wartime summers and travel along the edge of the ruler, through the trees at the end of the garden, up the hollow past the whistling factory, out of the city to Hamilton and Van Wert and then Jackson and Lansing and Alma and Clare and Gaylord and Wolverine. Soon the land begins to dip and roll and the air smells of pine. And then I am turning toward the lake, past Harbor Springs on the Shore Drive and down the last hill, around the sumac bend into the deepshaded woods with oaks and maples like the ones at the end of the garden at home. Home? I am not so sure of where that is, now that I am north again in Michigan. Nor do I care, for I am running now, around the side of the log cabin with the moose head over the great stone fireplace, down the steep bluff and across the footbridge and through the cedars in the lee of the dunes. And then the wide golden beach at Seven Mile Point, and beyond it the cool infinity of Lake Michigan.

For me there were seven summers like that. They ended for reasons I did not understand at the time, such as the delayed effects of a long Depression; and so my father, who had hired Indians to build the cabin on the bluff in 1922, sold the place and consigned us all to the long hot Indianless summers of Southern Ohio. That was in 1938. Four years later he took a shovel to the backyard and, in hostile yeoman defiance of Hitler and Hirohito, proceeded to plant okra and chard. It never occurred to me as I watched him from my window that he, too, might be capable of vicarious and sentimental journeys. It never occurred to me because, for a long time after 1938, no one in our family ever mentioned Michigan. But we remembered. Through all the dreary yard-bound, weed-pulling summers of the early Forties, the flavors of that other place stayed skulkingly with me; and even after the end of the war, as the availability of gasoline and family cash made motoring possible once more, the remembered pleasures of Seven Mile Point survived against the competing realities of Pikes Peak, Colorado; Lookout Mountain, Tennessee, and Mt. Washington, New Hampshire. I revered those high places and soon developed a proper taste for mountains, but at the same time I found them lacking, for none had what Northern Michigan had: the gold beach running wide to blue water, and the water rolling off to meet the edge of the sky.

The Uplands

Emmett County is part of what the regional planners in Lansing call the "Little Finger Country." Actually, it is the top joint of the third finger, the little one being the Leelenau Peninsula, the thumb being the bulge between Saginaw Bay and Lake Huron, and the whole unlikely hand being the Lower Peninsula of Michigan. Emmett County runs north from Wallon Lake to the Straits of Mackinac and east from Lake Michigan almost halfway across the tip of that peninsula to Huron. The county seat and principal marketplace is Petoskey (pop. 6,342) on Little Traverse Bay, directly across from Harbor Springs (pop. 1,662), the Second City. In addition, there are a number of scattered villages and townships, such as Alanson and Bliss and Carp Lake and Cross Village and Levering. Overall, the population of Emmett County has been growing at a faster rate than that of the United States, the State of Michigan, and the Little Finger Country as a whole.

Despite the proliferation of humankind in parts of Emmett County in recent years, it is not what you would call a crowded kind of place. Not yet, anyway. If you could spread every one of its 18,000 permanent residents around a little, back from the shore and into the hinterlands, each would have about seventeen acres all to himself, except on three-day winter weekends when the skiers come winging up from

Detroit and Chicago, and except for the time from June to September. Then, overrun with tourists and summer people, those individual seventeen-acre fiefs would erode substantially, along with the forests of Emmett County.

The forests are considerable. By official estimate they cover about 62 percent of the total area—a somewhat misleading figure because it is based on U.S. Forest Service criteria, which exclude from "forest" designation just about everything arboreal except what an owner, public or private, may readily sell off the stump whensoever he has a mind to. So, if you make allowances for such nonsense, and start adding cedar swamps and spruce bogs ("adverse sites," according to the Forest Service) and places like Wilderness State Park on Sturgeon Bay ("productive public forest land withdrawn from commercial timber use") and all the old tortured pastures running to yellow-birch insurrection and jack-pine vagrancy—well, then you *have* something. Not official but considerable, like about 75 percent.

That there are any trees at all in Emmett County and elsewhere in the Little Finger Country is something of a miracle, if you believe in such things. If you do not, then you must chalk it up to the crankiness of natural succession and to the scar-tissue quality of the moist sandy loam soils of Northern Michigan, resilient yet after nearly a century of merciless logging. On the porches of Petoskey there are white-haired folk with robust tales and remorseless memories, and they will tell you that their daddies and granddaddies hoisted twenty-pound double-bits in the white pine forests that covered so much of the region before the turn of the century.

The pines were huge, 200 feet tall and as much as seven across at the base; and from 1870 to about 1900 the loggers addressed themselves to these giants so persistently that Michigan led the nation in the production of lumber. And then one fine morning early in the new century, the loggers rolled out of their blankets, shoveled down their flapjacks, hoisted their heavy axes, and marched off into the forest only to discover that it wasn't there any more. The pine forest was gone, under the roofs and into the walls of a million new homes in the growing cities of the American Mid-west. So the pine loggers bade farewell to the Little Finger Country and, crossing the Straits of Mackinac, proceeded to repeat their astounding performance in the forests of the Upper Peninsula. Meanwhile, a new interest developed in the virgin hardwood forests south of the Straits. These presently were scalped as well, so that by the time my father staked his claim on the bluff at Seven Mile Point, in 1922, most of the big trees, hard or soft, were gone. Fortunately, no significant commercial use had been assigned to the white cedar. My father was convinced that white cedar would yield superlative logs, which it most assuredly does. And that is what the hired Indians felled for the rambling cabin where I spent the first seven summers of my life. When I got there, the logs of the cabin had weathered to a husky gray, and the surrounding woods were deep and cool and mysterious. And seemingly so wild that I never dreamed they might once have been wilder. Had I known, I suspect I would not have cared much anyway. Lost or intact, virginity did not loom large then among my private fascinations.

The woods back of Seven Mile Point—as I perceived them once with no botanical specificity, remember them now, and have sorted out with a little formal reading here and there—fall within what is generally known as the northern hardwood forest region, with occasional overlapping intrusions of boreal conifers. The predominant species was and is maple, both red and sugar, in mixtures with beech, yellow birch, oak, ironwood, white ash, and hemlock, each and all presiding somewhat arbitrarily over an understory of gooseberry, viburnum, elder and assorted other shrubs and such. Along the edge of the bluff, rising from it at bizarre angles, are tall white birch as well as aspen and cedar; and the slope of the bluff itself is held in place by a bit of one thing or another, including low juniper and buffalo berry, not to mention profuse blooms of poison ivy into which, it is said, I habitually crawled with willful negligence even as the last application of brown soap and calamine lotion was drying on my vulnerable extremities.

Of my first tentative exploratory sorties into the woods, I

have scant recollection, for most of my activity was oriented toward the beach. But I do remember long twilit evenings of hide-and-go-seek, or hidenseek as we called it, and how I always ran to the watercress spring behind the ice house and buried myself in the bracken there as large and menacing cousins clumped through the woods yelling *ollie ollie oxen free*; or how, if they didn't, and everything suddenly became very still except for the trickling of water over moss, I would begin to feel uneasy and alone in my green lair until presently the discomfort was too much to endure. Then, terrified that I had somehow been abandoned to the darkening woods, I would leap from the bracken and run as fast as I could to the security of the cabin clearing. I was no Mowgli wolf child. Like so many others of my impressionable generation, I had been weaned on the woodland terrors of Grimm and Walt Disney. I fancied that evil lurked in the heart of the forest, according to the word of the True and Holy Mother Church. We live and learn.

And I remember walking along the edge of the woods on the loose gravel of the Shore Drive. The Drive is paved now, a bloody *bona fide* two-lane highway. But then it was a high-crowned trail for occasional vehicles, and we would follow it north a mile or so to the cabin of an old woman who sold fudge from her front porch. And on the way home, we would stop at the Crooked Tree. Now here I must tread carefully between the shards of memory and the truths of recorded American history, such as there are, for I cannot say with infallibility that ours was the *real* crooked tree, the fabled *L'Arbre Croche*, the wind-tortured pine that was a landmark to early voyageurs out of Michilimackinac. We were given to understand by my father that our twisted ancient pine on the bluff was the real item, but I have since learned from others who have delved more seriously into the literature of the Old Northwest and the fur-trapping days that *L'Arbre Croche* died of old age in the 1830s, and that in any event it wasn't a pine at all, but a tamarack. Be that as it may, we believed, as obedient children always do; and believing, I would place my hands against the gray deep-grooved bark of that venerable dog-legged giant and, looking down over the edge of the high bluff to the lake below, fancy canoes filled with fierce bearded men in stocking caps, and paddles that flashed orange in the sunset. But today in Emmett County, do not seek to know from whence the tree crooks or paddles flash. Ask any knowledgable resident where *L'Arbre Croche* is and he will sensibly direct you to a real estate development by that name at the butt end of Little Traverse Bay.

In the summer of 1974 I returned to Emmett County and rented a small cabin in the woods east of Cross Village. The cabin was constructed of prefabricated pine logs, a feature I noted with some minor disappointment despite my understanding that one simply cannot go through life expecting Indian-felled, axe-hewn white cedar every time. Nevertheless it was a good place to sit out infrequent August showers, to think a little in isolation from telephones and mail deliveries and daily newspapers. And because it was not among the greater estates on Lake Michigan's shore, it afforded me an opportunity to see a bit of the backcountry I had missed as a child. I should add that I had already been back to the area, briefly, in the early 1950s, in the company of rowdy beer-drinking collegiates. But I had been too busy socializing to discover much about either the country or myself.

Among other things, this time around I discovered that it must take a lot of guts and patience and pig-headed perseverance to be a farmer in Emmett County. It is, as Aldo Leopold once observed of his own Sand County region in Wisconsin, "lean, poor land, but rich country"—land in Leopold's view being where "corn, gullies, and mortgages grow"; country being "the personality of the land, the collective harmony of its soil, life, and weather." Everywhere I poked throughout that resource-wealthy country north from Harbor Springs, I saw poor lean land growing mortgages. I do not mean to slander the efforts of so many hard-working people, or to imply that here or there in the backcountry you cannot encounter a fine patch of corn or a handsome herd of cows. But overall, the agricultural leanness shows through, as it does in New

England and Appalachia and wherever else family-farming people are trying to keep up with inflation on marginal, inadequate acreage. It shows in the great sway-backed barns that are tumbling down into kindling under time and the snows of winter, in the fields reverting to jack pine and brush, and the gaunt shells of houses abandoned reluctantly after years of unprofitable toil and doughty trust in the gods of fortune. And in Petoskey, a bit of rooting around at the county office building turns up the fact that between 1964 and 1969 the total acreage classified as farmland in Emmett County decreased by some 30 percent, a decline greater than that of any other Little Finger county save Kalkaska; and that with 57,000 acres of farmland remaining in 1969, only half of it was being farmed; and that with 248 individual farms operating that same year, only half were reporting sales of $2,500 or more. "It was marginal to begin with up here," said Keith Lamkin, the county agricultural extension agent, "and it's been sliding ever since. The small fellow can't swing it. It's easier to go off the farm and make a better living somewhere else."

I asked Lamkin about the even-aged, even-spaced stands of pine and spruce I had seen up-country in Pleasant View and thereabouts. "That's something else that didn't work out," he said. "Those are Christmas trees, or were. They were planted extensively in the 1940s, and just about the time they were ripe for harvest, the market got flooded with cheaper trees from Canada. Some people are just born to bad luck."

And others aren't, I guess, if you figure that for every ploughed-over tract succeeding to forest there is another somewhere that is going the other way, or will soon enough. For Emmett County is growing something in addition to trees. Namely people and houses. And the closer you get to big water, the thicker those crops tend to be.

I can't say I wasn't warned. The real estate broker who arranged the cabin rental near Cross Village had asked me, when I phoned him from New York, if I had ever been up that way before; and I told him, with emphasis on the Thirties. "Well," he said, "you'll hardly know the place." And as

I came down from the Mackinac Bridge that first morning, along the Shore Drive from Cross Village toward Seven Mile Point, I hardly did. About eight miles separate the village from the point as the road turns; and in all that distance, going back to the Thirties, I don't think there were half a dozen homes, including ours and an uncle's and the fudge woman's and one or two other shadowy places tucked back among the birches; and maybe twice that many by the early Fifties. This time I stopped counting at thirty-six, before I was halfway down the road. Then, just north of the point, I passed the first new development: Surfwood, with a fancy arch over the entrance and a sentry box for the security guard. Next, not wanting to stir up too many fragile memories in one swoop, I passed the driveway to what I remembered as our old place, unseen behind the trees, and turned down the Shore Drive Cutoff, an unpaved road to Five Mile Creek. All along it were mailboxes and side roads going off to new houses at the edge of the dunes. And then I was back on the main drive at the red barn and silver silo of the dairy from where we had fetched milk in the old days. The barn and silo were still intact, which did not surprise me, for they were substantial structures and the dairy had been a thriving one. But its thriving times were over now. Spreading in every direction from the barn were the manicured lawns of Birchwood Farm Estates, complete with motel and restaurant and the sun-decked, plate-glassed façades of expensive vacation homes straight out of Sea Ranch, California.

Later, in Harbor Springs, I called on the broker to pick up the keys to my cabin. "Did you come down the Shore Drive?" he asked.

I said I had.

"What did you think?"

"I think I like it better the other way," I said. "I think I'm wondering now if there's any place left to get to the beach."

Drift Zones

It was a different sort of place, once—the beach. I mean it was free and open and wild and wide, and now it is owned and posted and pinched. But as beaches go these days—as measured by the texture and color of sand, the clarity of the water, and the visual impact of uplands and water and sky all merging along the shore—I would still stack this one, the stretch from Five Mile Creek north to Sturgeon Bay, against the finest in North America, or anywhere else for that matter.

In the old times, brown as walnuts, we would spend entire days there, poking around in the dunes, building castles, roasting weenies, collecting treasured stones, such as the pocked gray petoskey, chasing shorebirds and gulls, tumbling in waves that came tall with the west wind and a hundred miles of open water behind them. It was a cloistered world, then. Days or weeks would pass without our seeing a single stranger. When one did appear in the distance down the shore, a moving splinter on the sand, we would run down the beach to look him over and make sure he was not some pitiful shipwrecked survivor, or a man overboard, or perhaps one of those bearded voyageurs in stocking caps. No such luck. And when strangers, alone or in groups, passed across "our" part of the beach or paused in the dunes nearby for a picnic, no one cared one way or the other. Permission to pass or pause was neither requested nor granted, for ownership of sand did not matter much in those guileless days before off-road vehicles, disposable containers, and the no-trespass signs of the summer gentry.

With reciprocal prescriptive rights, we too were at liberty to roam the beach, and the best part of that was the hike down to Five Mile Creek. We would start fresh and early in the morning, following the wet sand for a way, then cross back over the wide drifts to charge whooping through the sea rocket and beach grass at the edge of the dunes. There were long still pools back that way in shallow depressions behind the drift zone, and the slime in the pools felt good between the toes; except sometimes the smell of organic decay was too much, and with ghastly visions of leeches fastened to our gory ankles we would flee again to the cleansing waters of Lake Michigan. Of course there were no leeches, or anything else of a menacing disposition, though occasionally we did see deer tracks and the print of some canine wanderer which my brother, with face averted, proclaimed to be no less than a wolf. I suspected he was purposely in error even then; and to my everlasting discredit I must confess I was relieved to learn one day that my skepticism was well founded, wolves long since and without necessity having been extirpated from the Little Finger Country.

Five Mile Creek was no gushing torrent, but it was clear and cold where it came down from the cedar woods over polished stones and out across the beach to the lake. A trail led upstream to a staircase of shallow pools with undercut banks. After the long walk in the sun and the wind, the shady woods were inviting; and my cousins and I would lie on our bellies, each of us assigned to a different pool, each with just his head showing over the edge of the bank, watching for speckled trout. If we were patient and still, we would see two or three every time, magnificent fish with dark wavy lines on their backs and red spots on their sides and sometimes, in late August before spawning, with bellies the color of a Lake Michigan sunset. It was a good thing for the trout we were not yet wise to the ways of angling, though I suppose my older kin, inadequately equipped, may have tried from time to time without success. I do recall, however, that there was a friend of my father, a man known to us as "Uncle Bill." I remember him with a battered felt hat covered with tiny feathered hooks, a wicker creel, and a long thin pole like a coach whip. Uncle Bill went alone to Five Mile Creek and always returned with a heavy creel. I have no idea how many times over how many summers he did that, or whether there were others of equal proficiency who also stalked those shady pools. I only know, after recent wistful investigations, that the wild native brookies are long gone from Five Mile Creek, and that what we once were privileged to see there will never be replicated, hatchery stockings by the State of Michigan notwithstanding.

Curious and downright antisocial things happen to me nowadays when I approach a stretch of sand and water. I have been spoiled. My pleasure diminishes in direct inverse proportion to the accretion of human flesh on a beach. I have been known to turn away from what the waterfront planners call a "backup area" without even counting the bodies, a count of the cars having sufficed. One hot summer holiday I was enticed to Jones Beach on Long Island: a minefield of bosoms and buttocks and styrofoam coolers; and I watched children knocking their heads together in the surf in order to satisfy the lifeguard's notion of safety. *Safety in numbers. The more the merrier. Move over, I'm diving in.* Well, I suppose some people like it that way, and they are welcome to it wherever they can find it, which is almost everywhere these days. But there are still a few of us left who prefer our beaches lonelier, without lifeguards and peanut vendors and children with wounded heads. Actually, there are more than a few. There are millions of us. We are desperate. We are scurrying up and down the shores of America searching for lonely beaches, and we are not finding very many. I am scurrying up and down the shores of Emmett County, and I am not finding very many. It is not enough to remember. When propinquity comes at last to Northern Michigan, can Jones Beach be far behind?

Beaches were much in the local news in the summer of 1974. After picking up the key to my cabin that first day in Harbor Springs, I also picked up a copy of the *Harbor Light*, Emmett County's bright, readable weekly newspaper. The front page featured the last of a series of articles entitled "Paradox of Plenty," in which reporters Kevin O'Neill and Kendall Stanley explored the uses and abuses of private and public beaches and found the paradox in "an almost endless supply of shoreline that for a number of reasons doesn't seem to be enough." Later, I talked to Stanley in the *Light's* one-desk newsroom, chatted with others here and there, and moseyed around the beaches I remembered, as well as some others I had never seen before. The shore sure enough was in trouble.

Part of the problem was, and is, the level of the lake itself. All of the Upper Great Lakes are said to be higher than at any time since people started measuring such things. Nine or ten lavishly wet years have swollen the streams of the lakes' watersheds, especially along the north shore of Superior. And when the greatest of the Great rises, it is inevitable that Lake Michigan must also rise. We are informed it is a cyclical circumstance and that someday the beaches of the Little Finger Country will be wide again, as they were in the Thirties and as I remember them even after allowing for the distorted perceptions of youth. In any event, the water is high. It has pinched some Emmett County beaches back almost to the edge of the dunes, and has taken a few others altogether, so that to follow the shore one must swing from cedar to cedar, or wade. Nevertheless we can live with this deprivation, as we must, for it is only temporary. Aside from drowning a few piers, the risen waters have done no damage that will not be repaired one way or another in the course of natural events. And besides, the lake's high level is but a small part of the problem. The larger part is inadequate public access to the beach.

The paradox of plenty, as O'Neill and Stanley saw it, is that here is this county with some one hundred miles of shoreline, and about twenty of that in public ownership, yet *still* people are compelled to trespass, creating confrontations and angry uptight feelings and causing the landed gentry for the first time ever in 1974 to call out the militia—namely the agents of Polestar Security of Harbor Springs, unarmed but attired nonetheless in awesome uniforms calculated to make them look like State Troopers. (I never saw a man from Polestar in my two weeks' of beach-bumming and occasional trespass; but I saw a picture of one and that was enough. Thereafter, no trespass.) But why confrontations and Polestar when almost 20 percent of the beach is public? Why, because most of the people who prefer loneliness to propinquity do not want to stray too far from their cars to find it. They want to have their empty beach and park there, too.

Emmett County's relative wealth of public beachfront is deceptive. On the surface, it would seem that twenty miles should be more than enough; and it *would* be if you could spread the beaches around to achieve idyllic distribution, which you cannot. So let us begin on the south shore of Little Traverse Bay and work north, taking inventory. First off is Petoskey State Park, with about 300 acres and a mile of magnificent dune-rimmed beach convenient to the center of greatest summer population. If Jones Beach does ultimately descend on the Little Finger Country, this is the likeliest place for it to appear first. And God help Petoskey. Next, we are coming around the butt of the bay and it is solid wall-to-wall no-trespassing territory all the way into Harbor Springs. The Springs itself has a small municipal beach, but the best of the shore here is locked within the formidable private premises of Harbor Point, a sanctuary for midwestern tycoons and proprietors of inherited fortunes. And now we are out of the bay and moving north on the Shore Drive to Five Mile Creek.

At the time of my interim visit in the early Fifties, Five Mile was still sometimes a lonely spot, but it was also beginning to develop a reputation as *the* spot for beach parties—those shady pools being as good for caching beer as for catching trout, though I suspect the trout were gone even then. Well, it was indeed an excellent place for beer and bonfires, and I confess that my collegiate friends and I spent a good part of our time there depleting both the supply of available driftwood and our chilled six-packs of Champagne Velvet and Frankenmuth, the brews that made Michigan infamous. It did not occur to me then that we might have been squatting on private property, as in fact we were, or that our all-night raucous performances might have helped to establish a pattern for future trouble. The long-suffering man who owns the beach at Five Mile still permits public access, though from time to time I understand he has been forced to close it off in consideration of complaining neighbors, not to mention accumulations of beer cans and other artifacts abandoned on the beach. There were also reports not long ago that long-haired "nudies" were frolicking near Five Mile. The disclosure does not particularly distress me, except insofar as it indicates that, however free and natural we had it in the Thirties and Fifties, we sure as hell didn't have everything.

From Five Mile north to Cross Village, the best of all possible shorefronts is now virtually sealed off by the private ownership of sand, by cottages and cabins and assorted domiciles falling into neither category, such as the elegant, if not extravagant, alabaster fortress which sits cantilevered over the bluff a half mile north of my father's former place, like a rectilinear glacier on the green escarpment. Along this stretch there are no public beaches. That is, no beach is officially classified as such. But with some discretion and questions politely put to the right people, one can find a place or two to flop on the golden sand without fear of harrassment by naked ladies or beer-soused rowdies. A bit of patient exploration is all that is necessary. Trouble is, the vast majority of Emmett County's summer visitors don't have time for patience. As they drive along the shore, looking for lonely beaches, they see gaps between the domiciles and no-trespass signs; and assuming that where there's a gap there's a way, they park their automobiles and proceed to the beach. Whereupon the gentry reaches for the telephone and calls out the militia.

North of Cross Village, development is spotty and sparse. There is a fine township beach at Bliss, backed by superb dunes, and beyond that, where the Shore Drive ends, is Wilderness State Park—8,000 acres and eighteen miles of shoreline running the inside of Sturgeon Bay to Waugoshance Point, then back across the flat top of the peninsula toward Mackinaw City. Wilderness lives up to its name. It is as fine and wild a state park as I have seen anywhere. But it is not doing much to alleviate the problem of public access to the beach. That is not the park's fault. The park is there. Its beaches are there and they are accessible—to people who are willing to walk. But most people nowadays do not want to walk. "Why won't they walk?" I asked a ranger one day. He fixed me with a dour eye and said: "They've forgotten how."

Across the country I hear the purr of distant engines. I cannot escape the purr of engines coming closer. And closer. And now I hear a piercing *brrrrraaap* as the wheels go by, kicking sand in my face, and I am reminded of the muscle-bound bullies who used to appear on the beach in the Charles Atlas ads in order to humiliate the 98-pound weaklings. ORVs, we call them. Off-road recreational vehicles. Trail-bikes and scooters and motorcycles and beach buggies and little fat go-carts for little fat goggle-eyed boys who have forgotten how to walk, who may never have learned how to walk in the first place. I can see them now, roaring across the dunes at Bliss, racing toward the wilder shores of Wilderness State Park.

There are a good number of people in this country who have had it with ORVs. They are fairly rational folk, by and large, given to cool level-headedness and the democratic process, and they do not go around generally advocating infringements of fundamental liberties. But just get one of these persons going on the subject of ORVs and you are in for a full-scale demonstration of apoplectoid schizophrenia, complete with ominous exhortations, threats, and recriminations. I exaggerate only a little, for I know the strong emotions that can overcome one when, afoot on a wilderness trail or supine on some lonely beach, one discerns the sound of off-road engines coming closer.

They came to Bliss on a gorgeous azure day of wind-filled silence. I stood on the beach and watched them—two trail bikes bearing blue-helmeted riders. They were a hundred yards away where the dunes bunch up into long 45-degree slopes of sand held loosely by clumps of low juniper. For nearly half an hour, the two riders tried to mount the steep-est slope, smashing across the juniper for better traction, spinning their rear tires in the sand, losing momentum, backing off, revving up, charging again. Finally they gave up and rode away to the south, and I returned to my beach towel at the edge of the lake. Bliss. And then I heard them coming again. Up the beach. Small and purring and faraway, following the curve of the shore, and now large and brrrrraaaping and straight on with the sun glinting off their plexiglass face masks. I thought they would stop, turn off somewhere into the dunes, since the beach was narrow and there were four of us, all relatively tall, stretched across it. But no, they were coming by. *Brrrrraap*. Three feet away. *Brrrrraap*. Two feet away. Blue helmets and black bikes and the sand flying out behind them. And for a long time after they were gone, I sat there marveling at their supreme arrogance and the intensity of my loathing for them and for all the motorized morons who in so little time have managed to spoil so much of the outdoor experience everywhere.

They would even spoil Wilderness State Park, if the Michigan Department of Natural Resources would only let them. At the time of my last visit, the department had just ratified a master plan placing most of the park under protective zoning for primitive and natural area uses, with walk-in, backpacker campsites on the shore and a formal ban on motorized access along the beach at Sturgeon Bay. The ORV people didn't like that. They claimed prescriptive rights—a half century of beach-buggying along the bay to the mouth of Big Sucker Creek. The beach, they said, by long established tradition, was a highway for their vehicles. And at one hearing, an ORV practitioner from Harbor Springs went so far as to claim that he and his associates had been performing a high public service at Wilderness State Park. How so? Why, by routing from the beach "those hippies with their long hair and funny cigarets." Brrrrraaap.

Namaycush

If anything dominated my thoughts of Northern Michigan over the years, it was the lake itself. Big water has a way of getting at you, even at landlubbers like myself who like to sit on the sidelines and watch. I got in it enough, I guess.

Enough to learn how to swim anyway. There was a raft at Seven Mile anchored out in front of the beach fifty yards or so, and I think I managed unaided to get out there once or twice that last summer before the place was sold. Dog paddle, probably. And I remember once between the raft and the shore I felt the sudden touch of something else in the water, a soft bumping of my ankle. When I turned to see what it was, a dark shadow flicked across the clear sandy bottom. I suppose I was frightened to discover then that other things besides people were swimming around in Lake Michigan.

"It was big," I avowed from the safety of the beach.

"It was just a fish," someone said.

"How do you know?"

"Probably like the ones at Five Mile Creek."

"In the lake?"

"The lake is full of fish."

"And sharks," said my brother.

We checked it out with Uncle Bill and he said nothing in the lake was quite as mean as a shark, but there were still some pretty big fish. We wanted to know what kind.

"*Salvelinus Namaycush*," said Uncle Bill.

"That's a funny name for a fish," someone said.

"Well, it's better than most," Uncle Bill said. "You don't like the sound of it, try lake trout. Same fish."

I finally met *Salvelinus Namaycush* later that summer on the dock at Harbor Springs. After the ice cream parlor, the dock was my favorite place in town. It was long and wide and always busy, and at the far end of it were moored the great white yachts of the rich folk who lived in the great white houses of Harbor Point. Or perhaps only the women lived in the houses, for the men seemed always to be on their yachts, sitting in deck chairs, sipping cocktails, each with one sneakered foot crossed precisely over a white flannel knee, and each with a Clark Gable mustache. Those haughty sailors had been my heroes until, walking back along the dock one day, I noticed for the first time a small fleet of open, shabby gray boats with blistered paint, and the sun-bleached spars from which the gill nets hung drying, and the men in faded overalls and wool caps and black rubber boots. Large pine boxes filled with ice were stacked on the dock beside the boats, and the men were lifting big fish out of the boats and putting them down on the ice. The fish were gray like the boats, with deeply forked tails and mottled backs and ivory bellies. And I knew what they were without asking, because Uncle Bill had said that if you want to figure how a lake trout looks, think of a fish in Five Mile Creek, take away its red spots, put a notch in its square tail, and blow it up maybe four or five times. And since the description fit, I was pleased to meet *Salvelinus Namaycush* at long last, even if he was a little stiff.

I was equally delighted to meet these rough and crusty men in rubber boots, and I remember thinking that they must surely be even more heroic than the gentlemen in white sneakers at the snootier end of the dock. That impression was soon confirmed. The film *Captains Courageous* came to the theater in Harbor Springs, and as I sat there munching pop-corn, all previous allegiance to Clark Gable shifted irrevocably to Spencer Tracy, the intrepid Portuguese trawlerman who, as he hauled in his catch, would murmur, "Don't cry little fishie, don't cry any more." This, I think, was in 1938. I didn't know it at the time, but insofar as the lake trout of Michigan were concerned, there already was reason for tears. The magnificent native gray trout would weep at the dock in Harbor Springs for another ten or twelve years and then no more; for in ten or twelve years there would be no more trout. When I returned to Harbor Springs in the summer of 1950 and walked out along the dock, the pine boxes filled with ice were gone. So was the flaky gray fleet.

"What happened to the fishing boats?" I inquired of an old man who looked as if he might once have had some first-hand knowledge of such things. His face was the color of cured leather, and he was wearing rubber boots.

"What happened?" said the old man, staring at the water. "What happened is eels."

The lake trout is distributed across the top half of North America from Alaska eastward to the Labrador Peninsula, south to Northern New England, and west through the Finger Lakes of New York, the Great Lakes, parts of the Upper Mississippi watershed, and in scattered lakes of the Far West where the water is deep and cold at fifty degrees through the heat of the summer. Nowhere in this vast range was old Namaycush more abundant than in the Upper Great Lakes in general, and Lake Michigan in particular, from Little Sable Point north to the Straits of Mackinac. The outstanding laker of record was a Michigan fish, an 88-pounder caught off Grand Haven in 1864. And from 1890 to 1944, lakers provided the State of Michigan with a lucrative commercial fishery unsurpassed before or since by that of any other inland state. Every port had its flaky gray fleet: Mackinaw City and Manistique and Petoskey and Charlevoix and Traverse City. And all the Spencer Tracys of all those fleets, it once was estimated, handled in aggregate enough gill net to reach halfway around the circumference of the earth. It was lucrative all right; perhaps too lucrative. For the first thirty years of the harvest, the catches were huge—eight million pounds or more each year. Then the curve on the graph of the harvest began to slide—in 1926 to seven million pounds, in 1939 to 5.5 million pounds. Finally, in 1944, the harvest took a nosedive and the curve fell down through the years, so that by 1955 it had broken through the bottom of the graph and there was nothing left to measure. Well, there was something. That year there was thirty-four pounds. And everyone blamed it on the eels.

So much has been written about the eel-like sea lamprey and its invasion of the Great Lakes, presumably by way of the Welland Canal, that it does not bear too much repeating here. Except to say that the three-pound lamprey, with its toothed vacuum of a mouth, consumes an average of eighteen pounds of fish tissue and blood during its one-year life as a parasitic adult. And except to say that it most assuredly did contribute to the demise of the lake trout in lakes Huron and Michigan in the Forties and Fifties. The lamprey, in short, is an ugly and venal creature. It is a rat with fins. I wish it the worst of luck, and I am delighted to hear that after only partial success with electrical weirs in its spawning streams, Great Lakes biologists now have the parasite about 80 percent under control—killed off, that is—with a chemical called TFM, which is toxic to ammoecetes, the lamprey's larvae. The lamprey is so easy to hate that one is tempted to blame it for everything that has gone wrong with Lake Michigan since it was first sighted there in the mid-Thirties, perhaps the very same summer I heard Captain Courageous urging the fishies not to cry any more. But to do this, to hate so completely, one must forget about the curve on the graph of the lake trout harvest, which had begun to slide some ten years earlier. And one must forget as well the men in the black rubber boots, my early heroes, day after day, year after year with their nets in the water, and no limit on what they might take from the lake for the markets of Detroit, Chicago, and Cleveland. "Hell," says Bob Ryan, a sport-fishing charterboat captain in Harbor Springs, "there weren't any lamprey to speak of up here until the late Forties, and the trout by then were damn near gone."

It seems perfectly natural that the commercial fisherman should put the blame on the lamprey for what happened to the native trout of Lake Michigan, which ultimately was extinction; and that the sportsman should blame the commercial fisherman. Everyone loves to hate an adversary and hates to love ambiguity. But by the end of World War II, and increasingly thereafter, other things besides lampreys and nets were getting into the deep and nearly empty lair of Namaycush. The trouble with these newcomers to the lake was that they were hard to hate. And they were hard to hate because, except for the alewives and the algae, you couldn't see them.

I mean even in the clear blue-green water of Lake Michigan, DDT is invisible, and though its use is now largely prohibited, I use the present tense advisedly; this is one pesticide with the habit of hanging around for a long time. Polychlorinated biphenyls are invisible, too. And arsenic and cyanide and mercury and lead and a score of other toxins that poured— and to some extent still pour—from the outfalls of industry. I mean you cannot see nitrates and phosphates and Vitamin

B12, the by-products of human waste remaining even after treatment in most municipal sewage plants—and a ring of 300 encircles the lake. Nor can you see and therefore hate the nutrients that flow down the natural drainages of the mid-lake coastal counties, where dairy farming is big business and where the operators are in the habit of spreading winter manure on the frozen ground.

In 1967, *Newsweek* magazine posted me to Chicago to report on the aftermath of a dreadful Lake Michigan summer. I found the *Chicago Tribune* daily imploring its readers to "Save Our Lake." I found Chicagoans still shaken from the sight and smell of alewives rotting on their beaches and, after that, from the wispy green algae called Cladophora—a product of nutrient enrichment, a precursor of eutrophication—which also washed ashore in windrows of slime and even clogged the intake screens of the city's water filtration plant. And I found an ecologist in Madison, Wisconsin, who opined that, Lake Michigan being saturated with DDT and dieldrin, one could extrapolate by what had happened to the trout of New York's Lake George when certain levels of these pesticides were found in the fry. "They failed to reproduce," said the ecologist. "It's likely the same thing is happening now to Lake Michigan's trout." Of course, he was referring to the anadromous Rainbow, for old native Namaycush was crying no more. I filed my story by Western Union, announcing with Cassandran solemnity and no small amount of personal regret that the big waters of Lake Michigan were, in effect, beginning to die. Like Lake Erie's.

There was, however, one significant flaw in that report. In my eagerness to establish the necessity of an early death-watch, I devoted too much attention to the bad news and neglected to look for the good. Had I made an effort to seek out those with some faith in the future of the lake, I am sure I would have been directed to the Michigan Department of Natural Resources (though it wasn't called that then) and the United States Bureau of Sport Fisheries and Wildlife, which even then were two years into an ambitious program to establish in the deteriorating waters of the world's fourth largest freshwater lake, where the pestilential alewife already represented three-quarters of the fish biomass, a new and enduring recreational fishery. And I don't mean the coho salmon, which has been a good part of it—the most visible part of it—since that species was first introduced in the lake in 1966. Nor do I mean the Chinook and Atlantic salmon, planted in subsequent years. I mean Namaycush itself, a hybrid cousin to the long-gone native, out of Superior and Crystal Lake, Michigan: the brood stock stripped of their eggs and milt at a Marquette hatchery and the fingerlings planted thirty to the pound—800,000 that first year between Suel Choix Point and Epoufette off the Upper Peninsula, 100,000 each at Grand Traverse Bay, Kewaunee (Wisc.), Northport, and the reefs of the Beaver Island archipelago. And in 1966 another 1.7 million trout fingerlings, some as far south as the Milwaukee reef and Ludington. And in the dreadful Summer of '67, 2.4 million more, all the way down to the toe of the lake off the Great Lakes Naval Training Station in Illinois. Madness? Incredible madness. Magnificent madness. And the craziest thing of all is that it seems to be working. People are catching one hell of a lot of trout.

Mryl Keller is supervisor of the Great Lakes Fish Station in Charlevoix, Michigan, where the Department of Natural Resources monitors the pulse of its trout and salmon programs, where everyone tells you to go if you want to find out how Namaycush is doing. I went there on a stormy August afternoon and we sat by a window overlooking the white-capped lake. It was not a good day to be fishing.

The coho, Keller told me, is still the leading gamefish of the Upper Great Lakes. That is, in terms of the total catch. But the laker is gaining fast. "This is the bread-and-butter fish of Lake Michigan," he said. "You can take the lake trout any month of the year. When the salmon aren't hitting in the summer, he's down there waiting for the deep troller. Mid-October to late November, you can take him spin-casting in twenty-five feet of water. You can take him through the ice in the winter, and in the spring he's up near the surface, ready to strike. Now he's not as spectacular at the end of your line as the salmon or steelhead. But he sure is good eating." Yes, I said. I knew about the eating, but not about the end of the line. There was still some unfinished business between Namaycush and me.

We talked about the planting program. Keller said the state was now supplying the U.S. Bureau of Sport Fisheries with 11 million trout eggs annually. The Bureau raises the fry to fingerlings and, when they are about fifteen months old, plants them at selected sites in each of the three Upper Great Lakes. About two million fingerlings go into Lake Michigan each year. "And with all those alewives to feed on," said Keller, "they grow fast." After three years in the lake, the trout is averaging twenty inches; after five years, it is more than twenty-six inches and close to ten pounds. Keller said sportsmen are now taking some 300,000 lakers a year, averaging out at about seven pounds each. Some, however, have already come in as heavy as eighteen pounds. Keller did some fast math on a scrap of paper. "Sport-fishermen," he said, "are now taking from the lake a volume of trout that is equivalent to what the commercial operators were taking in the late Forties, right before the end. The difference is that now we are putting in more than are coming out." Put-and-take no doubt will continue until such time as the new trout proves that it is capable of reproducing on the old spawning shoals or in the feeder streams of Lake Michigan. So far, it hasn't.

It was not exactly as I had imagined it might be. There were no overalls or rubber boots, nor a Captain Courageous in a flaky gray boat. We went out from Harbor Springs on the *Islander I*, which was white and well-scrubbed like the fancy yachts at the end of the municipal dock, only smaller at twenty-eight feet and rigged in a very particular way for trolling. The skipper was Bill Schoenith of Alanson, who is quite capable of courage, having spent much of his life as a career paratrooper. But courage at the helm is no longer as necessary as it once was out on the big lake, except in sudden unforecasted storms, which still do occur in Northern

Michigan with occasional bottoms-up fury and callous disrespect for the science of human survival.

Out past the Harbor Point Light, Schoenith set his course toward the cement plant at Petoskey, throttled up the twin 183-horse engines, and shared with me some of his thoughts about the practice of dredging lake trout out of 150 feet of water. "It's a good bright day," he said, squinting into the sun. "And at 150 feet, you need it that way. It can get pretty dark down there when it's cloudy." In addition to its depth, Schoenith explained that Little Traverse Bay is visited by a strong circulatory current saturated with small organisms of a kind alewives feed on. And because lake trout like their water deep and cold, especially in August, and because they also like to eat alewives which are plump and well-fed, Little Traverse Bay is just about the most productive fishing hole in Northern Michigan. Schoenith didn't mention it, but I will. Little Traverse Bay is especially productive because that is where the fisheries people have planted nearly one million trout since 1966.

As practiced by Schoenith and other charter-boat operators, and by some well-endowed individuals with their own boats and a strong addiction to taking big fish in deep water, summer trolling can be an expensive and sophisticated endeavor. There are, for example, such sweet little thousand-dollar devices as the *Vexilar Sona-Graf*, which operates on the sonar principle, except that instead of detecting submarines it detects fish and conveys their depth to you on a graphic printout. A trained eye—Schoenith's, for one—can distinguish chubb from trout, and sometimes trout from salmon, just from the way the blips read: the chubb massed dark and scribbly like clouds on the bottom, the trout off the bottom in singles or clusters of arcs like upended parentheses. Then, if you prefer to play your fish without the encumbrance of a heavy sinker or metal line, there is that ingeniously malevolent Great Lakes device called the downrigger. The stern-mounted downriggers on the *Islander I* are equipped with 100 yards of steel line, fed off a wheel. At the end of the line is a 10-pound cannonball. Above the cannonball, a dropper line is attached by a release pin to the fishing line, which is 40-pound monofilament (in case you latch onto a Chinook) off a modified salt-water reel and trolling rod. The favored late summer lure is a flash fly or a blue-and-white spoon behind a large herring-dodger attractor. With a solid strike, the pin releases the fishing line from the downrigger line, and the rest of it is strictly between you and Namaycush. Of course, not everyone afloat in Little Traverse Bay, or in the Upper Great Lakes for that matter, goes about the business of killing trout (and salmon) with such methodical efficiency. I'm told, in fact, the majority of anglers go out without benefit of either sonar or downriggers, and do quite nicely chugging with bait.

We were watching the rods now. The rods were arched tight over the downriggers, bent almost double by the weight of the cannonball sinkers. On the *Sona-Graf*, trout blips were showing up at 150 feet, about ten feet up from the bottom.

"The lake trout is different from other gamefish," Schoenith was saying. "Most fish come up on their prey from below. The laker attacks from above. So if everything is going okay down there, our lures should be coming along right between those fish and the bottom."

We had been out for an hour, lolling around on gentle swells, with not much wind and a hot sun dazzling the surface of the water. There were three of us aboard, not counting Schoenith and his son Bill Junior, and we began making bets on which of the rigs would get hit first, the one with the flash fly or the one with the Dardevele spoon. I bet on the fly. And no sooner had I committed myself than the one with the spoon snapped straight up, with a quivering tip. We were into a fish.

We had five hits that afternoon, losing three near the bottom and bringing two fine fat ones—a twelve- and a ten-pounder—to net. There is no great drama, one must admit, in the playing of a lake trout even that large when it is hooked at 150 feet of depth. After setting the hook, you are dealing with a reluctant weight in the water. You are horsing it in with brute strength in your forearm and wrist, and there is so much line out you begin to think after a while that possibly you are reeling in nothing less than the other side of Lake Michigan. And then it is finally up at the surface, rolling on its white belly and sometimes fighting a little, as our ten-pounder did—just to show that it still has an ingrained genetic preference, however archaic, for the kind of freedom that prevailed for trout before lampreys and men.

We killed the larger fish with a club on the deck of the *Islander I*. Schoenith hoisted it toward the ice chest. Above the anal fin on its left side was a white scar the size of a tennis ball.

"Lamprey?"

"Yes," Schoenith said. "Going back a few years."

"Well," I said. "He's still a fine fish. He survived."

"Not quite," said a literal member of the party.

The commercial sale of lake trout taken from Michigan waters has been prohibited by state law since July 1974. Six months later the state banned the use of large-mesh gill nets. Together, these two measures may well give the hybrid Namaycush a new lease on life in the deeps of Lake Michigan. But still there are reports from time to time of unlawful shenanigans, of gill nets cached in the pine woods of Hog Island and other remote northern hide-aways, and of poachers in high-speed boats outrunning the fishery rangers and somehow managing to bootleg to the markets of Chicago some five to ten thousand pounds of lake trout a week. I do not know all this to be a fact, but I suspect it may be, plundering ways of yore having a tendency to pop up now and then, like recessive chromosomes.

The night before I left Michigan, I dropped by a backcountry saloon north of Harbor Springs and asked the friendly proprietor if he would give my two fresh-caught lake trout a fast overnight freeze for the trip back to New York. He was glad to oblige, and so I sat for a while at his bar and sampled his whiskey as we talked about fishing in Emmett County. I mentioned I had heard it had been a good year for brown trout.

"Browns?" said the proprietor. "You want to know about Browns, there's your man." And he pointed to a ruddy-faced customer at the end of the bar. "He knows more about Browns than about people."

"Browns been good, all right," said the expert.

"Whereabouts?"

"Around."

"He knows where they spawn," said the proprietor. "But he's not saying."

"Hell no," said the expert. "Nor how I git 'em, either."

"He goes in at night and takes a bundle," the proprietor said.

"How many's a bundle?" I asked, knowing the statutory limit was five fish.

"Maybe thirty," said the expert. "Forty on a good night."

"You better be quiet, fella," the proprietor said.

The man at the end of the bar took a pull on his bottle of beer. Then he looked at us with the fierce conviction of a man who can do no wrong. "Sure I violate," he said. "Don't everyone?"

"Not quite," I said.

"That's their tough shit then, mister," said the expert. "Me, I know what I'm doin' and I use it good."

I wanted to tell the man that his logic was remarkable. I wanted to say that this is how the old loggers felt about the white pine, and how the men in the flaky gray boats felt about the wild native lake trout. They used it good, too. And used it up. But I said nothing of the sort because the man at the end of the bar was full of beer and I think he would not have understood, and besides, he was a big man with hands like cannonball sinkers.

In the morning I closed up the cabin I had rented, gathered my gear, and drove down to the saloon, where I retrieved the two frozen lake trout and packed them with ice in a cooler in the back of the car.

"Do you think they'll spoil?" I asked the proprietor. "It's two days on the road to New York."

"Spoil hell," he said. "They're froze so tight they'll last forever."

I said I doubted they would last *that* long, thanked him
for his help, and wished him luck at the fall fishing. "But
that's only for you," I added. "Some people around here
should have rotten luck."

"You mean the Pole."

"I mean the one who takes thirty Browns in an evening."

"That's the Pole," the proprietor said. "Actually he's Irish
but everyone calls him the Pole. Short for fishing pole. Come
to think of it, he don't deserve that name."

"Why not?"

"The sonofabitch never uses a pole."

"What does he use then?"

"Everything there's a law against," said the proprietor.
"And other things the law never heard of, nor me either."

My second and final stop that morning was the place at Seven
Mile Point, which had run through one or two different owners since 1938 and was now in the hands of an attorney from
Bay City, Michigan. I had telephoned the day before, asking
permission to trespass nostalgically, and the attorney's son
said everyone else had gone and it would be fine if I wanted
to drop by. And it *was* fine, after poking around the rest of
Emmett County and finding so much of it changed, to discover that the old place after all those years was pretty much
the way I remembered it. The unpaved driveway circling
around to the kitchen breezeway. The original white cedar
logs antiqued by sun and snow and rain. The great stone fireplace intact with my father's New Brunswick moose head,
near bald after more than half a century, still presiding over
the livingroom. And the penciled lines on the door sashes of
the bedrooms, lines and initials recording the annual growth
of the summer children who came after me, our own ancient
family marks having long since faded into the rough grain of
the unfinished wood.

"You have a good place here," I said.

"Yes," he said. "And so did you. You remember it?"

"Well enough to know I'll never forget it."

"That must have been something else."

"What?"

"Being here then."

"It sure was," I said. "You would have liked it."

Then I went down the steep trail through the cedars and across the footbridge and the dunes to the beach. It was almost gone, the beach. North, I could see the new white fortress hanging down over the side of the bluff and the shore beyond running on to Mackinac. The lake inshore was dark under cloud but bright and blue farther out. Waves like feathers floated at the edge of the sky. I would have spent the full day there, watching the waves and the clouds, and remembering, and feeling too much at home. But I couldn't. As I turned back up the trail to the car, it occurred to me that if I didn't get a move on, those two fine trout in the cooler were going to spoil.

THE SELLING OF THE SHELF

The continental shelf of North America, or rather the part extending from the coastal United States into the sea to a subsurface depth of two hundred meters, encompasses an area of some 850,000 square miles. In width, the shelf varies from roughly five miles off certain stretches of the California coast to upwards of three hundred miles off New England and Alaska. The bed of the shelf consists of sediments eroded from the landmass of the continent over millions of years and deposited seaward in layers as thick as five or six vertical miles. Above the seabed, lazy currents stream across the shelf, gathering nutrients from the rivers and wetlands inshore. The chemistry is rich and the waters teem with great schools of fish. Pelagic birds and marine mammals feed on the fish, as do men.

Below the seabed is a different kind of wealth altogether. Locked within the sedimentary substrate are reservoirs of fossil hydrocarbons. This stuff which we call "crude" currently sells for eleven dollars a barrel; with refining, for about fifty to sixty-five cents per gallon at the neighborhood gasoline pump. No one knows exactly how much petroleum, not to mention its associated gases, lies beneath the continental shelf. Estimates vary greatly. But it is probably safe to say that there is enough of it to sustain the status quo for another decade or two. Enough so that the profligate consumer, if he so desires, may continue to spin wheels. Enough so that the oil companies may continue to reap huge windfall profits until such time as there is no more oil anywhere, and oil executives are free at last to retire on pensions to solar-powered homes in the suburbs of Houston.

The question that is now before the nation—as reflected in policy statements by President Gerald Ford and former Secretary of the Interior Rogers C.B. Morton, in subsequent counterproposals by a number of coastal governors, in public hearings, and in decisions now pending in the courts—is not whether America should ever develop the petroleum resources in "frontier" areas of its continental shelf. Even the most radical environmentalist, if he or she has any claim to sanity, can hardly doubt that someday there will be compelling need and justification to tap selectively these offshore reserves. Fossil hydrocarbons have many uses in our society aside from spinning wheels. When the day of the nonconsumptive energy alternative arrives (as one suspects it will out of sheer good sense—and some panic), when our gas gulpers have been relegated to the recycling depot and our homes are indeed heated and cooled by the sun, we shall still need petroleum for food packages and pharmaceuticals and cosmetics and a hundred other kinds of goods. So the real question is not whether, but when and where and how much and under what conditions we shall drill for new gas and oil offshore. And who should control the exploration of these seabed reserves. And how large a voice localities and states should have in the decision-making process, and how large a share of Uncle Sam's bonuses and royalties they should receive to help minimize the social and environmental impact of onshore refineries and pipelines and deepwater ports. And what kind of solid baseline criteria must be developed, for example, before one can determine whether the risk of a major oilspill is going to be "acceptable" to the seaside resort where the slick has a good chance of coming ashore.

There are a lot of questions, actually. Good ones. But very few answers. And there are a lot of people, especially in the Atlantic states and California, who have a gnawing suspicion that some of these questions may be academic; that, in fact, the decision has already been made in Washington to open the frontier areas to rapid development; that as far as President Ford and Secretary Morton are concerned, there is no turning back. *Not so!* say the official guardians of our public domain: "It's an option that's being pursued, but a decision that has not yet been made." And yet the record shows that on January 23, 1974, former President Richard Nixon directed Secretary Morton to increase leasing of the outer continental shelf, the deepwater OCS beyond state-owned tidelands ending at the three-mile limit. And not just increase but *triple* it by opening up, in 1975 alone, ten million acres of untouched seabed, as vast a domain as the aggregate of all federal leases granted for offshore drilling over the previous twenty years. Any thoughts that the new president might pursue a less ambitious course were dispelled when Ford, in his first State of the Union address, detailed how his administration planned to move the nation away from dependence on uncertain sources of foreign oil toward total reliance on domestic oil and gas reserves.

Between the Nixon directive and the Ford commitment, a curious mission began to unfold for Secretary Morton and his aides in the energy/minerals field. At the Office of Oil and Gas, the Bureau of Land Management (caretaker of the OCS), and the U.S. Geological Survey (assessor of OCS resources as well as regulator of its lessees), the most important task, the highest priority soon became the selling of the shelf; and before long eager administrators at almost every level of command and at every opportunity were echoing in public the official Morton line. For example, it is said in the sales presentation that transport of oil by tanker represents an environmental hazard far greater than that posed by pipelines from wellheads offshore. This, however, is a rather strange admission, for what is left unsaid is that all of the oil that might be sucked from the Gulf of Alaska—the richest and riskiest of the potential OCS frontiers—would travel to West Coast refineries not by pipe but by tanker. Next it is claimed that the industry's safety record has vastly improved since the infamous blowout at Santa Barbara in 1969. With more than seven hundred new wells punched into the Gulf of Mexico and Santa Barbara Channel OCS areas over the intervening years, it is said there have been only—*only*—nine major spills. ("Should we be grateful," asked one reporter hearing this, "that there haven't been seven hundred?") And so it goes, this effort by the Department of the Interior (DOI), hustling along with all the verve and vigor of a major ad campaign and sounding, not infrequently, as if the copy had been written by some creative huckster from Exxon or Mobil. Which, I tend to think in my darker moments, is not at all beyond the shadow of a giant possibility.

In the early phase, Interior concentrated much of its effort in California, where public resistance was expected to be stiffest. Rumors were already circulating in the press that Interior would soon announce a massive leasing program for OCS waters off Santa Monica and other southern coastal cities, and that additional leases might later be sold off the state's scenic central and northern coasts. Thus a donnybrook was in the making, for environmentalists are highly organized in California. And though the electorate as a whole is generally schizophrenic about natural-resource issues, the coast is one resource almost every Californian reveres with militant proprietary interest and sanguine prayers that "Santa Barbara" shall never happen again.

Two incidents are illustrative of the attempt by Interior to soften this opposition. To the conference room of the California Resources Agency in Sacramento in summer, 1974, came Jared Carter, a deputy undersecretary of Interior. Carter, who has since left the government, sat there with representatives of various state agencies. They discussed the implications of an accelerated leasing program for the Southern California coastal region. Later, in an affidavit filed with the state attorney general (who was preparing to file suit to block the OCS leases), one of the participants in the Sacramento conference recalled what Jared Carter had said about the purpose of his mission to California. "He stated in substance," wrote Assistant Attorney General Robert H. O'Brien, "that he was sent to California to do a selling job with the citizens, convincing them of the feasibility and merits of OCS development."

In another instance, Interior's evangelistic posture was undraped by Philip Fradkin, the crackerjack staff writer who specializes in environmental affairs for the *Los Angeles Times*. Digging into the affairs of the Bureau of Land Management's new oil and gas office in Los Angeles, Fradkin uncovered a remarkable memo authored by BLM area manager William Grant. The document proposed an expensive ($1.2 million) research study, including $50,000 for "reaction analysis and identification of local political power structure." An additional $43,000, Fradkin reported, "is proposed for a public relations program 'to soften negative public opinion.'"

Evidence that the U.S. Department of the Interior is playing a heavy advocate's role in the unfolding drama of the OCS should come as no surprise to those who are even remotely familiar with the agency's stance on resource issues over the years. Department secretaries have come and gone and, with few and recent exceptions, most have tackled their jobs with the pragmatic belief that God created Interior to enhance the Gross National Product. Morton was not an exception, which perhaps explains why he is now the Secretary of Commerce. Naturally, in the course of pursuing such a goal, some lasting relationships have developed between Interior and certain elements of the private sector which also contribute hugely to the GNP. Notably, Big Oil.

The love affair between DOI, as we shall hereafter call Interior Department, and Big Oil (henceforth BO), is a long one. Morton did not create the romance; he inherited it, along with dozens—perhaps scores—of departmental employees who, having served their apprenticeships in BO, now serve as stewards of gas and oil in the public domain, or as regulators of their former mentors. I do not mean to impugn the motives or integrity of individuals I do not know, or of those I do know, for I have met a few of these regulators in the field, and I believe by and large they are honest people trying to do a decent job for Uncle Sam. By the same token, one hopes the regulators do not impugn the intelligence of the private citizen when he sometimes wonders whether it is possible for men apprenticed in BO to serve without bias in DOI. There is something to be said here about old dogs and new tricks— and this is as true of ex-oilmen as it would be if the Geological Survey, for example, were suddenly to recruit its offshore inspection staff from the membership roster of Friends of the Earth.

It could be argued that cynicism is unproductive in these trying times. Perhaps. And yet one's suspicions must surely be alerted when pronunciamentos from the highest sources confirm the citizen's darkest thought—that Satan created DOI to enhance BO. None other than Rogers Morton himself has been quoted widely as having told a group of oil industry leaders at a White House briefing in 1973: ". . . the Office of Oil and Gas is an institution which is designed to be your institution, and to help you in any way it can." And Morton added: "Our mission is to serve you, not to regulate you. We try to avoid it."

At least one other member of the Ford cabinet shares Morton's talent for playing to such an audience. Even as DOI and the White House were preparing to "brief" Atlantic coastal governors on an accelerated OCS leasing program, more than two thousand oilmen assembled in New York City for the 54th annual meeting of the American Petroleum Institute. Among the session's leading speakers was Secretary of the Treasury William E. Simon, the onetime Nixon energy czar. Simon got right to the point. "A nation that can tame the wilderness," he said, "is not going to surrender to a small group of blackmailers." Thunderous applause and the turning of many well-trimmed heads—possibly to ascertain if there were any Arab observers in the back of the ballroom. Too much reliance on energy conservation, said Simon, could cause "economic disruption." He was gravely concerned, he said, about "environmental restraints of questionable validity." Again, the applause. Then the secretary looked out across the sea of friendly faces and announced that it was the administration's goal to lease ten million OCS acres a year, starting in 1975. There was no hedging here about "options." The secretary was speaking of an administrative decision to go for a specific goal. "I have bright hope for the future," Simon concluded with obligatory good cheer. "I assure you we are committed to developing . . . (these) resources fully."

As the happy conventioneers departed New York on the

following morning, American Petroleum Institute publicists summoned reporters to a press conference to announce the results of a timely study. Timely, because one must bear in mind what was happening in Washington that very same day: President Ford was meeting with the governors of coastal states to tell them how important the OCS is to the nation's security, and Secretary Morton was releasing the specific details of an accelerated OCS lease-sale schedule through 1978, with all the target frontier areas appropriately shaded on a map in solid black ink. But more on the lease-sale later, for it is The Study that is now before us at the press conference. And what does The Study show? Why, it shows, in the words of the Institute's covering news release, that "despite their environmental concerns, nearly three-fourths of some 500 community leaders interviewed this summer in eight U.S. East and Gulf Coast cities favor offshore drilling for oil and natural gas." Could it possibly be? We read on.

We learn that the Institute has commissioned the New York opinion research firm of Oxtoby-Smith, Inc., to study "how influential citizens in East and Gulf Coast cities view offshore drilling: trends in sentiment since 1972." We learn that the polling was conducted in Portland, Me.; Boston, Mass.; Long Island, N.Y.; Atlantic City, N.J.; Dover, Del.; Norfolk, Va.; Mobile, Ala., and St. Petersburg, Fla. We learn that 71 percent of the respondents were either "strongly" or "somewhat" in favor of OCS drilling—up from 65 percent in 1972, partly because of the Mideast oil boycott and the memory of long lines at the gas pumps. We see that 62 percent believe strongly or somewhat that the U.S. should "speed up its leasing of offshore waters, so oil companies can get on with the job of trying to find new oil and gas reserves." As for the respondents—the "influentials"—we learn that all belonged to or attended meetings of at least two community organizations, about half had written on public affairs to an elected official, and a third had addressed a public gathering; that most had incomes exceeding $15,000 annually; and that one-quarter were members of groups "specifically concerned with ecological or conservation issues."

Could it possibly be? We read on.

And we discover, among other things, that the methodology as well as the specific elements of this questionnaire commissioned by the American Petroleum Institute leave something to be desired, for nowhere in the entire report is there an indication that the influentials responded to anything but a generalized hypothesis. Favor offshore drilling? Yes? But off *whose* shore? The questionnaire lacks geographic specificity. There is no immediate perspective. The respondents in Portland, Maine, for example, were not informed that in April, 1974, the President's Council on Environmental Quality (CEQ) listed that city as one of several possible "receipt" areas for onshore development of refineries, petrochemical complexes, and related industries that could "strain existing public services, bring additional land under commercial, residential, and industrial development, and add to air and water pollution." The respondents in Massapequa, Long Island, were not advised that the same CEQ report predicts that oil spilled at the north end of the Baltimore Canyon—the Middle Atlantic region's OCS frontier —has a high probability of coming ashore, on *their* shore, in stormy spring seas. The influentials of Atlantic City and Dover apparently were not apprised of CEQ's finding that while offshore oil and gas production might "impact" biologically valuable wetlands and intensively-used recreation areas, local energy supplies would still have to be supplemented from sources outside the region. And so we nitpick on through the Oxtoby-Smith report and into the supplemental tables, to the one labeled "G."

Though the Institute and Oxtoby-Smith have heartily disagreed with me personally, in my opinion "G" sums it up. "G" is the clincher. "G" appraises the influentials' "awareness of specific offshore accidents." And what is that awareness? It is incredible. If we are truly speaking of influentials, or what the Institute prefers to call "community leaders," it is impossible. Though some respondents mention *California, Gulf Coast, Santa Barbara, East Coast,* or *Other,* only one in two of the influentials was able to say he or she was aware of a specific accident in any of those areas. Worse, eight in ten of these alert, active, *au courant* individuals—"sophisticated and knowledgable" is how Joe Smith, president of Oxtoby-Smith, describes them—were unaware of the most notorious offshore accident, the most widely-publicized environmental disaster in U.S. history. That the event occurred five years earlier, and may therefore have been lost to some memories, in no way allays one's suspicion that something here is amiss. Because *more* than eight in ten of Oxtoby-Smith's respondents were unaware of this accident when queried in 1972.

"What I want to know," a reporter from Boston is saying from a press conference chair behind me, "is how can anyone in America be sophisticated, knowledgable, influential, and in favor of offshore drilling—and never have heard of the blowout at Santa Barbara?"

The gray drilling platforms at Santa Barbara seem unreal in flat water. From the cockpit of a helicopter, you can look west and see them strung out like pawns advancing across the chessboard of the sea—Standard's four in state waters off Carpinteria, then Phillips's pair just over the line on the federal shelf, then Sun's Hillhouse, and, farthest out, the twin towers of Union's A and B platforms. North and inland, the Santa Ynez Mountains hunker mistily behind the narrow coastal plain. Seaward loom the Channel Islands—Anacapa, Santa Cruz, Santa Rosa, San Miguel—beyond which lie the unleased squares of other chess sets where petroleum is king. Oilmen are eager to anchor new drilling platforms behind these wild, unpeopled islands. The way they figure the citizens of Santa Barbara, aesthetics are half the battle. If it's out of sight, it's out of mind—at least until the next blowout brings a black tide again to Leadbetter Beach.

In the interest of forestalling such an occurrence, the Division of Conservation of the U.S. Geological Survey maintains a busy staff of inspectors at its field office in Santa Barbara. The inspectors spend much of their time in boats and helicopters traveling between the mainland and the drilling platforms in the channel. A platform such as Union A, for example, has some 260 safety devices aboard, set up in redundant systems inspired by The Blowout and dependent on the smooth efficiency of many moving parts. It is the job of the inspectors periodically to make sure that the systems are smooth and the parts moveable. It is also their job on occasion to conduct guided tours for visiting Washington officials and journalists curious about the mysteries of BO on the OCS.

"We're in luck," Leon Bray was saying as we flew up the channel in a chartered helicopter. "With this overcast, you'll be able to see some of the seeps." Bray is the Geological Survey's chief petroleum technician at Santa Barbara. And he knows oil. Before joining the government, he was with Standard of California for seventeen years.

Bray had told me about the seeps earlier when we were ashore. There were two kinds—natural seeps like the one we would see later off Coal Oil Point, and induced seeps from fissures in the seabed that buckled in the blowout of 1969. Bray said that the worst offenders, in terms of the volume of released oil, were the natural seeps. I asked what had been done to plug the other kind.

"They've tried everything," Bray said. "They even poured cement into the fissures. Tons of it. But nothing worked. Ever since the blowout, it's been leaking maybe five, ten barrels a day. You'll see." And we did. As pilot Sandy Wheeler brought the bubble-nose chopper around to windward of Platform A, Bray pointed down at the gray-green sea. Three thin slicks oozed shoreward, glistening like streamers of grease in a kitchen sink. "If you think that's bad," said Bray, "wait until you see the gusher at Coal Oil Point."

Beneath the 'copter pad, where Union's 76 symbol is emblazoned in bright orange, Platform A is an intricate and imposing structure. On the main deck, seventy-three feet above the water, are forty-five wellheads, of which all but two were in production the day I was there. The wells are 1,200 to 4,000 feet deep and, having been drilled from the platform at various angles, are scattered some two hundred yards to a half-mile out from the rig itself. On the bottom deck are huge tanks where the gases and petroleum liquids are separated from subterranean brine and then pumped through pipelines to the Rincon Refinery in the coastal hills west of Ventura. A meter in one of the control rooms clicks off "barrels" produced as the oil enters the pipelines. It is Union's dashboard, measuring both the rate of production and the cumulative barrelage. At 11:50 A.M. on 4 February 1975, Union's A and B platforms jointly were producing at the rate of 23,000 barrels a day. Total production from both platforms was then about 75 million barrels since the first wells were drilled in January 1969. This, of course, does not include the more than 100,000 barrels of oil that blew out of the uncased bore of Well A-21 and up through the ruptured seabed and out across a thousand square miles of water and more than fifty miles of coastline during the first five months of A's operational life. Those barrels are lost forever, as are a number of other things that came in contact with the slick.

Union Oil is negotiating with the government for permission to anchor a third platform—C—on its leaseholdings in the Santa Barbara Channel. "There hasn't been a failure out here in five years," said Dick Gillen, Union's superintendent of production. "With Platform C we could throw half a million gallons of gasoline each day into the Southern California market."

I allowed as how perhaps a lot of people in Santa Barbara would rather do without their share. Gillen looked out across the water toward shore. Even from six miles out, with visibility shrinking under a ceiling of rainclouds, we could see the Spanish-mission whites and tile-roof reds of the city beyond the beach and the yacht basin. "Yes," he said with a wry smile, "I suppose some people are like that."

And then we were flying away, platform-hopping from Union to Phillips to Sun; to the barge CUSS I, where Continental, Union, Shell, and Standard were driving exploratory drill bits into the OCS nine miles off Port Hueneme near the Channel Islands National Monument at Anacapa; and then on to the seep off Coal Oil Point. We could smell the escaping gas even inside the plexiglass cockpit, and below us the seep surfaced in a froth of turquoise bubbles from which lambent streaks of blue and purple radiated in every direction. "There's mother nature's own oilspill," said Leon Bray. "She's pumping 75 to 125 barrels a day." (In Santa Barbara later, Murray Lewis of the Los Padres Chapter of the Sierra Club agreed with Bray's assessment—up to a point. "Yes, there are some natural seeps," he said. "But since the drilling started out there, the seeps have been appearing over a larger area, and more oil is getting loose. Oldtimers say the beaches were cleaner before the action offshore.")

On our way back to Ventura, hugging the coastline, we passed the campus of the University of California at Santa Barbara and the posh seafront homes of the Hope Ranch district. Bray stabbed his finger rapidly toward one large rooftop where members of Get Oil Out, Inc., the city's most militant anti-OCS group, had painted its acronym *GOO* in public mourning for their blackened beaches. I don't know why, but for some reason the style of Bray's innocent gesture—stiff wrist, hand cocked, index finger jabbing downward —struck a terribly familiar note. It reminded me of the cliché aerial scene in the war films of the Forties, where the squadron commander is hand-signaling *six o'clock low* from his cockpit, just before the Spitfires roll over and down on the roofs of the enemy.

Six o'clock was about the time the Department of Interior's public information man walked into the west-wing pressroom of the White House. It was November 13, 1974. The information man carried a thick stack of press releases announcing the Bureau of Land Management's "tentative" OCS lease-sale schedule through 1978, and as he passed them out he also passed along the word that Secretary Morton and the governors would be with us shortly. Some of the details in the release had already leaked out in newspapers around the country. And of course by now everyone—everyone, perhaps, except for Oxtoby-Smith's influentials—knew that the federal goal was the leasing of ten million acres a year. But what wasn't known until now was exactly where and when the government hoped to sell its leases, and the speed with which it expected to bang out baseline studies and impact statements and public hearings and notices of sale, and how the frontier OCS areas lined up off cities and seashores whose people had long assumed that the ocean would forever remain the one inviolate feature of their environment. To wit:

In the Atlantic, four areas are designated. The northernmost is the Georges Bank Basin, a 175-mile-long trough of sediments curving southeast and east off Nantucket and Cape Cod—"Cod" because of the predominant commercial catch of the Bank's fishing fleet. Target sale: June 1976. Just in time to take the edge off Boston's Bicentennial tea party. Next, the Baltimore Canyon, stretching from Long Island nearly to Cape Charles, Virginia—some fifty miles off the busiest resort beaches in America, two national seashores, six national wildlife refuges, and some of the most spectacular salt marshes remaining in the world. Target sales: December 1975 and August 1977. Now, jumping over the bulge of Cape Hatteras, we come to the Southeast Georgia Embayment—from Georgetown, South Carolina, to Cocoa Beach, Florida—snuggling all this length against the gold coast of Dixie, including the fabled isles of Ossabaw, Sapelo, and Cumberland. Target sale: July 1976. And seaward of here, the Blake Plateau three thousand feet beneath the ocean surface, a drilling depth, according to CEQ, that is "beyond current technology." So let's have a jolly sale anyway, say about May 1978.

One might be tempted to dismiss the lease-sale schedule for the Gulf of Mexico, inasmuch as drilling has been going on there—mainly off of Louisiana—ever since the mattress of the federal seabed was first pressed in 1953. But, as archdruid David Brower likes to wonder, because the lady has slipped once, must she go professional? For now it is not just the Central Gulf, but all of it, from the Ten Thousand Islands off Everglades National Park, on past Sarasota and St. Petersburg and Crystal River and Cedar Key, all the way around the crescent to Corpus Christi and Brownsville and the lonely beaches of Padre Island National Seashore, where West Texas wildcatters splash in the surf to purge themselves of the lingering stink of upland petroleum. Target sales: 1975 through 1977.

In the Pacific, the scale of the OCS proposal is so staggering that the Santa Barbara Channel begins to appear as a drop in the barrel. From Dana Point, near San Clemente, to San Pedro Bay—280,000 acres. From Palos Verdes Point to Malibu, across the full seascape of the Los Angeles basin—163,000 acres. Off Santa Catalina Island—180,000 acres. Seaward of the Channel Islands—290,000 acres. And farther seaward yet, at drilling depths "beyond current technology" —a tract large enough to swallow the state of Rhode Island. Target sales: July, 1975, September 1976, and May 1977. And so on up the coast, from Point Conception past the Nipomo Dunes and Big Sur and Monterey to Half Moon Bay; from Cape Mendocino on past the Gold Bluffs of Redwood National Park almost to Coos Bay, Oregon; from the Columbia River's mouth at Astoria past Olympic National Park to the Strait of Juan De Fuca, where the supertankers from Valdez will soon be turning down into Puget Sound with their cargoes of Alaskan crude. And not just the crude from the North Slope. The crude from the Gulf of Alaska OCS. The crude from the Kodiak Trough and Cook Inlet and Bristol Bay and the Beaufort Sea and the Norton Basin off Nome—from millions of seabed acres whose harsh arctic physical properties are not only beyond current technology but beyond existing scientific knowledge as well. Target sales: 1975 through 1978.

So there it is, the entire package. Of all the coastal states, only two—North Carolina and Hawaii—are spared the perils of OCS development. In any event, it is going to be quite a show as Uncle Sam trundles his auction block up one coast and down the other, from tract to tract. From sea to shining sea.

And back in the pressroom now, the towering figure of Rogers Morton loomed above such flanking governors and governors-elect as Edwards of Louisiana, Carey of New York, Longeley of Main, Thomson of New Hampshire, and Byrne of New Jersey. Morton was wearing a dark pinstripe suit, the type morticians occasionally don for special open-casket affairs. His blue eyes twinkled in the klieg lights as he told the assembled newsmen that the governors had his assurance of an OCS program that would be both "orderly and environmentally safe." Figuring at least five years from sale to full production, he said, the OCS, plus reserves in Alaska, would make the nation almost totally self-sufficient to meet its petroleum energy needs through the 1980s. The proposed leasing schedule, he said, was essential so that government and industry could allocate resources and prepare the appropriate environmental protection measures.

Of the state leaders present, two—Edwards and Thomson —were clearly eager to buy Morton's message. Edwards, of course, represents a state in which oil has long shouldered a large share of the economy, and where offshore activity has been officially encouraged since 1937, when a Pure-Superior Oil combine sank the first paying Gulf well one mile out from Cameron Parish in fourteen feet of water. At the press conference, Edwards articulated his belief that it was the moral, humane, and patriotic duty of every coastal state likewise to embrace offshore activity; for supportive logic he cited the imperatives of foreign policy, unemployment, and world famine, among other things. Meldrim Thomson of New Hampshire did not speak, but was recorded in favor. Thomson is a mountain man, hailing from the high hills of Orford far from the sea. Moreover, Thomson presumably has scant cause to worry greatly for the shore of his state: it is only twenty miles long. He is more concerned about bringing BO to New Hampshire in the form of a large refinery which would theoretically employ hundreds of the resident unemployed—few of whom have skills relevant to a refinery's manpower needs. In his disregard for the finer points of environmental quality, the governor preaches what he has practiced. Once, on his Orford farm at the foot of Cube Mountain, in a fit of proprietary pique, Meldrim Thomson ordered his own trees chopped down across the Appalachian Trail to discourage occasional hikers from crossing his land.

For the other side, Brendan Byrne spoke briefly and unhappily of the Bureau of Land Management's month-old draft environmental impact statement on the OCS program. Byrne found it lacking. Hugh Carey, only recently elected governor of New York and still serving as a member of the House of Representatives, was more cautious. Both of them, as well as Longeley of Maine, seemed to be holding back. They were, after all, guests of the White House. It was Ford's and Morton's show. The skeptical governors would save their own lines for later.

Nature played a trick on humankind when it fashioned oil from the decay of marine organisms and vegetable matter. Instead of being straightforward, nature slyly cached the sticky stuff in secret hiding places. This amuses no one except geologists, who get restless in their lecture halls and long to be out in the good fresh air. Having been out there for nearly a century now, poking around in synclines and anticlines, the geologists are presently in a position to say that only 667 billion barrels of liquid petroleum remain in the known and recoverable fields of the world. They are not saying that this is the end of the hunt. There undoubtedly are other caches and better ways of extracting what is in them. But 667 billion barrels is all they are promising at this time. And since the people of the world currently consume about 20 billion barrels of oil each year, that isn't very much of a promise. In fact, when you start looking beyond 1999, that's *nothing.*

The known oil reserves of the United States contain about 48 billion barrels. Current annual consumption is about 6.2 billion barrels—or 17 million barrels a day, of which 6.4 million are imported from foreign producers. If the U.S. suddenly were to stop these imports and lock its geologists back in the lecture halls, the nation would then have to rely solely on its known reserves. At the current rate of production and consumption, the known reserves would last eight years. Obviously, this is not going to happen. What *is* likely to happen, according to government forecasts, is that the U.S. will somehow supplement its known domestic supplies and continue to consume oil, in greater or lesser amounts, through the

1980s. Exactly how the reserves may be supplemented over the next decade and a half is a question of some significance, especially to tidewater Americans from Nantucket to Nome.

Among the various energy scenarios making the rounds these days, two in particular seem relevant to the future of the OCS. One is a "high" forecast for petroleum supply and demand in 1985. It was prepared by Walter G. Dupree and James A. West of the Department of the Interior. It assumes a population growth rate of 1 percent, a 20-fold increase in nuclear generating capacity, an annual energy growth rate averaging 3.6 percent, and negligible efforts at energy conservation. The other scenario is a "low" forecast for petroleum supply and demand in 1985. It was prepared by the staff of the President's Council on Environmental Quality. It assumes continuation of the present population growth rate of 0.7 percent, major reliance on coal and nuclear fission, an annual energy growth rate of 1.8 percent, and substantial conservation efforts. The high DOI forecast projects a demand in 1985 for 25 million barrels a day, up about 35 percent over current needs. Of the 25 million barrels, some 13.8 million will have to come from sources other than proven domestic supplies on Alaska's North Slope and in the lower forty-eight states, including existing offshore production areas in the Gulf and Santa Barbara Channel. And what other sources might be available? CEQ lists them in its low forecast: foreign imports, synthetic oil from shale or coal, and, last but not least, the frontier areas of the OCS. This forecast projects a need in 1985 for 13.2 million barrels a day, of which only 4.7 million will have to come from imports, synthetics, or the OCS.

Yet straightaway we are being advised by more pragmatic minds in Washington that some of the options are unrealistic. Rogers Morton, for example, tells us that while energy conservation is indeed a worthy goal, it simply isn't going to make that much of a dent in the rising curve of demand. So, if one wants to believe him, we must rule out the low forecast of CEQ and stick with the high of DOI, or at least a facsimile thereof which may lie somewhere on the upper side of in-between. Now the question is: where in 1985 will the U.S. come up with 10 to 14 million barrels a day to supplement production of its proven domestic supplies? From imports? Possibly, but don't count on it. Who knows what evil lurks in the heart of the Mideast, or what the Venezuelans and Canadians might be up to ten years hence? Besides, self-sufficiency is now the goal, as was the moon in the 1960s. And we made it. So no imports. Synthetics? "Very little potential before 1985," say the oil and gas men at DOI. In fact, in one interview, the deputy assistant secretary for energy and minerals, King Mallory, dismissed liquefaction of oil shales as a "popcorn process." With shale, he told me, "you end up with more spoil than you start with—and who wants that?" I said I didn't, and guessed the people on the western slope of the Rockies didn't either.

"And with coal," he went on, "you pollute the air."

"That doesn't leave us with much."

"Only the OCS," said Mallory.

Vincent McKelvey is the director of the U.S. Geological Survey. Nathaniel Reed is DOI's assistant secretary for parks and wildlife. On November 14, 1974, both were among a score of federal officials, including Rogers Morton, who assembled in the DOI auditorium to explain further details of the accelerated OCS program announced at the White House the previous evening. Reed, of course, had nothing to explain; it was not his program. He sat, as an observer, in a side aisle near the wall, a long arm draped over the back of the empty seat next to him, listening attentively as his departmental colleagues addressed the audience of newsmen and gubernatorial aides from the coastal states. McKelvey sat with Morton, facing the audience across a felt-covered table flanked by charts and easels. After Morton, McKelvey was the man with the most to say, and he was there to say how much oil and gas were thought to be contained in the seabed deposits of the OCS frontiers.

For perspective, one must first understand that estimating undiscovered, yet presumably recoverable, quantities of oil beneath the sea is not an exact science. The estimator might do better standing at the edge of an unfathomed lake trying to calculate its storage capacity in acre-feet. Thus, in recent reports, the Geological Survey has issued estimates of total OCS oil resources that have fluctuated from the range of 80-150 billion barrels downward to 58-116 billion barrels. For the Atlantic and Alaskan OCS frontiers alone, government estimates have ranged all the way from a high of 45 billion barrels down to a meager 8 billion, or about a fourteen-month supply at the nation's present rate of consumption. All of which has caused a number of observers to wonder whether the government actually has any accurate idea of OCS potential—or is simply playing a game of mathematical roulette.

McKelvey was speaking now in the DOI auditorium and his choice of words amused the audience. "Does the poke contain a pig?" he inquired, gesturing toward the OCS areas shaded on the map behind him. "We think it does." And from there McKelvey went on to count off the Survey's latest, most conservative estimates for the areas scheduled for lease-sales in the coming years.

In the Gulf of Alaska, said McKelvey, "7 to 15 billion barrels." (*In the eastern Gulf of Alaska area,* the CEQ had reported earlier in its April, 1974 environmental assessment of OCS development, *probabilities for a spill coming ashore . . . are no lower than 40 percent in winter and exceed 95 percent in the summer. . . . Major earthquakes of Richter 7 magnitude are common. . . . Tsunamis also are frequent and . . . would create damage at fixed berth tanker sites.*)

In the Baltimore Canyon, said McKelvey, "2 to 4 billion barrels." (*Oil spills in the northern part of the Baltimore Canyon,* said the CEQ, *would tend to beach in northern New Jersey and Long Island, impacting some of the nation's most intensively used recreation areas. . . . Oil reaching . . . salt marshes would persist in marsh biota and fine sediments for a number of years.*)

Outside the auditorium later, someone was saying how much he liked the part about the poke and the pig. "Actually,"

said the man, "you couldn't come up with a more appropriate symbol."

And then I was talking with Nathaniel Reed, who looked
grim and tired. "With all this talk about billions of barrels,"
he said, "what no one here wants to admit is that we have
finally come to the end of the petroleum era."

I asked him if he was worried about the impact on parks
and wildlife, inasmuch as so many places under his jurisdic-
tion are directly inshore from likely drilling sites.

"You bet I'm worried," he said. "Mainly about Alaska.
We're ahead of our technology. We don't know enough about
waves up there. We don't know enough—" and he stopped,
with a hopeless shrug of his shoulders, as if the list of un-
knowns might go on forever.

DES is bigspeak for Draft Environmental Impact Statement.
Each year, in accordance with the National Environmental
Policy Act, various government agencies prepare and circulate
for comment at public hearings thousands of DESs on dams,
highways, airports, bridges, tunnels, sewage plants, new factories, timber harvests, pest control programs, and other such
appurtenances of our lives and times in these United States.
Among the more interesting DESs of 1974 was a Bureau of
Land Management document prepared not to assess but to
justify accelerated leasing of the OCS.

The OCS/DES—1,300 pages in two volumes—hatched in
October, 1974. In November, hearings in Anchorage, Trenton, and Santa Monica were hastily announced for early
December, even though the appropriate agencies in several
key coastal states had not yet seen a copy of the document
to which they were expected to respond. Officials from
California pleaded for a postponement. Rogers Morton refused, whereupon California prepared its own document—a
lawsuit seeking injunctive relief and naming Morton as defendant. On the advice of his solicitor general, Morton backed
off and rescheduled hearings for early February. And the
Santa Monica site was shifted to Beverly Hills, presumably
in the hope that an inland auditorium would attract fewer

surfers, sunbathers, and other antagonistic intertidal riffraff.

Perhaps the most interesting thing about the OCS/DES was the conflicting manner in which people reacted to it. Oilmen loved it. Environmentalists laughed at it. State and municipal officials generally loathed it. Typical of industry's high praise for BLM scholarship was the statement of H. Edward Wendt, Getty Oil Company's manager of offshore exploration and production. Said Wendt in Trenton: "The environmental impact study that already has been judiciously prepared and evaluated, plus prior industry experiences, amply demonstrates that the environmental risks of offshore drilling are minimal." To which the president of Brooklyn Union Gas Company, Eugene H. Luntey, added: "No thinking person who carefully reads these two volumes can help but be impressed with the careful attention to detail and the objectivity of this report." And in Beverly Hills, John H. Silcox, vice-president of Standard of California, after addressing himself to the petty annoyances of "professional obstructionists" who would delay exploration offshore, complimented the BLM for its "comprehensive" work on the DES. His only regret was that more wasn't said about the "positive" aspects of seabed development.

Yet aside from Big Oil and its ancillary champions, few other speakers in Trenton or Beverly Hills found the DES judicious, objective, or comprehensive. In fact, virtually everyone not connected with gas and oil or the Department of Interior found the study to be, if not wholly uninformed, at least purposely naive. Consider such admissions in the OCS/DES as these:

"We believe that the plankton . . . will be able to absorb the impact of a major oil spill and recover fairly rapidly. This is based partly on the lack of evidence that plankton populations are catastrophically impaired by oil spills."

Or, "Although we have no conclusive evidence, it is our opinion that a major spill would affect sport fishing adversely."

Or, in assessing the impact of oil on marine mammals, the presumption that the effect of a major accident "will be negligible as long as the mammals are able to escape the area of the spill."

Or, in the course of devoting but one page of the 1,300 to the potential impact of OCS development on coastal recreation, the remarkable concession that such interference as a spill would be "generally" distasteful to beach users.

Or, in glaring confirmation of Nathaniel Reed's gloomiest doubts, the confession that "there are large gaps in the scientific information that cause problems in analyzing and predicting the impacts of OCS (development). . . ."

And yet in Trenton, leaning into the live microphone and speaking for the record, Roger Babb of DOI directed this question at Gerald P. McCarthy, administrator of the Virginia Council on the Environment. "Mr. McCarthy," Babb said, "can't we just say we have a pretty good (DES) statement?"

"I'm glad you asked me that," McCarthy replied. "In Virginia we would not even release a statement like this. It is just too unprofessional. It is not simply inadequate. It is woefully inadequate."

Across the continent in Beverly Hills, U.S. Senator John Tunney of California took the matter of the DES more gravely. It was, he said, a "nightmarish blueprint for disaster."

And then, the letter from the United States Environmental Protection Agency:

> Mr. Curtis J. Berklund
> Bureau of Land Management
> U.S. Department of the Interior
> Washington, D.C. 20240

> Dear Mr. Berklund:

> The Environmental Protection Agency has reviewed the draft environmental statement on the proposed increase in acreage to be offered for oil and gas leasing on the outer continental shelf. We acknowledge the need to expand domestic energy supplies, and especially OCS oil and gas resources. However, the protection of the

environment is of equal concern. The increase in OCS leasing and the means by which the OCS development is managed may be among the most critical energy decisions to be made in this decade. . . .

. . . . While we are cognizant of the immensity of the task of examining the programmatic options relative to this proposal, we do not feel the statement succeeded in the analysis. Therefore, in accordance with the EPA rating system for environmental statements, we have classified this statement as Category 3, Inadequate. . . .

. . . . The impact statement fails to evaluate or justify the necessity for this size offering, and the need to simultaneously enter Atlantic and Alaskan virgin areas. Nor is any consideration given to data derived from Project Independence studies which seem so clearly to refute the expediency of this size offering. . . .

. . . . Some of these areas, especially the Gulf of Alaska, contain unique and vulnerable natural resources combined with significant natural hazards that would make precipitous development highly undesirable from an environmental standpoint. The . . . plan . . . takes no cognizance of this assessment and further disregards the recommendations of the CEQ study. . . .

Sincerely yours,

Sheldon Meyers, director
Office of Federal Activities, EPA

Attachment B enclosed: Inclusion of Alaskan OCS Areas in the Leasing Schedule. . . . DOI has not been able to demonstrate that the benefit in oil development outweighs the environmental cost. . . . EPA's position is therefore that leasing in Alaskan waters should not be considered at this time and that substantial technical and biological research is required. . . . [A]n immoderate acceleration policy will be economically and environmentally costly. . . . [P]roduction by 1985 in the Gulf of Alaska can be surplus to the nation's need and should, at a minimum, be preserved for future years. . . .

Strong stuff, I was saying to Kenneth Biglane, the EPA's resident expert on oil pollution.

"They must have known it was coming," he said of the DOI. "This whole OCS thing has been like a bullfight. They hold the cape here, and when we charge, they move it over there."

Yes, I thought, and what a marvelous way to get gored.

If it accomplished nothing else, the OCS/DES brought out the horn-tossing instincts in everyone. Even before the hearings, senators Tunney and Alan Cranston moved to introduce a bill that would open the Naval Petroleum Reserve at Elk Hills, California, to full production (300,000 barrels a day by 1977, a step the Ford Administration likewise advocates in addition to accelerated OCS leasing). "It makes no sense," Tunney told the Senate, "to begin a massive OCS leasing program at this time when we have naval petroleum reserves which can be developed and produced more quickly and in an environmentally safe manner." Another bill was introduced later in the House by Alphonzo Bell, the Republican congressman from West Los Angeles. It would amend the Outer Continental Shelf Lands Act to provide for congressional veto-power in the granting of offshore leases. In Beverly Hills, Bell appeared on the first of three days of hearings with 400,000 signatures on petitions opposing new drilling. "You should know," he said to the hearing examiners from DOI, "that there is a general belief in Los Angeles that these hearings are meaningless; that the decision to lease . . . has already been made in Washington; and that no amount of testimony, scientific or otherwise, will reverse that verdict."

Despite such dour suspicions, the adversaries of accelerated drilling turned out in force in Beverly Hills, and their attack was spearheaded largely by the Seashore Environmental Alliance and the Los Angeles City Attorney's office. The Alliance, said its president, Shirley Solomon, is "the nonpartisan coalition (that) Bill Grant (BLM manager in Los Angeles) referred to as a 'vocal minority.'" Ms. Solomon paused, smiled, and then went on to explain that the Alliance was comprised of ninety-one affiliate organizations with an aggregate membership of 700,000 individuals, including four congressmen, two state senators, three assemblymen, and four county supervisors, not to mention the mayors of Beverly Hills, Santa Monica, Manhattan Beach, Hermosa Beach, and Rancho Palos Verdes. Having established the magnitude of this minority, Ms. Solomon turned to the problem of seismic activity in Southern California.

Oilmen and their friends do not like to talk about earthquakes, and like it even less when others do. Of the 1,300 pages of OCS/DES, only two are devoted to this hazard as it applies to offshore development in Southern California. When I put the question to Darius Gaskins of DOI in Washington, his answer was: "Sure, there's some seismic activity out there. But it's not too risky. Matter of fact, it's a cupcake." In Beverly Hills, Harry Morrison of the Western Oil and Gas Association likewise dismissed the risk. "We don't mind saying we live in earthquake country," he declared with True Grit spirit, "because we don't fear them."

Ms. Solomon, on the other hand, as well as the Sierra Club's Mary Ann Eriksen and other witnesses, felt somewhat less courageous about the seismic risks. Since 1812, Ms. Eriksen noted, there have been six major earthquakes of Richter 6 magnitude, or greater, "whose epicenters were in the offshore area of Southern California." She reminded the hearing examiners of the Good Friday earthquake in 1964, when the Alaskan port city of Valdez slid into its own harbor and a tidal wave associated with the quake smashed across Crescent City, California. And Shirley Solomon, referring to Robert Easton's book, *The Black Tide*, recalled that Union Oil's Platform A "is situated directly over an angular fault . . . about four miles from the epicenter of a 3.0 Richter magnitude quake which occurred a few months before it was erected." Which raises the question, Ms. Solomon concluded, "of whether or not seismic activity had anything to do with the blowout in January of 1969."

The most impressive statement in opposition—and clearly the most comprehensive—was submitted by Los Angeles

Mayor Tom Bradley and City Attorney Burt Pines on behalf of the Southern California Council of Local Governments, a coalition of eleven counties and municipalities ranging from San Diego to Santa Barbara. Compared with New York City's see-no-evil speak-no-evil fence-straddling seven-page testament in Trenton, the Los Angeles document was a blockbuster—nearly four hundred pages, plus one hundred more in an appendix of reports from the city's scientific advisory committee. The report covered all the bases, but none so well or so cogently as the possibilities of energy conservation and the potential of nonpetroleum energy sources as alternatives to accelerated leasing of the OCS.

The Los Angeles report found that the OCS/DES failed to consider alternatives; that, in fact, the OCS/DES virtually ignored the conclusions of the Federal Energy Agency's *Project Independence Blueprint* and the Ford Foundation's energy policy project (*A Time to Choose*), both of which had indicated that true "independence" could never be achieved unless conservation measures went far beyond those currently popular with the Administration. Indeed, the Ford Foundation study indicated that strong conservation measures, enforced by legislation, could preclude the need for new offshore drilling for at least ten years—"without affecting economic growth." But what measures?

The Los Angeles report notes that transportation consumes a quarter of the nation's energy budget and that three-quarters of *that* quarter is attributable to automobiles and trucks. BO and the auto industry, of course, blame fuel inefficiency on environmental constraints. Los Angeles, among others, places a larger share of the blame on vehicle weight, automatic transmissions, and air conditioning. In 1973, it is recalled, CEQ Chairman Russell Train, who is now the boss at the EPA, reported that a thousand-pound increase in auto weight could result in a 30 percent decrease in fuel efficiency. And yet, laments the report, that year the new Chevrolet Impala was 1,500 pounds heavier than the 1958 model, and presumably doing worse on mileage by about 45 percent. Further, it is reported that manual transmissions can save up to 15 percent on gasoline consumption. And according to the Ford Foundation study, altering a few characteristics—manual transmissions, reduction of rolling resistance through radial tires, and a redesign of configurations to reduce aerodynamic drag—could boost average performance by eight miles per gallon by 1980, even without smaller cars. . . . And so on—from the design of better insulated buildings to the elimination of continuous pilot lights in gas-heated homes, which pilots consume more than 200 billion cubic feet of natural gas annually. "With conservation," said Assistant Los Angeles Attorney Jan Chatten-Brown in Beverly Hills, "we don't have to lower the quality of our lifestyles. We just might improve it."

As for the development of solar, geothermal, wind, or organic waste resources, these also were treated lightly in the OCS/DES, as if they were science-fiction schemes appropriate only for the Year 2000. The Los Angeles report, noting that the period required for full OCS development is a minimum of six to eight years in any event, wonders why DOI is so down on the sun when the American Society of Mechanical Engineers finds "no technical barriers to wide application of solar energy to meet U.S. needs." Perhaps part of the answer lies in the federal budget. Of $643 million allocated in 1973 for energy supply, research, and development, less than $10 million was spent on solar or other nonconsumptive energy alternatives. Things improved a bit in 1974. Some $12 million was allocated by the government for solar research and development. But Lorna Salzman of Friends of the Earth, speaking in Trenton, didn't think $12 million was good enough—at least not from the same federal budget that made $30 million available for the development of a more sophisticated hydrogen bomb trigger.

To the DOI, Trenton may not have been as educational as Beverly Hills, but it was certainly as aggravating. Even as departmental hearing examiners were checking into hotel rooms on the eve of the opening session, officials from Long Island's Nassau and Suffolk counties filed papers in federal court alleging that the OCS/DES violated the decision-making processes of the National Environmental Policy Act. The papers named Rogers Morton as defendant and accused him of nothing less than a "conflict of interest." The titular trustee of the continental shelf, the lawsuit seemed to imply, should not also serve as its principal sales promoter. As if that were not enough, New Jersey Governor Brendan Byrne led off the roster of speakers by declaring: ". . . . We refuse to bend to the pressures of the federal government and the big oil companies who have advocated the precipitous . . . policy that your draft environmental impact statement attempts to justify unsuccessfully." Byrne was on home ground now, and he was furious: that morning's *Federal Register* contained a published invitation to oil companies to nominate in the Baltimore Canyon the specific drilling tracts which they might bid on later—the first step in the leasing process.

This call for nominations irritated Byrne for several reasons. First, so sudden and unexpected an action was a blatant show of federal force, possibly originating in the White House itself, a reaction to opposition expressed in Anchorage and Beverly Hills. Second, it came at a time when the U.S. Supreme Court was preparing to hear arguments in the case of the United States vs. Maine, a jurisdictional dispute in which Maine and eleven other Atlantic coastal states were claiming ownership of seabed resources beyond the three-mile limit. And finally, it disturbed the governor because it violated Rogers Morton's prior agreement to defer all offshore tract nominations in the Atlantic until the court had ruled in the Maine dispute. "The (DOI) is now attempting to renege on that commitment," said Byrne, his apple cheeks flushing brighter. "I have instructed the attorney general of New Jersey to take whatever legal steps are necessary to insure that the (DOI) keeps its word—or has it kept for it by the courts." Morton backed off. But shortly thereafter the Supreme Court rejected the states' claim to the seabed—whereupon Morton reissued his invitation to the oil companies to start playing chess on the Atlantic OCS.

It has been said by the proponents of OCS development that

their adversaries do not fully understand and appreciate the "drastically rearranged economic environment" which we all now inhabit. I take no great exception to this statement, for I cannot even begin to appreciate, for example, the full economic and political impact of our current dependence on foreign oil and the stress it places on our balance of payments, or how much it may ever matter that in 1974 24 billion American petrodollars flowed from U.S. banks to the coffers of such faraway places as Caracas and Kuwait. The drastic rearrangements that bring me greater heartache are closer to home, I am afraid, and far more puzzling. Such as the flow of my own dollars to the coffers of Getty and Texaco, notwithstanding the inherent economy of a battered station wagon with manual transmission and fuel performance that is better than 20-miles-per-gallon; or the rearranged environment of Big Oil, and the windfall profits that allowed Exxon, for one, to clear $2.3 billion after taxes during the first nine months of 1974—up 130 percent over the same period in 1972, and richer by five-fold than the earnings of General Motors. No, I do not understand such things, and appreciate them even less.

Among those who are not ecstatic about accelerated development of the seabed but who nonetheless do understand a thing or two about BO's new economic environment are Los Angeles Mayor Tom Bradley and Kenneth Cory, the state controller of California. Drawing on reports by the House Subcommittee on Regulatory Agencies and the Federal Power Commission, Bradley and Cory have shed some interesting light on the fiscal follies of the OCS. On the matter of shut-in wells, for example, and why the oil companies may be sitting on them. On whether industry can actually absorb the leasing of 10 million frontier acres in a year, and what kind of fair return, if any, the U.S. taxpayer can expect from industry—if competitive bidding should be undermined by a market that is glutted with leases.

At the time of the hearings in Beverly Hills, Bradley and Cory reported that wells on 168 leases in the Gulf of Mexico were currently shut-in. That is, they were capped, or plugged, or not even yet drilled, and therefore not producing. The leases covered almost 800,000 acres of seabed. The wells and leases were officially classified as being capable of producing "in paying quantities." Industry, however, claimed there were mechanical problems, or production failures, or shortages of materiel, and that therefore the leases could not be made to bring gas and oil to the market. The House subcommittee had found some of these excuses to be legitimate; but as Mayor Bradley recapitulated the subcommittee's findings, "in the majority of instances the classification of 'producible shut-in leases' was sought as a means of holding on to a lease beyond the original primary term of five years. One obvious benefit of such a maneuver is to allow oil and gas companies to produce valuable resources in the future when demand-market prices have increased." Federal Power Commission economist David Schwartz, in testimony before the House subcommittee, was less kind to BO in his choice of words. "It is this type of withholding which assures higher prices," said Schwartz of the shut-ins, "and unless we are able to effectuate public policy to bring about attachment of these reserves, our current supply posture will worsen and prices will rise and profit margins will increase for the individual producers."

Profits aside, the presence of so many shut-in leases in the Gulf of Mexico raises a rather large question about the rest of the OCS. As Kenneth Cory puts it: "If the oil industry is not now working this acreage under existing leases, how rapidly and how effectively can we expect them to develop an additional eight or ten million acres on the OCS frontier lands?" Cory's answer: Don't hold your breath. Some researchers, in fact, noting the very real constraints of insufficient skilled manpower and shortages of such crucial materials as tubular steel goods, believe that industry at this time is incapable of exploring and bringing into production more than 2.5 million OCS acres a year—about 100,000 acres a year more than the Ford Foundation energy study indicates we might have to lease annually to meet domestic oil requirements under the *highest* growth scenario.

So why ten million acres? Or even eight million, the figure

to which Rogers Morton retreated on the eve of public hearings? Because, in the words of the Ford Foundation study, ". . . the apparent guiding principle behind this decision (to lease) was to release as much of the resource as could be sold, with little concern . . . that the market for leases in coming years is apt to be flooded. Revenues to the government will probably drop as competition decreases." Those revenues are already ridiculously low. DOI spokesmen boast of the billions of dollars in cash bonus bids that will accrue to the U.S. Treasury as the frontier areas are placed on the auction block. Yet Kenneth Cory wonders if the taxpayer is going to get a fair return. Using industry's own projections for the Pacific OCS, which indicate a "recoverable" pool of about 14 billion barrels, Cory figures that under the best of bidding situations, and with the traditional 16.67 percent royalty in effect, the U.S. could expect to receive $2.17 per barrel over the life of leases (while the producer would pocket the $8.83 in change). By comparison, Cory adds, Indonesia is scheduled to receive $4.20 per barrel from its offshore contractors until their basic investments are fully recouped, and $7.00 for every barrel thereafter.

No one in the U.S., of course, is suggesting that we raise the ante for Big Oil on the OCS. It wouldn't be democratic. It might even disrupt the entire political process because, if we upped the ante substantially, how could an oil company afford to contribute to political campaigns, as the Securities and Exchange Commission recently accused Gulf of having done in concealing on its books the existence of a $10 million slush fund? In any event, it is likely, though not sure, that other changes distasteful to BO will come about in the years ahead. There is the possibility of the creation of a Federal Oil Exploration Authority, to help Uncle Sam begin to understand what he owns beneath the seabed, so that Uncle would no longer have to make leasing decisions based on industry's profit-oriented assessments. Perhaps there will be some kind of incentive so that industry will stop lobbying to drill new wells into frontier areas, and return instead to its old ones, where secondary and tertiary recovery methods, such as caustic waterflooding and air injection, could begin to extract the oil that is still there (enough, say some experts, to satisfy 40 percent of domestic oil requirements even in 1985). And finally, something even BO agrees with: a new federal formula for sharing the revenues from bonus bids and production royalties with the coastal states, so that vulnerable shore communities can begin to gird themselves for the inevitable impacts of OCS—OCS being, it seems, the only sure bet in the whole grab-bag of petroleum possibilities.

By car from New York City, being careful to observe the 55-mph speed limit which is strictly enforced on the Garden State Parkway, one can cover the 150 miles to Cape May Courthouse in just under three hours. Nearby are the City of Cape May, the Town of West Cape May, the summer colony of Cape May Point, as well as the Wildwoods, Stone Harbor, and Avalon, all of which are within the County of Cape May in the State of New Jersey. The cape is at the concourse of Delaware Bay and the Atlantic Ocean. One hundred and thirty miles due west are Washington, D.C., and the offices of Rogers C.B. Morton. Sixty miles due east are the Baltimore Canyon and an estimated two-to-four billion barrels of liquid petroleum.

According to local historians, Cape May was discovered by Henry Hudson, the explorer who first sailed into Delaware Bay in 1609. I suspect some error here, for it is more likely that the Indians discovered Cape May before Hudson did. In any event, the English soon replaced the Dutch, and the American colonists replaced the English and Indians. And blessed with safe harbors behind the cape's outlying islands and barrier beaches, the colonists built ships, smelted bog iron, and occasionally sallied forth to engage in piracy on the high seas. There was also a time when the seafarers sallied forth in pursuit of whales, in order to extract from the blubber a substance called oil, to be used in lamps. And then, about the time geologists spread the word that the carboniferous residue of long-dead marine organisms would do just as well, if not better, than the blubber of living ones, someone in Cape May discovered the beaches. And the sun. And the surf. And the salt air. And ever since then, though the county has produced prodigious crops of tomatoes and lima beans, and processed textiles and canned seafood, Cape May has nonetheless staked its fame and fortune on the claim that it is "The Nation's Oldest Seaside Resort."

They say that over the years six U.S. presidents, including Lincoln, chose Cape May as their spa. Some landmarks survive: sprawling Congress Hall, all yellow brick and black shutters, with an *1879* chiseled on the cornerstone; the Windsor, with red scalloped shingles below the roof; the Huntington House; gingerbread Victorian mansions here and there behind the sycamores and replicated gaslights of "Center City," as South Jersey citizens acculturized to Philadelphian ways call their downtown areas. Yet between the sagging artifacts the cape is also cultivating more contemporary tastes. Motels with saunas, pools, and picture windows are edging in along the shore. Condominiums have risen in the Wildwoods. Custom ranches are now clustered from Stone Harbor to Avalon along Seven Mile Beach.

On a weekday in the dead of winter, Cape May County is a quiet sort of place and, considering its location at the tip of the nation's most densely-populated state, not what you might call overly crowded. The county, 267 square miles, is divided about equally into three parts: one part for woods, mostly pine and oak and holly and cedar; another for the salt marshes; and the leftover third for people, of which there are some 70,000 regulars in all seasons. But because of the wide sandy beaches and the surf and the sun and the salt air, the county's census undergoes a radical change just about the time the oaks and sycamores are coming into full leaf. So that, by the Fourth of July, for example, the 70,000 will have increased tenfold to nearly three-quarters of a million. "We're the recreational backyard of Megalopolis," says William Diller, an Avalon builder and chairman of the county planning board. "More than 90 percent of the economy here is attributable to the resort industry. That industry is our economic base, grosses more than $185 million annually, and generates a cash flow in excess of $400 million." And that base, adds Diller, "is inextricably bound to a high-quality natural environment."

Unfortunately for Diller and the other regulars of Cape May County, not to mention all the tourists from New York and Philadelphia, the recreational backyard of Megalopolis before too long could become the industrial frontyard of the Baltimore Canyon. Under full leasing and development schedules, thirty-eight offshore drilling platforms are projected for the Middle Atlantic OCS by 1985, and thirty more by 2000. The extracted petroleum will come inshore for processing. It could go by tanker or pipeline directly to existing refineries in Northern New Jersey or the Camden-Philadelphia area. Most theoreticians in and out of government think it will not. Most think it will come ashore somewhere in Southern New Jersey—somewhere, for instance, like Cape May or Cumberland County, northwest of the cape on Delaware Bay. What's more, Cape May has already been designated as a likely location for a deepwater tanker port. The CEQ has speculated that if a deepwater tanker port is dredged in the Cape May area, there will also be a refinery. If there is a refinery, there will be pipelines and tank farms and pumping stations. And, quite possibly, petrochemical installations. And storage yards. And boat facilities to service the offshore platforms. And bases for the drilling crews. The CEQ assumes for the Cumberland-Cape May region an investment of some $118 million in new industrial construction by 1985, should both the deepwater port and "high" OCS development materialize. The CEQ assumes that such developments would create 30,000 new jobs in the region by 1985; that 30,000 acres would be required for new housing as well as for the industrial infrastructure; that the OCS impact alone could require the equivalent of five new 1,000-pupil high schools in the area, also by 1985.

Such assumptions as these do not make life easy these days for Elwood Jarmer, who is planning director of Cape May County. It was winter when we talked. Outside the courthouse, the streets were quiet and uncrowded, and large assumptions were difficult to perceive.

"If it happens in a big way," Jarmer said, "it will be the death of the resort industry and of the environment of this county as we know it. I'm not saying they shouldn't ever drill in the Atlantic. I'm saying they should give us some time. We're less than two years away from completing our coastal zone management plan in this state, and until we can say, 'This area is hands-off, that one over there is okay,' then there should be no production drilling."

On paper, one of the best and the brightest pieces of environmental legislation to emerge from the Nixon years was the Coastal Zone Management Act of 1972. The measure was enacted to help coastal states inventory their shorefront resources and draw up long-range plans to manage those resources wisely, lest the people wake up some fine morning and find all the shores of America cast in concrete. The act provided that planning grants should be made available to qualifying states by the National Oceanic and Atmospheric Administration, which Nixon placed under the umbrella of the Commerce Department, insuring that the new agency would behave itself and not rock too many proprietary boats. NOAA's good behavior in the eyes of the White House was further assured by the fact that, for more than a year, no funds to speak of were allocated to enable the agency to implement the Act. As a result, only a few of the coastal states had even begun to assess their shorefronts when Rogers C.B. Morton announced the federal government's intent to accelerate development of the OCS.

Of all the artful dodges and sleights-of-hand that have so far been utilized by BO and the federal government to hasten a final closing on the OCS, none was quite so transparent as the effort to obfuscate both the intent of the Coastal Zone Management Act and the potential onshore impact of offshore drilling. The OCS/DES, for example, found the socioeconomic ramifications of onshore development to be so significant as to merit only thirty pages of discussion. And a good deal of that was cribbed selectively from the CEQ's April 1974 report—a fact that was duly noted at the Trenton hearings by none other than Robert W. Knecht, NOAA's assistant administrator for coastal zone management. Said Knecht of the OCS/DES:

"Unfortunately, those (CEQ) passages selected seem mainly to be the ones which suggest that positive or beneficial onshore socio-economic impacts will occur. Sentences which indicate the opposite are largely ignored. For example, the (OCS/DES) states: 'The significant demands for labor of all kinds would lower a local or regional unemployment rate relative to other sections of the nation.' With the exception that the 'would' is a 'could,' the same sentence exists in the CEQ report, which, however, then continues: 'But low unemployment will not always result because publicity often attracts more workers than are needed and unemployment remains high.' Similarly, the (OCS/DES) concludes that in areas of OCS operations 'the average per capita income of each locality would also rise.' The similar sentence in the CEQ report, however, is followed by the qualifier that 'However, income benefits may not always accrue to current residents of the area but may instead go to imported labor.' . . . These departures from the CEQ study would seem to represent rather broad license in reporting these potential impacts."

Yet the warnings of men like Robert Knecht and Elwood Jarmer fall on deaf ears when the listeners happen to represent BO or the DOI. Charles D. Matthews, president of the National Ocean Industries Association, has stated in effect that the only thing coastal planners really need to know is where the oil's at. "Incomplete state coastal zone plans need not be a hindrance to accelerated leasing," says Matthews. "Actually, exploratory activity by the ocean industries could help state employees and officials to devise and approve coastal zone plans, and decisions would not have to be made in an informational vacuum." (Matthews fails to add, however, that oil companies consider their exploratory data privileged information—and do not share it freely, not even with the USGS.) As for the DOI, it seems to regard coastal zone planning as if it were some kind of bad dream. The states, Secretary Morton magnanimously explains, are under no obligation to complete coastal plans. Waiting for a state to do so, he says, "could, in an extreme case, give an important veto power over an extremely important national decision to a very limited number of people."

So Elwood Jarmer, not unlike many coastal planners elsewhere, sits pensively in his office at Cape May Courthouse with a half-finished plan, and thinks about all the fine woods and marshes and beaches where the hands-off signs should go up, and wonders where the big fist is going to fall, and what it will do to these places—and to him and his neighbors, and the tourists from Philadelphia—should it fall on Cape May. Outside, in the quiet streets, there are rumors. One rumor has it that "holding" companies fronting for BO have already acquired enough vacant land to turn "The Nation's Oldest Seaside Resort" into the industrial armpit of America.

It is the winter of YEA and I am walking alone on the beach. YEA, in case you haven't noticed the full-page advertisements paid for and copyrighted by the Mobile Oil Corporation, is bigspeak for The Year of Energy Action, the year we get into the swing and give offshore drilling in the Atlantic and Pacific the go-ahead. The beach I am walking on is the wide one with dunes at Cape May Point, at the concourse of the Atlantic and Delaware Bay. The summer homes behind the dunes are empty. I am truly alone on the wide beach except for the solitary figure of a stranger, far-off but coming my way. The sand is smooth and flat at the water's edge. The tide is coming in. I have a stick in my hand and I start writing with it on the beach. I write

OCSDESDOIBLMUSGSBOYEA WAS HERE

and step back to admire the sharp clean letters in the sand.
    "Hello."
    I look up and see that the stranger is upon me. "Hello," I reply. "Fine morning."

The stranger is staring at the letters in the sand. "Who's that?"

"That?" I am embarrassed. I say it is nothing, a personal sort of joke about oil and the ocean.

"You mean the Baltimore Canyon?" says the stranger. "I heard about that."

We stand there talking about the Baltimore Canyon and Arabs and petrodollars and the price of gasoline as the tide comes higher on the beach and begins to pull apart the letters of my message in the sand.

After a while, the stranger says: "I'm glad I'm not in business around here."

"You think it'll hurt?"

"You bet I do."

"The oilmen tell us not to worry," I say. "The Western Oil and Gas Association, in fact, tells us business will be better than ever once we give the go-ahead to offshore drilling."

"Go on."

"No, I'm serious. They tell us people will flock to the shore just to gawk at the rigs. Just like the Indians came out of the woods here to gawk at the first explorers."

"I heard about that," says the stranger. "And look what happened to the Indians."